A THEOLOGY OF THE PARISH

A Theology of the Parish

The Face of the Church in Challenging Times

William A. Clark, SJ

Foreword by Austen Ivereigh

Paulist Press
New York / Mahwah, NJ

Imprimi Potest: Very Rev. Joseph M. O'Keefe, SJ

Scripture quotations are from New Revised Standard Version Bible: Catholic Edition, copyright © 1989, 1993 National Council of the Churches of Christ in the United States of America. Used by permission. All rights reserved worldwide.

Cover image by faak/Shutterstock.com
Cover design by Sharyn Banks
Book design by Lynn Else

Library of Congress Cataloging-in-Publication Data
Names: Clark, William A. (Associate Professor), author.
Title: A theology of the parish : the face of the church in challenging times / William A. Clark.
Description: New York / Mahwah, NJ : Paulist Press, [2022] | Includes bibliographical references and index. | Summary: "The Face of the Church answers skepticism about the pastoral role of theology by presenting a case for "Theology of the People" as an important tool for empowering whole communities at the local level of the Church"—Provided by publisher.
Identifiers: LCCN 2022015945 (print) | LCCN 2022015946 (ebook) | ISBN 9780809155620 (paperback) | ISBN 9781587689604 (ebook)
Subjects: LCSH: Parishes. | Church. | Catholic Church—Doctrines.
Classification: LCC BX1746 .C53245 2022 (print) | LCC BX1746 (ebook) | DDC 262/.02—dc23/eng/20220801
LC record available at https://lccn.loc.gov/2022015945
LC ebook record available at https://lccn.loc.gov/2022015946

ISBN 978-0-8091-5562-0 (paperback)
ISBN 978-1-58768-960-4 (e-book)

Published by Paulist Press
997 Macarthur Boulevard
Mahwah, New Jersey 07430
www.paulistpress.com

Printed and bound in the
United States of America

This book is dedicated to
the memory of
Dan Gast (1946–2022)
Trusted Colleague,
Cherished Friend,
and Devoted Member of
the People of God

The Church is a people with many faces, and expresses this truth in countless different ways, according to each culture. That is why I like to think that evangelization must always be in the dialect of each place, with the same words and sounds that a grandmother uses to sing lullabies to her grandchildren.

Pope Francis
Let Us Dream: The Path to a Better Future

CONTENTS

FOREWORD

Austen Ivereigh

PERHAPS THE MOST apt of Fr. Bill Clark's many potent quotes from Pope Francis comes at the head of his final chapter, "Parish: A Vision Forward." It is from Francis's apostolic exhortation *Evangelii Gaudium*, "the Joy of the Gospel," which burst onto the Church in November 2013, just a few months after the new pope's election. "The call to review and renew our parishes," Francis wrote in paragraph 28, "has not yet sufficed to bring them nearer to people, to make them environments of living communion and participation, and to make them completely mission-oriented."

By the standards of papal documents, this was direct language indeed.

In the western world, the parish had been in crisis and decline—or so it felt; and there were always numbers to back up the feeling—for well over two decades. There was no lack of diagnoses: progressives blamed patriarchy and authoritarianism, traditionalists scapegoated liturgical changes, while academics called attention to modernity's crisis of belonging.

Nor was a prescription lacking. For thirty-five years Popes John Paul II and Benedict XVI had sought to calm the post–Vatican II turbulence by giving a firm direction to the Church through a clear interpretation of the Council. But parishes continued to shrink and close throughout that time in Europe and America. Some concluded the parish was over and the future lay now in church movements, in "events," networks, and "fresh expressions"—charismatic, traditionalist, or prophetic—that appealed to the young and to the beleaguered. Meanwhile diocesan bishops put faith in the latest expensive renewal program, centered almost always on training small groups of able "leaders." As Clark observes, some of those initiatives bore fruit, but often only until the next change of pastor or until the leaders moved on and the parishes were left to continue their atrophy.

Now here was a new pope, from Latin America, daring to suggest that all this *Sturm und Drang*, all those costly renewal initiatives, had failed. They had not led to parishes offering the experience of missionary communion portrayed in the Acts of the Apostles: compelling, life-filled, evangelizing. But rather than lament that the secularization of culture had led people to leave the Church, Francis asked the Church to take responsibility for leaving the people. Far from being outdated, he said the parish was amazingly flexible, changing shape in accordance with "the openness and missionary creativity of the pastor and the community."

In other words: if parishes had become remote, distant, and clerical, too often lacking the elements of loving fellowship and vigor that so marked out the early Christian communities, there was a lack of openness and missionary creativity. As Clark notes in chapter 7, the Church has been especially vulnerable to the wider cultural trend of popular alienation from institutions. Indeed, in so far as the Church has taken on the worst characteristics of modern institutions—impersonal, functionalist, corporate, self-referential—it has suffered more than most.

In the language of Ignatian discernment of spirits, parishes—and not just parishes, but the Church in general, at least in the rich, northern lands of former Christendom—were in desolation. As *Evangelii Gaudium* made clear on almost every page, it would take the fire of the Spirit to turn them outward again. The pope invited us to trust in that Spirit, abandoning the corporate and ideological securities that were incapable of giving life. He invited us to live from the consolation of an evangelizing Church in which missionary disciples shared the joyful responsibility of making known in words and actions the good news of a God who had undergone death out of love for his creatures and risen to bring them new life. For this, a pastoral and missionary conversion would be needed: to become poor in spirit, humble, open; to live from gift, not power; to serve, not dominate; to preach the reckless mercy of God, not a rulebook. We would need not just to understand the kingdom of God, but to enter it.

In the months after *Evangelii Gaudium* came out, it was clear that it had been misunderstood, ignored, even opposed. Even when people saw the need for the conversion, they had little idea how to go about it. *Evangelii Gaudium*, bursting with the signs-of-the-times discernment of the Latin American Church at Aparecida in 2007, was too strong a tonic, too much for most of the northern Church to assimilate. There was no shortage of commentaries and essays showing its genesis in Paul VI's *Evangelii Nuntiandii* and Aparecida, but what was needed was theological reflection on the praxis Francis was giving us, one rooted in concrete experience of parish life, that could put flesh on its vision. And there, I figured, was the rub because theologians in the English-speaking world are not much interested in parochial life.

Then Fr. Bill Clark got in touch. A soft-spoken U.S. Jesuit theologian with a passion for parishes, he had been inflamed by *Evangelii Gaudium* and wanted to capture its vision. What is such a parish like? We met in Buenos Aires, where he talked to bishops, pastors, and laypeople who had been engaged with facilitating the pastoral and missionary conversion of the Church of that city after Aparecida. Later, we continued to correspond, and I read some early chapters of *A Theology of the Parish*. But only now that it is out do I see just how international is its scope, how comprehensive is the research behind it, how varied is the long list of parishes and people he thanks, and how persuasive and compelling is his articulation of the vision of *Evangelii Gaudium*.

Clark insists that this is not about offering a blueprint or model. A good parish is always inculturated in time and place; it carries a unique culture, a tradition—one might say a "soul"—formed by the lives and prayers of the faithful people who make it up, present and past. Clark approaches parishes with respect, even reverence, always attentive to this culture; and rightly, he reserves his harshest words for a clericalist, bureaucratic, functionalist leadership culture that sees the parish as a "a tool for the ministry of the ordained" rather than a community to be cherished, a family of God rooted and grounded in love. Parishes, of course, must be organized and funded, and sometimes clustered or even closed. But to make those decisions remote from the faithful people themselves—as Clark recounts happened in Boston in 2004—is to do violence to the very nature of a parish.

Although Clark only mentions synodality in detail toward the end of the book, it is possible to read every chapter in the light of Francis's call for a "wholly synodal Church." In the years since *Evangelii Gaudium*, in fact, it has become increasingly obvious—including to Pope Francis himself—that a pastoral and missionary conversion must begin with a synodal conversion, which is what, in his famous October 2015 speech, Francis said God expects of the Church of the third millennium.

A Theology of the Parish implicitly concurs on almost every page with that discernment.

A parish comes alive, for itself and for others, when the ordinary people of God are allowed to express the gifts that the Spirit has poured out equally on all the baptized: when they listen, are heard, and are involved in the making of decisions. As Clark puts it in chapter 4, this communion—which should be the Church's hallmark, the sign it belongs to Christ and not to the world—calls for "a continual deepening of the habits of attentive presence to one another and to Christ in their midst." As Francis writes in the new apostolic constitution on the Roman curia, *Praedicate Evangelium*, communion "gives to the Church the face of synodality: a Church, that is, of mutual listening, in which everyone has something to learn."

That is how a parish remains deeply rooted in one place, yet constantly on the move; how it can transform relationships of trust and belonging free from the commodifying market and the stifling impersonalism of the state, yet be turned outward, in confident service of the wider community. It is how the parish embraces the mission as a task for all the faithful, to be lived out primarily in family and workplace, but also in the collaborative ministries within the parish, under the leadership of the ordained ministry but not dependent on it.

The road to this revitalized Church is marked by the path of synodality, which is a method for always starting in mission. What is the Spirit asking of us? How do we need to change, and what must we do to carry out that mission? As Clark puts it, "Let the mission—prayerfully discerned—seek out the tools by which it can be accomplished, rather than letting whatever tools we have handy tell us what the mission is." For the mission is what Christ founded the Church for: to preach the gospel by witnessing to the mercy we have received, through acts and words of humble service. And while there are many vehicles for that mission, none is as vital or as ubiquitous or as flexible as the parish. For it is still mainly here that the gospel—if we allow it—makes its home among us.

PREFACE
On Method and Style

THIS IS A WORK of pastoral theological reflection. While this designation should not in itself suggest a less rigorous consideration of the topic—the meaning and purpose of parishes—I have very intentionally written with a general audience in mind rather than addressing my theological colleagues exclusively. By this I mean that I have taken care to spot assumptions that I might otherwise make about terms, sources, and standard interpretations, and have provided further explanation when I thought it would be helpful. I have further favored arguments and approaches that I am convinced will help parishioners, pastors, and pastoral professionals receive and consider the viewpoints I am offering in the following chapters. In my research and reflection on parishes over many years, and particularly over the past decade and a half, I have learned most from the generosity, dedication, and welcome of those directly engaged in the life of parish communities. It has been my intention, therefore, to speak most directly to them, even while taking up many of the studies, insights, and suggestions made by many excellent theologians, sociologists, and other fellow academics who have brought breadth and depth to the field of local ecclesiology in recent years. With these considerations in mind, I offer these opening notes on the ways I have built the discussion you are about to read.

Observations and Research of Specific Parishes: Each chapter of this book opens with a vignette, more or less extended, of one particular parish community, meant to provide a concrete point of contact with the issues in that chapter. I have also frequently referred to and drawn examples from other parishes in the main body of the chapters. Unless noted otherwise, all these parishes are among the many that I have visited, observed, worked in, or studied methodically (using some basic ethnographic tools) over about thirty years of focused interest in parish communities. In some cases (explained in the chapter notes), I have chosen to use pseudonyms when describing situations that I judged to be either unresolved or too complex to deal with thoroughly within the context of the point I was highlighting. In every case, whether or not I have employed a pseudonym, it is important to remember that parishes are living, developing communities. Every description or example is, therefore, merely a snapshot—through the lenses of my own history and theological perspective—of an ever-evolving social and ecclesial situation. These snapshots were taken in several different countries under widely varied circumstances, but ultimately and unavoidably my perspective has been shaped by my experience as a U.S. citizen and member of the Society of Jesus. It remains my hope still that what I have drawn from my many parish encounters will be interesting and useful to readers with quite different experiences of church communities.

Use of Scripture: In keeping with the overall style of the book as described above, I have employed what might be called a "homiletic" style in my frequent references to Sacred Scripture. My intention is, once again, to present biblical passages as important points of contact, now between foundational Christian tradition and the needs and circumstances of local church communities in our own time. With due attention to the general conclusions of recent commentary, I attempt to apply the Scriptures to the subject and situation at hand. Along the way, I may employ some passages in unusual ways, in hope of keeping the witness of early Christian communities close to our contemporary discussion. None of this should be taken as a claim to any special expertise in detailed biblical scholarship on my part.

Use of Church History: Historical consciousness is an essential tool in the study of theology and the Church's tradition. A great deal of clarity can be gained by knowing something of the story of a person, a place, an institution, a culture. Accordingly, I have made use of historical development and historical example in a number of key places in the book. I have found reflection on the early Church to be particularly useful. Beyond such references, I have not tried to write a "history of the parish." I have attempted, instead, to stay focused on what I believe to be particularly relevant to the task of reflecting on the meaning and mission of the parish in the Church of the twenty-first century.

"Mission," "Proclamation," and "Evangelization": The international context of many of my parish examples, as well as the intense awareness in much contemporary scholarship of the impacts of colonialism, slavery, and racism, call for a comment on my frequent use of words like *mission* and *proclamation* throughout the book. I am aware, and urge readers to remain aware as well, of the ways in which the concepts behind these traditional Christian terms have been distorted and misapplied—not only in the past, but in our own time as well—to justify military, political, and economic domination; dismissal of the dignity and natural rights of fellow human beings; and the impoverishment, enslavement, suffering, and death of countless persons. I endeavor throughout the book to place such terms back into what I consider their original context in the *hope* inspired by the encounter with Jesus and in the *love in action* called forth by this hope. This is my primary intention in putting such emphasis on the "theology of the people" that has been so consistently applied by Pope Francis.

The Impact of the COVID Pandemic: When I first formally proposed this book, the onset of the COVID-19 pandemic was still some months away. In the many ensuing months of struggle, loss, heroism, and adaptation, incalculable social changes have taken place. It is already clear that some of these will be permanent and profound, even as their long-term consequences remain to be seen. Parishes are certainly not least among the communities that will be dealing with the effects for a long time to come. Although discussion and new research began almost immediately, it is still impossible to anticipate all the changes that may come about in the environment and circumstances of local church communities due to the impact of the pandemic. Although I have referred to the situation as often as it seemed relevant and prudent, there is still a lot of observation and adaptation to be made. My hope is that the whole approach I present to the meaning and purpose of parish would suggest an *attentive openness* to evolving circumstances that will guide Spirit-filled development far into the future.

Fr. Bill Clark, SJ
December 31, 2021
Vigil of the Solemnity of Mary, Mother of God

IN GRATITUDE...

THE TARGETED RESEARCH, drafting, and finalizing of the manuscript for this book took about three and a half years, spanning a sabbatical year, five teaching semesters, and the COVID pandemic. In that time, I have accumulated debts of gratitude to an extraordinarily long list of people whose generous help has been indispensable. The full truth of the matter makes the task of acknowledgment even more daunting, and well-nigh impossible to complete: my professional interest in Catholic parishes has been growing for decades, and rests on foundations laid at the beginning of my life and built on by family, friends, and colleagues ever since. By rights, I should be naming literally hundreds of people here. Among those who will inevitably not be included will be many whom, when I think of them individually, I will regret having left off the list. In the spirit of the "pilgrim people" whom I've tried to describe, though, I will begin here a happy task of thanksgiving that will surely have to be completed in eternity.

My remarkable extended family introduced me to my first parish community and has both fed and challenged me in faith ever since. Here I will name only my late parents, William H. and Theresa R. (Laflamme) Clark, remembering their quiet support and extraordinary love. Their nine and ten siblings, respectively, gave my sister, Paula, and me fifty-five first cousins. So, to the Clark/Edgerly and Laflamme clans, my love and respect and deep gratitude!

For the past twenty years, I have been privileged to work with outstanding colleagues in the Department of Religious Studies at the College of the Holy Cross in Worcester, Massachusetts. I am indebted to them all for the atmosphere of collegiality and serious scholarship that has inspired and challenged me, and for their deep dedication to our students. I would like to thank especially Profs. Matt Eggemeier, Peter

Fritz, and Bill Reiser, SJ, for their practical help, thoughtful reading, and enthusiastic encouragement of this project.

I began to organize my research on visits to several destinations during my sabbatical year of 2018–19, made possible by the generous assistance of both the College of the Holy Cross and the Holy Cross Jesuit Community. In June 2018, I was hosted in Rome by the Jesuit community at the Church of the Gesù while I met with members of the faculty at the Pontifical Gregorian University. My special thanks for the success of that visit go to Jim Corkery, SJ, Orlando Torres, SJ, Gerry Whelan, SJ, Miguel Yañez, SJ, and Paul Mueller, SJ.

For two weeks in July and August 2018, in Argentina, I was the guest of the Jesuit communities at the Colegio del Salvador in Buenos Aires and the Colegio Maximo de San José (now Centro Loyola) in San Miguel. Gustavo Morello, SJ (Boston College), Emanuel Vega, SJ (Colegio del Salvador), and the College of the Holy Cross's Study Abroad office (particularly Jimena Collingwood in Worcester and Leonardo Grana at Universidad del Salvador) were instrumental in organizing this trip. (Landon Cass, Holy Cross '20, later took time during his semester abroad to track down books by Rafael Tello for me.) Dr. Austen Ivereigh (Campion Hall, Oxford) not only read and commented on parts of the draft later on but was an indispensable guide and interpreter in Buenos Aires. We had wonderfully engaging meetings with Auxiliary Bishops Juan Carlos Ares and Gustavo Carrara, Padre Pepe Di Paola, and Virginia Bonard (who had worked closely with Archbishop Bergoglio). The late Juan Carlos Scannone, SJ, Jorge Seibold, SJ, and pastors Rafael Velasco, SJ, and Julio Merediz, SJ, were also very generous with their time and tolerant of my rudimentary conversational Spanish. Dr. Emilce Cuda (now of the Office of the Pontifical Commission for Latin America) graciously welcomed me to her home in Buenos Aires for conversation about "theology of the people." *¡Muchas gracias a todos!*

During a frigid four weeks in January and February of 2019, I availed myself of the resources of the Raynor Memorial Libraries at Marquette University in Milwaukee, courtesy of my brothers in the Marquette Jesuit community. My thanks go especially to Joe Mueller, SJ, and Fred Zagone, SJ (then, respectively, rector and minister of the community), for their hospitality. While in Milwaukee, I had helpful conversations with Jim Flaherty, SJ (pastor of Gesu Parish), Tom Sweetser, SJ (director of the Parish Evaluation Project), Fr. Curt Frederick (vicar general of the Archdiocese of Milwaukee), Fr. Tim Kitzke (pastor of "Three Holy Women" Parish), and with Peg Flahive ("Companions in Ministry," Marquette University) and Susan Mountin ("Pastoral Leadership in a Cultural Context," Marquette). I so appreciate your time and your insights!

Thanks to the assistance and hospitality of Dan Gast (my colleague and former director at Project INSPIRE at Loyola University and the Archdiocese of Chicago, who passed away just as these thanks were being written) and Dan's wife Kathy, I arranged working visits back to Chicago from Milwaukee. Thanks to Frs. Ken Simpson and Bob Heidenreich (a longtime companion in this work, who also read drafts of the text), for their organizing of a very fruitful roundtable discussion with chancery staff and pastoral workers and priests of several parishes, including Lorie Crepeau, Cathy Walz, Carol Fowler, and Frs. Manuel Durantes, Rodolfo Ramirez, Thulani Magwaza, and Simon Burganza. Many thanks to all for making time for me!

On a short visit to Germany at the end of February 2019, I was hosted at the Center for Applied Pastoral Research (ZAP) in Bochum by my friends and associates through the "Crossing Over" pastoral exchange program, Prof. Dr. Matthias Sellmann, Dr. Andreas Henkelmann, and Dr. Benedikt Jürgens. During a busy week, I had stimulating conversations with all of them, as well as with ZAP research associates Veronika Eufinger and Matthias Kuchnowski. The ZAP staff also arranged another roundtable discussion for me with pastoral workers of the Diocese of Essen, where I was generously received by Dr. Nicolaus Klimek, Thomas Halagan, Michael Diek, Norbert Lepping, Marcus Minten, Fr. Ludger Molitor, Dr. Herbert Fendrich, Dr. Ann Elisabeth Meiers, and Annabelle Reim Gonzalez. At the end of the week, a day trip to the city of Hildesheim allowed me the privilege of a too short but intense conversation with Dr. Fr. Christian Hennecke, director of the Pastoral Office of the Diocese of Hildesheim. My sincere thanks to you all for a visit much more productive than I ever hoped for!

I spent two months in London as guest of my longtime friends Rev. Jennifer Smith, superintendent minister of Wesley's Chapel in City Road, and her husband Rev. Keith Riglin, now bishop of Argyll and the Isles in the Scottish Episcopal Church. Their far-above-and-beyond hospitality was awe-inspiring! While in London, I benefitted greatly from the facilities and collections at the British Library, found a pastoral home in the twinned parishes of St. Mary Moorfields and St. Joseph Bunhill Row, and in conversations throughout my visit, benefited greatly from the insights of Fr. Chris Vipers (St. Mary's), Martin Pendergast and Michael Winter (St. Joseph's), Andrew Cameron-Mowat, SJ (St. Ignatius, Stamford Hill), Rev. Dr. Michael Moynagh (Wycliffe Hall, Oxford), and Bishop John Inge (Anglican Diocese of Worcester).

Many other colleagues in the academy and the Church have contributed, in important ways both direct and indirect, to the successful completion of this project. I would like to thank, in particular, Dr. Brett Hoover (Loyola Marymount University), who generously read portions of the draft; Fr. Simon Smith, SJ (Weston, MA), for his encouraging comments; Michael Rogers (former chaplain at the College of the Holy Cross) for his introduction to Austen Ivereigh and other key contacts; Dr. Paul Lakeland (Fairfield University), for his invitation to present an early overview of the work as the 2020 Bellarmine Lecture at Fairfield; Dr. Rafael Luciani (Boston College), for conversation about his book; Dr. Charles Zech (Villanova University) and all associated with the 2018 International Festival of Church Management, for the brilliant exchange of ideas we had there; Pfarrer Bernd Wolharn, Fr. Troy Bobbin, Fr. Des Panton, and Joe Owens, SJ, for welcoming me to their parishes in Germany, Australia, and Honduras; Don Keegan, SJ (Weston, MA), for decades of friendship and pastoral wisdom; Dr. Phyllis Zagano (Hofstra University) and Prof. Alice Laffey (Emerita, Holy Cross), for their ongoing encouragement, support, and steady friendship. Finally, Donna Crilly, senior academic editor at Paulist Press, another longtime friend, has encouraged this project from the beginning and offered unfailing good cheer and patience when things were "going slowly," at best.

As the project comes to completion, I am also keenly aware of the many other dear friends and family members whose contributions were not to the research or writing, but to my own personal well-being as I worked. For their ongoing love and support, particularly in the months after March 2020, I will be forever grateful. If I named you all, there'd be no room for the rest of the book, so let me just say that you live in Maine, Massachusetts, New Hampshire, Connecticut, New York, Ohio, Illinois, California, Texas, Alabama, Florida, North Carolina, Washington, D.C., Jamaica, England, Scotland, Norway, Denmark, Italy, Australia (and undoubtedly other places that I am momentarily forgetting). You know who you are…love and peace to you all!

All day, every day, my brother members of the Society of Jesus in the community at Holy Cross embody for me the commitment that unites us. Representative among them are Fr. Jim Stormes, SJ—for the past six years our kind and wise superior—and Fr. Ed Vodoklys, SJ, a faithful companion since our novitiate days, a fellow member of the "evening hot-chocolate circle," and a Jesuit of unsurpassed dedication and loyalty. Thank you, thank you, thank you!

I conclude with a much-abbreviated list of parish communities by whose faith I have been fed and for whom this book was written. For lack of time and space, I include only those who are mentioned or alluded to in the text. There are *so* many more—all written in my mind and heart. Blessings on your common life and your work for the Lord and the people of God!

Blessed Sacrament, McKinley Park, Chicago, Illinois
Christ the King, August Town, Kingston, Jamaica
Corpus Christi, Waterville, Maine
Immaculate Heart of Mary, Fairfield, Maine
Liebfrauen Pfarrei, Bochum, Germany
Mary Immaculate, Newton, Massachusetts
Most Holy Trinity, Waukegan, Illinois
Nuestra Señora del Perpetuo Socorro, San Miguel, Provincia de Buenos Aires, Argentina
Patriarca San José, San Miguel, Provincia de Buenos Aires, Argentina
San Jorge, Olanchito, Honduras
San Juan Bosco, Villa Carcova, Buenos Aires, Argentina
SS. Peter and Paul, Liguanea, Kingston, Jamaica
SS. Peter and Paul, Norwich, Connecticut
St. Anne's, Fenway, Boston, Massachusetts
St. Barbara, Duisburg, Germany
St. Bernard's, Newton, Massachusetts
St. Ignatius, Rogers Park, Chicago, Illinois
St. Ignatius, Stamford Hill, London, UK
St. Joseph's Bunhill Row, London, UK
St. Joseph's, Biddeford, Maine
St. Mary Moorfields, London, UK
St. Mary's and the Western Mission, West Wyalong, New South Wales, Australia
St. Matthew's, Dorchester, Boston, Massachusetts
St. Patrick's, Waterhouse, Kingston, Jamaica

St. Patrick's, Milford, New Hampshire
St. Patrick's, Portland, Maine
St. Patrick's, Williamstown, Massachusetts
St. Stephen's, Worcester, Massachusetts
St. Thomas Aquinas, Papine, Kingston, Jamaica
St. Thomas of Canterbury, Uptown, Chicago, Illinois

Chapter 1

WHY PARISH? WHY THEOLOGY? WHY NOW?

An Introduction

> The parish...brings together the many human differences within its boundaries and merges them into the universality of the Church.[1]
>
> Second Vatican Council, Decree on the Apostolate of the Laity

OMPHALOS: MY HOME PARISH[2]

I was a week old when I was brought to Immaculate Heart of Mary, the church in Fairfield, Maine, that I would frequent for the next fifty years. It was two blocks away from my childhood home. Both my parents—my mother in her infancy and my father before their marriage—became Catholics there. Its community supported the elementary school that my mother and her ten siblings, and my own sister, had attended, as did I until it closed after my fifth-grade year. The parishioners were those people whom, as a child, I knew best other than my own family—the elders I was taught to respect and their children who were my friends and classmates. No holiday, no life milestone, was complete until it had included a visit to church for whatever sacrament was appropriate and whatever celebration was planned. My spiritual foundations were laid there, even if Immaculate Heart was not always the sole source of my deepest understanding of faith or of my greatest enthusiasm for Christian life. My family provided much of that, and later so did the charismatic prayer movement I was involved in as a teenager. But for as long as that parish community remained, it was what the ancient Greeks called the omphalos*—the navel, the center point—of my spiritual world. My growth or lethargy, my holiness or sin, my wisdom or foolishness, my "joy and hope, grief and anxiety"*[3] *were all gathered together there. That community taught me habits that would have been hard to break—if I had ever thought I wanted to break them.*

After leaving home, I continued to find it a very natural impulse to look for a spiritual base in the local parish church wherever I went. Although I was being spiritually nourished and educated through all sorts of events, associations, relationships, and eventually my commitment to the Society of Jesus, the parishes kept me connected to the concrete reality of "the Church," regardless of what else I was doing. In Williamstown, Massachusetts, the parish was one way to step out of the rarified world of academics. Back in Portland, Maine, during my first teaching job, it was a point of comparison between the day-to-day life of the Church and the religious community I was beginning to be drawn to. During my novitiate training in Boston, a nearby parish eased me into my first experience of visiting hospital patients. Novice "experiments" at parishes in Kingston, Jamaica, and Norwich, Connecticut, gave me a taste of working on staff and coming to feel "at home" in local church communities in two very different parts of the world. While studying philosophy in Chicago, volunteer work in one parish and frequent Sunday liturgies in another allowed me to witness economic disparity and the uncertainties of immigrant life, and to meet a community of young adult Catholics whose faith was leading them to seek a more just society. Many of the subsequent years found me immersed, in one role or another, at other parishes from Jamaica to New England to Europe to Australia, with shorter visits to many other communities in many other locations.

THE POWER OF local church community is at the heart of stories and experiences of Catholic faith that I have made my own in each of these places. With every encounter, I understood more deeply that a bond could develop among people, still to be felt decades later, by sharing nothing more visible than the sight of one another praying and receiving the Eucharist week after week. I was feeding what has become my permanent fascination with the distinctive character (and "characters"!) of each local community, and my growing appreciation of that treasure and its integral connection to the whole people of God. I began to realize that when I hear or say "the Church," it is not the pageantry of an episcopal liturgy or the dome of St. Peter's that comes first to mind, but the faces I have seen over decades and around the world in these many local church communities.

Innumerable believers from every region and era of the Church's life have shared in this same kind of experience. Strong, faith-filled local communities have always been an essential element of the collective lives of Christian people—that is to say, an essential element of the Church. The Gospel accounts suggest that even as large crowds were following Jesus, listening to his teaching, and wondering about its implications for their future as the people of God, his disciples were gathered around him in progressively tighter and more intimate circles of friendship, support, and trust. At the center of each of these circles, Jesus nurtured not only his disciples' growing faith and understanding of God but, just as insistently, their willingness to live that faith together. The reign of God, he taught them, "is among you" (Luke 17:21). As the universal Church grew from the communities the first disciples founded, and as its cultural contexts multiplied, many details of the local communities developed and changed, their meaning growing in depth and complexity along the way—the structures of leadership, the customs of gathering, the size and shape of the meeting places, and numerous other features.

Even today, what Roman Catholics and many other Christians all over the world call "the parish," in fact, varies greatly in form and function according to its location, specific history, and social circumstances. Yet the Church has never been without, and has generally sought to nurture and protect, local gatherings of believers. Members of such communities worship and receive the sacraments together, learn the life of Christian love from each other, and rely on each other to maintain, defend, and grow in their Christian faith. Shared faith, sacramental worship (essentially material, embodied, and therefore local), and the practices of Christian love are fundamental to the Catholic understanding of Christianity. That is why the local communities in which these things take place are likewise fundamental to Catholicism. Yet, for all its seemingly constant presence and influence, all is not well with this institution in the Church of the twenty-first century.

WHAT IS A PARISH?

Since the parish is, indeed, an institutional structure of the Roman Catholic Church, it is appropriate to begin—but only to begin—with a brief look at its canonical definition. In the canons on "Particular Churches," the Code of Canon Law describes the *diocese* as the "particular church" and, in canon 374, the *parish* as a portion (*portio*) of a diocese.[4] Since everything else in this title of the *Code* ("Particular Churches and the Authority Established in Them") pertains to the duties of bishops, it seems clear that this designation is meant primarily to call attention to parishes as one of the many essential responsibilities of a bishop toward his diocese, rather than chiefly to describe what a parish actually *is* in itself. That perspective is taken up in canon 515, under the heading, "The Internal Ordering of Particular Churches" (*CIC* 515).

> A parish is a certain community of the Christian faithful stably constituted in a particular church, whose pastoral care is entrusted to a [parish priest] as its proper [pastor], under the authority of the diocesan bishop.[5]

This canon, which opens a whole chapter on parishes and their ordained leadership, provides the lens for viewing the relationship that parishes establish within the Church between the Christian faithful and its hierarchical leadership. (This emphasis is original to the 1983 post–Vatican II revision of the *Code*; it takes up some of the focus of the Council's Dogmatic Constitution on the Church, *Lumen Gentium*, which is famous for placing its discussion of the Church as "the People of God" ahead of its description of the "Hierarchical Structure.") Parishioners are related to the whole membership of the Church as a *community* of the faithful. The parish priest is to them a *pastor*, expressing the care of Christ, and that of the whole Church, directly to this community. The bishop carries *authority* in this community because he shares *with* them, in Christ and by Christ's Spirit at work in the structures of the Church, the offices of sanctifying, teaching, and governing (Priest, Prophet, and King).

Through this legal lens we can thus glimpse the parish as a *pastoral* reality, organized toward the mutual nurturing of Christian faith and life, and the undertaking of the Church's mission to proclaim the reign of God. When, after Jesus's death and resurrection, the disciples began moving out in all directions from Jerusalem and Galilee,[6] they did not simply preach to large crowds and move on. They established relationships, communities whose new faith sustained them, and from which emerged the earliest forms of local Christian leadership. It was these communities that the Apostle Paul, from his earliest letter onward, referred to as "assemblies," using the same word (*ekklesia*) that comes to us in English as "church": "Paul, Silvanus, and Timothy, To the church of the Thessalonians in God the Father and the Lord Jesus Christ: Grace to you and peace" (1 Thess 1:1). Both parishes and dioceses in our modern sense are descended (by rather different routes) from these apostolic churches.[7]

By the end of the first century, as the writings later contained in the New Testament were being completed, the local communities were beginning to be described as *paroikos* ("sojourning"), an adjective applied in Greek versions of the Hebrew Scriptures to the patriarchs Abraham, Isaac, and Jacob, and to the children of Israel in Egypt. In the New Testament, this image helps to focus attention on the Christian community's longing for the return of Christ, its hope for the coming reign of God, and the need to endure rejection and suffering for Christ's name. All of this is clear in the First Letter of Peter, which uses the idea of "sojourn" in three distinct passages as it addresses communities that are clearly under great social pressure.[8] At around the same time, or perhaps slightly later, a letter to the Christians at Corinth from Clement of Rome (traditionally listed as the "fourth pope," from AD 88 to 99) refers in its opening address to both "the church of God which sojourns at Rome" and to "the church of God sojourning at Corinth."[9] It was a short step, taken over the next century, to begin referring to a local community itself as *paroikía*, a community of alien sojourners—a "parish."[10] The terminology and administrative arrangements continued to evolve, but these groups of Christian "sojourners" (or perhaps one might prefer "pilgrims") went on gathering. Their purpose was to receive the Spirit of Christ and to live in communion (*koinonia*) with the Lord, the apostles, the local pastors, and one another. Together, for nearly three struggling centuries before the Church became established as a legal institution, they embraced and passed along this new tradition, their Christian faith. In all the centuries since, albeit through a sometimes-bewildering maze of developments both local and Churchwide, parish communities have continued to be the way that most Catholic Christians first encounter the presence of the Church.

WHY PARISH?

Mortal Threats? "Parishes are dead! Why waste your time on them?" This was only the bluntest of several similar reactions that I received from some of my theological and pastoral colleagues responding to my interest in a theology of parish. While certainly not what I most hoped to hear, this attitude nonetheless taught me a great deal about important perspectives on the contemporary institution of parish. In the course of its constantly evolving history within the Church, the parish has faced crises and transformational moments many times. Today, after some centuries of relative stability, it again faces a plethora of challenges, seemingly everywhere, that sometimes seem to threaten the continuation of the institution altogether. The threats come from shifting demographics in many places, and new patterns of social interaction. They arise in the growth of cultural suspicion toward institutions in general, and in many places, particularly toward Western and religious institutions. Institutional responses to such attitudes are often inept, and varied spontaneous reactions give rise to incompatible strategies and prescriptions, which encourage greater divisions and shifts away from church life altogether. Thus, the challenges mount.

Typically, the approach of my skeptical colleagues would begin by discounting the notion of "parish as community" in a postmodern social context. On the one hand, it seems that perhaps the parish is becoming increasingly superfluous in this role. Today, there are many alternatives that also attract believers into more or less enduring face-to-face groups in which faith, loving relationships, and outreach can be sustained. Specialized chapels in retreat houses, hospitals, schools, and so forth, gather groups dedicated to the works they serve, who already have a shared context for their Christian service. Lay ecclesial movements such as the San Egidio communities, the Neo-Catechumenate, the Charismatic Renewal, and a host of others, are flourishing in their work of empowering and sustaining distinctive kinds of prayer, community life, and service. Many Church members also find their need for strong Christian relationships satisfied in more informal meetings for prayer, Bible study, and faith sharing, or as guests of welcoming congregations in other Christian communions, or simply by "praying on my own."

From a less positive perspective, these many options for fulfilling lives of faith, within or "nearby" the Church, exist within a larger context that currently includes great disruption in and distrust of official Church structures—not least the parishes themselves. The original 1917 Code of Canon Law discussed parishes from a thoroughgoing clerical perspective that was not unexpected in its day but that now quickly collides with suspicion of often-abused clerical authority and demands for more responsible roles for lay members of the Church. Notwithstanding what many consider the significant and very hopeful change of emphasis regarding "parish community" that has been noted in the 1983 Code, the law still quickly turns to clerical prerogatives, which in the final analysis give almost total control to the pastor and the bishop and too easily become "clerical*ism*." Processes followed in many cases of diocesan restructuring in recent decades (particularly in Europe and North America) have included the explicit reassertion of diocesan authority and ownership of parish infrastructure, often in direct opposition to significant elements of "the community."[11]

Doubt about the usefulness of parochial communities is also fueled by several well-known tendencies in parish life that seem particularly destructive within our current social situation. One could be called "localism" (or "parochialism," for that matter). This encourages the establishment of strong and intimate bonds among members of a community, but at the same time imbues them with a defensive insularity that narrows their vision and impedes their willingness to share either the spiritual or the material goods of the community. "Legalism," usually closely allied with the "clericalism" mentioned above, makes a community very strong in terms of its fulfillment of the Church's structural and procedural requirements, and therefore keenly aware of its universal dimensions. The accompanying rigidity, however, can rob such a parish of its witness to the empathy and mercy of Christ and gradually empty its activity of any relevance and larger purpose in the eyes of the vast majority of those who may be seeking a place to belong. Even some of the fullest and most active communities can wrestle with "integralism," the temptation to usurp control over all aspects of the faith and social lives of their members, failing to create space for and recognition of the functions and charisms of Catholic families, overlapping civic and societal memberships, and various "people of good will."

Such issues sharpen the awareness that in much of the Western world (at least prior to the COVID pandemic) attendance at formal worship and other parish events skews increasingly toward an aging, generally traditional, and often quite passive population. Observers and researchers point out that many of those who might be invited to turn this imbalance around—younger people with spiritual energies focused on building a better world—have simply not been interested in "going to church," and no amount of marketing of the "old product" is likely to change their minds. As the Pew Research Center confirmed regarding the United States in October 2019,

> The data shows a wide gap between older Americans (Baby Boomers and members of the Silent Generation) and Millennials in their levels of religious affiliation and attendance. More than eight-in-ten members of the Silent Generation (those born between 1928 and 1945) describe themselves as Christians (84%), as do three-quarters of Baby Boomers (76%). In stark contrast, only half of Millennials (49%) describe themselves as Christians; four-in-ten are religious "nones," and one-in-ten Millennials identify with non-Christian faiths. Only about one-in-three Millennials say they attend religious services at least once or twice a month....Indeed, there are as many Millennials who say they "never" attend religious services (22%) as there are who say they go at least once a week (22%).[12]

For the moment, although the downward trends are very clear, these figures still display the famously high level of American religious observance in comparison with Europe. In 2001, Scottish cultural historian Callum Brown argued that 80 percent of British citizens were effectively disassociated from the Church and concluded that "Britain is showing the world how religion as we have known it can die."[13]

Beyond Parish? With all this and more taken into consideration, a pessimistic appraisal of parishes on the part of some pastoral workers and theologians surely owes a lot to frustration with the struggles of the contemporary Church to nurture vibrant community institutions. The frustration, in turn, responds to a deeply held longing for the gospel to make a more marked difference in the world and in the practical lives of believers. Further, it is clear that Christians, too, have much to gain from listening more carefully to the world at large. Among some of my European colleagues, especially, these paths of thought have engendered great enthusiasm for more hopeful alternatives "beyond parish," such as the growing movement that in the Church of England has been called "Fresh Expressions."[14]

As the name perhaps implies, this movement operates "in the plural," without putting forward one preferred idea of how the local church of the future should be shaped. It does arise, however, from the shared conviction that local churches need to stop emphasizing the traditional model—the neighborhood center to which people come to experience and participate in "a certain community of the Christian faithful stably constituted in a particular church" (to carry the earlier quotation of canon 515.1 a bit further). Advocates of Fresh Expressions contend that available energy and resources should go instead into forms of ministry—particularly in urban areas—that rely on what is sometimes called "touch and go" contact with people in specific situations of contemporary life. Rather than focusing on drawing people to *its* space, the Church should be seeking ways to meet people in *their* space, everywhere from hospital wards to day care centers to the local pub. The goal would be to interact with whomever can be found in these spaces, in ways that suggest themes of Christian faith without soliciting a specific response or commitment.

Regarding this approach to local church, German Catholic pastoral theologian Matthias Sellmann, again taking as a point of departure the Church of England and Callum Brown's terminal prognosis for British Christianity, reports happily,

> Only a few years [after Brown's dire assessment], entire conferences in Germany and elsewhere are being dedicated to "fresh manifestations of church"; the German theologian Michael Herbst states that "the English patient" has improved a lot; English church leaders are reporting the founding of 2,000 new church congregations; and the entire semantic field of "pioneer ministry," "mission-shaped churches," "church for beginners," and "church planting" has become part and parcel of the vocabulary of new initiatives in innovative pastoral ministry, well beyond the confines of the English-speaking world.[15]

The "future-proof parish," writes Sellmann, "does not take itself as the point of reference for the secular space, but takes the secular space as a point of reference for itself."[16]

The argument, as well as the energy with which it is offered, is deeply impressive. Equally exciting are the ideas and successes of initiatives reported in conversation with these colleagues, discussed in materials they suggested, and observed in practice within the work of several communities to which they directed me. These outreaches display in concrete action two essential convictions of contemporary pastoral theology. The first is that the mission of the Church remains relevant in the world, despite new forms of indifference and opposition. The second is that Christians who listen carefully—even in the "secular" world—will always find the Spirit of God at work ahead of them in this mission. Despite the struggles of our times, there is still great grace and vitality given to the Church.

In the end, though, these new pastoral perspectives still leave some important questions, only heightened by the experiences of local communities during the COVID pandemic. Who is it that will continue to plan and offer these creative ways of "touching" our secular contemporaries as they "go" about their daily business? How and where will these initiators be nourished and sustained in *their* faith? What if some of the fruit that is borne by "touch and go" ministry takes the form of genuine interest and desire for *more*: to where will people be directed so that this desire can become "fruit that will last"? How does "informal encounter" become "Christian belonging"—*union* with the whole Body of Christ—for someone who is genuinely moved? Or is local Catholicism facing a future of professional "religion providers" who expect nothing in particular of their "customers"[17] (least of all, perhaps, a lasting commitment to a particular community of persons)? Such questions can provoke some genuine anxiety about the future of foundational Christian values—and at just the moment when human beings seem critically short of places to learn and practice commitment to one another's dignity and flourishing.

The Value of Parish. I conclude that the traditional parish still matters. It is the one structure of the institutional Church that has as its primary purpose the embodiment of the local, face-to-face, and day-to-day community of believers. As such, it witnesses to the Church's institutional commitment to some essential ecclesial components: opportunities, beyond the family and outside of vowed congregations of religious, for relationships that offer intimate sharing of faith; a living and mutual connection between clerical leadership and faithful lay Christians; possibilities of encounter between what is "local" and familiar, on the one hand, and what belongs to the vast diversity of the universal Church, on the other. All these features are essential because they animate the Body of Christ with sensitivity, flexibility, and genuine communion (see 1 Cor 12:12–31). The parish matters, then, not because it has an exclusive claim to these characteristics but as a practical *presence*, *witness*, and *intervention* in the "world at-large" that allows the *one*

Church to be seen in the *many* communities, and the *many* communities to be seen as *one* Church.

Vatican II's *Lumen Gentium* puts forward the basic principle:

> In these communities, though frequently small and poor, or living in the Diaspora, Christ is present, and in virtue of His presence there is brought together one, holy, catholic and apostolic Church. (*LG* 26)

In his apostolic exhortation *Evangelii Gaudium*, Pope Francis underscores the mission of these communities: "The Church which 'goes forth' is a community of missionary disciples who take the first step, who are involved and supportive, who bear fruit and rejoice."[18] In relation to other kinds of local expressions of faith—even when these come about in reaction to the failures of parishes, and when parishes clearly have much to learn from other pastoral practices—it is still the Church's institutional commitment to the *parish* that assures Catholics that the Church treasures the relationships and witness of face-to-face Christian community. As Pope St. John Paul II summed it up,

> The ecclesial community, while always having a universal dimension, finds its most immediate and visible expression in the *parish*. It is there that the Church is seen locally. In a certain sense it is the *Church living in the midst of the homes of her sons and daughters*.[19]

WHY THEOLOGY?

In a large American city, I was confronted with another challenge, equally blunt as the one regarding the focus on parish. "Why try to give us more theology?" a group of pastors and pastoral ministers demanded. "We are dealing with deeply dysfunctional parishes! We don't need *theology*; we need a *plan*!" This objection, too, raises some resonant questions. Can theologians really engage the gritty day-to-day problems of parish life? Are they even interested in the ways that the messy realities of people's pastoral need collide with the complex and unavoidable details of parish administration and church politics? After all, theologians often write to and for other theologians. Our books are not always easily read by, or even available to, many pastoral leaders and ordinary parishioners. Anyway, in the middle of a storm shouldn't we try to keep a boat from sinking before trying to analyze how well-constructed it was in the first place?

For years, there has been a lot of interest in books about parish ministry that describe "how we did it"—how a particular pastor or pastoral team helped parish ministry to flourish in what seemed like an impossible situation. Such works have had a great positive impact on "best practices" in parishes in North America and elsewhere. They have helped bring back a sense of liveliness that many parish ministers remember wistfully from the middle and later decades of the twentieth century. The renewed interest and optimism have been extremely important gifts in those places that have felt them. Although these approaches are not without theological foundations, their emphasis is on the practical. This suits especially the *American* temperament very well.[20]

Yet there is again something missing. There are innumerable parishes in which the leaders are so overwhelmed by day-to-day challenges—everything from the profound struggles of their parishioners' lives to literally keeping a roof on the parish church (or, just as likely these days, on *several* parish churches)—that the idea of trying to implement "one more program" of parish renewal is much more discouraging than empowering. There are places where some parishioners and leaders have gotten "fired up" about a particular approach (or, worse, about a series of promising approaches), but have quickly met opposition or indifference and the dissipation of their own enthusiasm. Even in parishes where a lot of good work seems to have led to positive results, the initiatives are, often enough, heavily dependent on the vision, talents, and energies of one or a few leaders. They struggle to survive a change of pastors or the retirement of a particularly able pastoral associate.

To a priest-theologian, what is missing often appears to be a community of parishioners with the twofold gift of knowing who they *are* and knowing that they are being *heard* by their leaders. These gifts, too, are apt to be approached primarily on a practical/procedural level. ("If only we could get the right structure for our parish council in place, then....") Yet, self-knowledge and attentive leadership *must* rest, for laity and clergy together, on a shared vision of their collective relationship with God in Christ, on mutual respect and mutual trust. Exploring and expressing these foundations, so that they can be truly accepted and shared, is the work of theology. Happily, this theological work does not and cannot belong exclusively to academic theologians! Each local community secures its foundation amid an ongoing conversation that asks, "Who are we as members of the Body of Christ, the people of God, the Catholic communion, the Church, here, in this place? How can we listen—to God, the larger Church, each other, the society around us? How can we come to know our mission more and more clearly and undertake it with greater commitment?" Growing confidence among the members of the local community that they themselves know how to respond to such questions can increase their ability to gain a hearing in the wider Church as well.

These general ideas of how theology can be the shared work of a parish community will be assumed in everything that follows in this book. By the same token, I have tried to make them the bedrock of my own method in the preparation and writing of the book itself. My intention has been to keep in mind an earlier time in the Church's history when theology often began with pastoral dialogue: Christian communities and their leaders reflecting on the real questions of their struggle to lead lives of faith in a challenging world. As we will see in chapter 2, the most crucial aspect of such an ongoing pastoral discussion is its continuing effort to receive every voice with respect and to face every reality squarely. It is in these ways that the community seeks both to hear and to proclaim the word of God.

WHY NOW?

The Church in the 21st Century. The Church is in crisis. What just a few years ago may have seemed an "edgy" proposition in need of a detailed defense is now virtually undisputed, even though how we got to this point and what we should do about it remain hotly contested matters. The seriousness of the situation is being oddly clarified by the rise of COVID-19. Pandemic conditions, as varied as they have been, have greatly affected the ordinary workings of parishes throughout the world. Interruption of routine participation by many members, inability of clergy to respond fully to the extraordinary pastoral need occasioned by the pandemic, uncertain financial futures, the new prominence of online "spiritual options," and the ever more obvious rifts within Catholic communities trying to cope are only some of the many effects that are being observed globally in the wake of the contagion.

All of this has been laid atop other issues that already constituted a critical situation. The more "familiar" problems have ostensibly clustered around the ongoing revelations of widespread sexual abuse of both children and adults by clerics of all ranks (as well as by lay church workers in various capacities) and the catastrophic loss of confidence that has followed. What may once have been read as an "ordinary moral failure" is now seen with much greater urgency, almost universally, in the face of its most disturbing characteristics. These include the targeting of some of the most vulnerable members of the Church by sexual predators in positions of power and trust. The scope of the problem across time and territory has been astounding, but scarcely less so than the failure of clerical leadership to recognize it and respond adequately. Most devastating of all has been the increasingly evident collusion of some bishops in hiding the truth, and even the direct participation in abuse by certain high-ranking clerics. For many, the Church's credibility as a moral authority has been utterly shattered, not just by the abuse itself, but by the pervading impression of a corrupt "men's club" deeply focused on its own prerogatives and pleasures and seemingly lacking in the most essential leadership traits.

The issue of sex abuse in the Church and its attendant abuses of power could hardly be more horrific. Yet these issues emerged just when the Church's attention most needed to remain on the growing number of signs that its position in the world is rapidly changing and calling for new ways of pursuing the gospel mission in the future. At the level of the Church's more traditional public presence, many parish buildings in Europe and North America are being shuttered, sold, or demolished as membership dwindles for reasons that range from the worldwide refugee crisis to internal economic migration to long-term cultural change. In other places, ostentatious building is in progress, sometimes indicating genuine growth and sometimes the presentation of a "brave face" on an increasingly desperate institutional reality.

It is hard to escape the conclusion that unease caused by these highly visible conditions of change has helped to sustain and strengthen a growing polarization and atmosphere of suspicion that began to appear as far back as the aftermath of the Second Vatican Council. Various factions within the Church have their own incompatible analyses of the new social and political conditions and attempt to implement their own mutually incompatible strategies for both internal renewal and external engagement with the secular world. Most strikingly, some of the most essential signs and supports of unity in the global Church have increasingly become battlegrounds. Prominent clerics seem ever less reluctant to contradict and undermine one another publicly, including in their attitude toward the current pope, endangering "in head and members" the unifying authority of the episcopal college. The sacraments, as well, the ritual backbone of Catholic unity, are increasingly employed as political weapons both internally and externally. Acrimonious debate among the bishops in 2021 about the appropriateness of offering Eucharist to the second Catholic elected to the U.S. presidency is one prominent example. In the United Kingdom, a somewhat similar spat arose at the same time over the Catholic marriage of twice-divorced Prime Minister Boris Johnson. Most prominently of all, Pope Francis unleashed a firestorm of denunciation and counterdenunciation in July 2021, when he issued new restrictions on the use of the "traditional Latin Mass,"[21] specifically citing concern about groups that refuse to recognize the validity of the post–Vatican II reform of the liturgy. Catholics readily wield standards of "orthodoxy" or of "faith and justice" against other Catholics in all these conflicts. In incidents that arise with seemingly increasing frequency, groups of lay parishioners are already refusing to receive the sacraments from priests who represent an opposing faction—usually by opting for a different parish or no parish at all. Amid increasing division and disruption, practical decisions with potentially long-term effects are reshaping the organizational, pastoral, liturgical, social, and political future of the Church.

Crisis in the Secular World. These problems and tensions have all become quite familiar to those who pay close attention to day-by-day developments in the Church. What is not as commonly noted is that the ecclesial crisis of leadership, credibility, and unity shares several significant characteristics with the widespread cultural and political crises that have been unfolding in the West, and even globally, over a similar span of time. Without attempting a detailed analysis of these wider crises, we can note some of their manifestations. The emergence of new authoritarian leaders in countries from the Philippines to Turkey to Brazil has been only the most ordinary of indicators of serious underlying global problems. Many observers have also found the crises embodied in the ongoing struggle of world leaders (and even refusal in some cases) to address together the increasingly destructive effects of climate change. Environmental problems have also been one factor in the worldwide refugee crisis. In turn, refugee issues have contributed to new political instability even in Western Europe and the United States. Part of this unrest has been due to the rise of nationalist parties and other populist political movements, such as the Brexit referendum and subsequent political chaos in the United Kingdom, or the rise of Donald Trump, the "border wall," and the reshaping of the Republican Party in the United States. (Both of these movements have also demonstrated, since their appearance in the mid-2010s, a staying power that belies attempts to pass them off as mere historical flukes.) Long-brewing American political, cultural, and racial tensions have now issued in a polarization that is shaping every political debate from election procedures to pandemic policy, which contributed significantly to racial clashes following a series of police killings of Black citizens in the summer of 2020, and that spawned an unprecedented attack on the U.S. Capitol building in January of 2021.

Increasingly, these fast-moving social and political events suggest recurring themes that do not seem so far removed from the internal crisis of the Church. Structural inequalities of power and wealth are foundational to the societies and organizations in question. Old patterns of racism, marginalization, and exclusion[22] join with the growing perceptions of powerlessness even among people once fairly content with their place in the established order. Discontent on many levels points toward a sense of alienation from a powerful elite who are seen to be the beneficiaries of these patterns of exclusion. In recent years we have been experiencing important initial results of this alienation. Widespread disinterest, skepticism, and distrust toward political structures and many other communal institutions has led to greater social isolation and political splintering. When "walking away" from institutions has been an option, it has been chosen by unprecedented numbers of people. A seemingly smaller number—certain Christians very much among them—have sought ways of escaping what is "impure" or "compromised" by forming small, closed communities that focus on a narrow "authentic" expression of a political, social, or ecclesial ideal.[23] Now, a further phase has been entered, exacerbated by the social disruption of the COVID-19 pandemic: when neither indifference nor isolation is possible either practically or psychologically, the disaffected (from many points of the political spectrum) turn toward more and more disruptive and violent action, more and more authoritarian styles of leadership, and, inevitably, increasingly destructive *reaction* to the violence of others.[24]

It may seem foolish indeed to be concerned about something as apparently inconsequential as parish church communities when democracy, political stability and peace, and the Earth itself may be on the brink of cataclysm. Yet this aligning of so many critical issues is creating a crossroads moment of immense significance for human history. Is it possible that this is precisely the right time to be concerned with exactly the sort of human community that a parish could come to exemplify? Could this be the moment for the Church to again recognize itself in small, intimate groups of people, bound together by shared faith, hope, and love? Could this be the time to reclaim the importance of local gatherings of believers, founded on a common relationship with Christ and committed to the dignity of every human person? Might the Church again hear in these communities a familiar call to all Christians: to follow our deep desire to live our relationship with Christ in the midst of the world, to muster the determination to live out the implications of this faith into our future, and to commit ourselves to the flourishing of the whole of creation? Aren't these the very gifts that the future of humanity most needs?[25]

CRISIS AS OPPORTUNITY, PARISH AS RESPONSE

What I am suggesting may seem an unlikely vision for the parish. We are, after all, used to thinking of the "parochial" as designating a narrow localism that defends its own borders and seems neither to seek nor to acknowledge the wider world, except in the formal connections to the larger Church that it takes for granted. Yet, it is my contention that the parish—carefully understood, both from its own roots and with reference to these contemporary "signs of the times"—can be, and in many instances already is, a vital part of a just and effective response from the Church to these critical circumstances. The parish can be a counterwitness to the cultural crises both within the Church itself and in the world at large.

Some of the parish's most essential characteristics—aspects that often get lost in the contemporary administrative role of parishes—are revealed in the root word *paroikía*, which I briefly examined earlier and to which I will return frequently in the coming chapters. This analysis provides a reminder that the parish was originally understood to be an identifiable community of persons with a particular spiritual significance, not primarily an organizational structure or territory. (Chapter 5 will, nonetheless, look carefully at the relationship of "parish" and "place.") To speak of the parish as a community is to invoke the essential Christian value of "communion" (*koinonia* in Greek: "what is held in common"), referring to the spiritual union that binds all the members together because each is in union with Christ, the head. As the Gospel of John demonstrates (especially 14:15–23), such a relationship with Christ also necessarily brings us into communion with the triune God. (This will be explored in chapter 4.) This chain of relationships suggests a vital role for the local community in maintaining the unity of the whole Church, as that unity was envisaged at Vatican II:

> Thus, the Church has been seen as "a people made one with the unity of the Father, the Son and the Holy Spirit."[26]
>
> ...In order that we might be unceasingly renewed in Him, He has shared with us His Spirit who, existing as one and the same being in the Head and in the members, gives life to, unifies and moves through the whole body.[27]

The roots of "parish" also remind us of the "sojourning" dimension of the local community. Rather than being settled in a permanent "spiritual home," members of the ancient Christian communities saw themselves as "pilgrims on the way." This quality precludes a strategy of defensive clinging to a static way of life or to an irreformable collection of rules or to an untranslatable way of telling their own story. Rather, these pilgrim communities—even while they hold fast to their goal and the identity it gives them—must for the sake of that very identity be dynamic, flexible, and missionary, open to every possibility of sharing the gospel in the changing contexts through which they pass. In *Evangelii Gaudium*, Pope Francis has said this:

> The parish is not an outdated institution; precisely because it possesses great flexibility, it can assume quite different contours depending on the openness and missionary creativity of the pastor and the community. (*EG* 28)

This characteristic flexibility creates space for many simultaneous variations on the structure and action of parish communities from one context to another. Such flexibility has helped local communities to be among the important drivers of growth at pivotal points in the Church's history. In them, the dynamic edge of the Christian encounter with the contemporary world has often been found. We need only to think of the value of witness and support in strong local communities during the earliest preaching of the gospel, or in its global presence to this day, or in times of severe persecution, from Rome in the third century to Nagasaki in the seventeenth to Krakow in the twentieth to Mosul in the twenty-first. The face-to-face encounter of Christian believers with each other and with the cultures of the world has depended on local communities, the subcommunities they contain, and the many other communities with which they overlap.

With these foundational ideals, and with its many forms and variations stretching back nearly the full two thousand years of the Church's existence, the parish's status as a basic institution within the worldwide Church gives it far more weight and potential than is often recognized.[28] Without insisting on the precise canonical form that (only since 1983) is described in canon 515, it can be said that the vast majority of Catholic Christians in nearly every age and place have been touched, and very often profoundly influenced, by local communities with the essential mission and function of the parish. This broad reach brings together "the *people*" (a term we will consider theologically in chapter 2) with essential elements of the Church's heritage (tradition, Scriptures, sacraments, stories, customs, etc.) and with its pastoral leadership (ordained priests and other Church professionals). As a canonical institution, the parish gathers all these relationships into communion with the universal Church, through the ministry of the bishops and an ongoing mutual exchange concretely promoted by many other works of the Church. (This complex of relationships will be considered further in chapter 6.) At its best, such a structure creates a space where all the members of the community can grow in understanding their mutual calling, discerning their particular contributions, and actively engaging in the mission of Christ. (The *mission* of the parish will be the focus of chapter 3.)

By reason of its location "in the midst" of the people, then, the parish is an essential element in the ongoing rebuilding of the Church's relationship with society. Both the longings and the hesitations common in contemporary life were of particular concern during the pivotal

Church renewal moment of the past century, the Second Vatican Council. By applying both the principle of responding to the times in which the Church exists (*aggiornamento*) and that of reexamining the roots of Catholic tradition and practice (*ressourcement*), the Council reflected in new ways upon the relationship between the Church and the world at large, and upon the role of the laity in the Church's mission. With these broad strokes, the Council set the terms for a reconsideration of the significance and potential of parish communities in our own time. Popes since Paul VI (1963–78) have worked to bring these insights into the practice of the Church, using the particular tools which their own cultures, studies, and experience have provided.

For his part, Pope Francis (elected 2013) has brought to this task the pastoral theological approach known as "theology of the people," which will be discussed more thoroughly in chapter 2. The intention is to begin "near to people," a phrase Francis has used often to describe his ideal for the Church.[29] This nearness is characteristic of a Church seeking to develop and deepen a familiarity with the cultures in which people actually live, work, pray, and attempt to lead their Christian lives. If it is genuine and generous, such familiarity with the whole "people of God" reveals much more than the well-known lives of those who are already comfortable and influential in society and in the Church. Rather, it leads these theologians to pay particular attention to the people who are often much less known, those who are on the margins away from comfort and influence, the poor and the socially rejected. Theology of the people begins to desire, as Pope Francis has said, "a church that goes out" to the margins (*EG* 20–24). What is more, this "going out"—already motivated by a desire to *listen* and so better to *proclaim*—begins to move the Church not only to teach, but also to learn. This mutuality uncovers a possibility that has always been the hope of Christians, but that many have presumed was lost during centuries of colonialism and empire: that the gospel of Christ not be imposed on its hearers, but rather heard, discovered, and embraced in the life of the people themselves. Implied, of course, is the rejection of structures of clerical domination and, in their place, the creation of genuine "missionary disciples" within the Church (*EG* 24).

As Pope Francis has made this theology the basis of his pontifical teaching, now is an opportune time to reconsider how local church communities might use it to learn to flourish in new ways. The Church can rediscover the parish as a community of missionary disciples, dynamic and attentive to the world within which it must bear witness to the gospel. In doing so, it can also find a powerful voice in response to the inequality, division, and fear in so much of contemporary society, and to the growing fascination with authoritarianism that these problems have engendered. Contributing to this project is the purpose of this book.

Chapter 2

THE PARISH AND A THEOLOGY OF THE PEOPLE

> Faith is called to be made real as an historical event within a people.[1]
>
> Lucio Gera (Argentinian theologian)

POPE FRANCIS'S PARISH

Padre Jorge Bergoglio, the future Pope Francis, was rector of the Jesuit Colegio Máximo de San José from 1980 to 1986, when it still housed the philosophy and theology faculties for Jesuits preparing for priesthood in Argentina. (The Colegio is located within the province of Buenos Aires, in the administrative district of San Miguel, about twenty miles from the city center.) As soon as he took up the position, Bergoglio "adopted" the adjacent parish of Patriarca San José (St. Joseph the Patriarch) and incorporated its activities into the work of training future priests. San José's original parish church—a traditional structure with seating for perhaps three hundred persons that stands within sight of the Colegio—had been completed only two years before.

While Bergoglio was rector, the students at the Colegio were deeply involved in the parish's outreach to the huge neighborhood it encompasses. The pastoral style they established can still be seen in the work of evangelization and social and material assistance at San José.[2] At the time of my visit there in August 2018, Pope Francis's connection with the parish was being commemorated with a large poster of the smiling, waving pope, proclaiming him "Our First Pastor." Signs of the Jesuit connection and themes from the Spiritual Exercises of St. Ignatius *(founder of the Jesuits) are everywhere in the church, including three separate quotations from the culminating exercise, the "Contemplation to Gain the Love of God": in the tower room set aside for the MEJ (Youth Eucharistic Movement), brightly painted murals include a portrait of Ignatius and the quotation "Love should be shown more in works than in words"; a spiral arrangement over the staircase displays the prayer "Take and Receive"; and a long banner hung between two pillars in the nave of the church reads "in all things to love and to serve."*[3] *Also on display in the church was a list of the "Characteristics of Jesuit Parishes," declaring that the parish should be a "community of communities" that have "faith in Jesus Christ and his Kingdom" and are "fraternal…in solidarity…missionary…liturgical." A flyer was also posted advertising a series of workshops in celebration of the fortieth anniversary of the Diocese of San Miguel (one of eleven associated with the Archdiocese of Buenos Aires), with these themes: "Always to choose encounter and fraternity"; "To learn from the piety of our people"; "To accompany the life of the people with a committed love," "To promote participation and co-responsibility in our communities."*[4]

Today, the canonical parish of Patriarca San José includes more than thirty thousand parishioners, encompassing a predominantly working-class population, with smaller groups of middle-class and long-term unemployed at either end of the socioeconomic spectrum. The main church, with an adjacent eight hundred-student parish school, is an important social center for the whole area. But the parish is also served by five capillas *(chapels)—some of them larger than the main church—in various other neighborhoods of the large parish territory. These are supervised by lay parishioners working closely with the pastor. Mass and other sacraments are offered frequently in these chapels, which are also used for various gatherings of parishioners praying, learning, celebrating, and working together. Additionally, at least two other "mission centers" serve as headquarters for parish organizations and projects that follow the preferred model of "the parish going to the people" and not the other way around—community kitchens, tutoring, legal counseling, justice advocacy, neighborhood fiestas, public evangelizing, and whatever else might be useful and possible. Another major manifestation of this approach is the annual "parish mission" conducted over four or five days by lay volunteers—mostly* los jóvenes *(older teens and young adults)—who spread out across all the neighborhoods and attempt to visit "every home in the parish."*[5] *Another banner on display in the main church seemed to celebrate this effort with its proclamation, "United in Christ we go out to meet the most needy."*

PATRIARCA SAN JOSÉ is by no means unique in its pastoral approaches among parishes in Buenos Aires. In another section of San Miguel, just a short bus ride away, I also visited Nuestra Señora del Perpetuo Socorro (Our Lady of Perpetual Help), where the pastor oversees as many as seventeen *capillas*. Earlier I had visited Parroquia San Juan Bosco in one of the *villas miseria* ("misery settlements" or shantytowns) closer to the urban center. There I met Padre Pepe Di Paola, well known for his work with crack addicts in another part of the city, which has gained him both high praise and death threats. The front of the small church building there is adorned with a huge mural of Padre Carlos Mugica, an advocate for the poor who was assassinated outside his church in another part of Buenos Aires in 1974. I also had the opportunity to speak with two auxiliary bishops of the archdiocese—Bishop Juan Carlos Ares and Bishop Gustavo Carrara—who worked closely with Archbishop Bergoglio and have been involved with urban pastoral initiatives ever since they became priests. In all these visits and conversations, the primary assumption was that the parish *is* the people, both those who "attend church" in the traditional sense as well as all those whom they encounter around the parish neighborhoods daily. The recurring pastoral themes included welcome, presence, and accompaniment of all these people in their varied struggles; broad participation of the people in all the works of the parish, especially its outreach beyond church walls; close listening, not only "to help" with material needs but most especially to *learn* from the ways in which others express their faith (or lack of it); action for charity and justice in whatever ways are possible.

Fr. Rafael Velasco ("Padre Rafa"), the Jesuit pastor who welcomed me to Patriarca San José, explained his conviction that the parish is the "real presence of the Church" and the *primera linea* (the "front line") of the Church's mission. As an embodiment of Pope Francis's call for *una iglesia en salida* ("a church going forth"), San José's ability to *recoger el universo*—to gather up the "whole universe" of human life within its sphere of influence—allows it to become a center of Catholic culture, particularly for *la base*, that is, the working class and poor at "the bottom of the heap," who also form "the foundation" of society. Those who make up *la base* have few other institutional connections to help them maintain those ties to the Catholic world that *los altos* ("the higher-ups"—those "at the top" of the social ladder) can take for granted.

A crystal-clear conviction joins these ideas about church and culture to the specific social and material issues that concern these parishes so deeply. The link was emphasized for me in a conversation with Padre Julio Merediz, who when I met him had been serving for decades as pastor of Nuestra Señora del Perpetuo Socorro. After listening to his long description of all the many services and programs offered by and for the people of his enormous parish, I asked how they had managed to function during the times of political repression in the 1970s and '80s. His answer put all the buildings and murals and activities into perspective: "We are a Christian community. Sometimes conditions are more favorable, sometimes less, but we carry on doing whatever we can for each other." These are words that could guide *any* parish, any local church community.

READING THE SIGNS OF THE TIMES

The fusion of pastoral action and theological reflection that is so evident in these experiences of community in Buenos Aires call to mind what we might consider the Church's warrant, issued by the Second Vatican Council, for the sort of theology the communities themselves must engage in:

> Inspired by no earthly ambition, the Church seeks but a solitary goal: to carry forward the work of Christ under the lead of the befriending Spirit. And Christ entered this world to give witness to the truth, to rescue and not to sit in judgment, to serve and not to be served. To carry out such a task, the Church has always had the duty of scrutinizing the signs of the times and of interpreting them in the light of the Gospel. (*GS* 3–4)

If the parish, the Church's institutional commitment to local Christian community, is truly the Church's "most immediate and visible expression" as Pope St. John Paul II claims,[6] then this work of the Church must also find "immediate and visible expression" in the local community. As trends in both pastoral studies and theology have underscored ever since the Council, discerning well these "signs of the times" requires careful attention to the ordinary lives of believers. In the "joys and hopes, griefs and anxieties...especially [of] those who are poor or in any way afflicted" (*GS* 1), crucial pathways for the Church's mission are revealed. In the lives of their sisters and brothers everywhere, Christians can see the light of the gospel reflected and can contemplate when and how to gather and mirror that light even more intensely. As much as Vatican II and John Paul II speak to the universal Church, they also direct local church communities toward this careful and deliberate reading of the signs of the times and of the shifting cultural paradigms they portend.[7]

In the years immediately following Vatican II, Argentinian theologians participated in the dynamic discussions that led up to the 1968 second plenary meeting of the Conference of Latin American Bishops (CELAM), held at Medellín, Colombia, which was intended as the continent's reception of the Council. Medellín has become iconic for producing truly revolutionizing documents on the Church's mission in Latin America, which both reflected and bolstered the pastoral-theological movement that became known as liberation theology. In Argentina, where the cultural and political context was in many ways distinct from countries such as Brazil, Mexico, Colombia, and Peru, Fr. Lucio Gera began describing "the People," carefully understood as an historical "event" of the Church, as a context for doing serious theology (a *locus theologicus*).[8] Fr. Rafael Tello began exploring the content, motivations, and implications of the deeply held spirituality of popular devotions in Argentina, referring to "the people's Christianity."[9] A meeting of Argentinian bishops and theologians at San Miguel in 1969, the year following CELAM's Medellín gathering, produced a declaration meant to be the Argentinian application of Medellín's approach to the Church's mission. This uniquely Argentine stream of post–Medellín theology went on to exert great influence over the whole Latin American church in the final documents of CELAM's third and fifth plenary meetings, at Puebla, Mexico, in 1979 and at Aparecida, Brazil, in 2007, and came to be called "the theology of the people" (abbreviated in what follows as "ToP") or, sometimes, "the theology of culture."[10]

THEOLOGY OF THE PEOPLE: LISTENING TO THE WHOLE CHURCH

The reference to culture serves to highlight one of the most crucial aspects of the concept of "the people." It also provides an important distinction between ToP and the literature of what might be called "classic" liberation theology (as articulated by theologians such as Gustavo Gutierrez of Peru or Jon Sobrino of El Salvador, and particularly prior to the end of the Cold War in 1991). Although their viewpoints are not mutually exclusive, the best-known liberation theology has been broadly focused on *economy* and *politics* rather than *culture.* ToP, for its part, takes culture as its point of departure, from which it is eventually able to comment on all the rest.[11] Culture is understood as the concrete embodiment of the judgments and values of a people, the thing that makes them distinct, "a way of acting and operating," as Rafael Tello explains. It is a concept that looks back to historical roots but also, "because it is social," involves the decisions and actions of individuals.[12]

The people are therefore the collective *agent* of culture and of its historical implications, by which they are shaped and which they themselves shape. The people engage in the human struggle to counter tendencies toward emptiness and death with a spirit of empowerment and life. They live and shape their culture with the values they hold, the choices they make, and the ways in which they change in response to the world around them. In all this, they also respond, whether knowingly or not, to the Spirit of God at work in the world. This conviction allows ToP to seek God's presence and guidance confidently by "thinking from the peripheries"—the edges of society, among the marginalized. This position is taken in deliberate contrast to constantly engaging in the sorts of "pastoral analysis" and "pastoral planning" that are done *for* (or, perhaps more cynically, "done *to*") those who are far from the seats of power in the Church and the world.

A people's day-to-day embodiment of its basic cultural values is not, of course, necessarily in coherence with the gospel. Most directly, all people are sinful and prone to making sinful choices. Also very important (but less frequently acknowledged) is that those choices are often distorted by the necessity of coping with or confronting great systemic injustice. Many of Pope Francis's writings and speeches challenge the morality of common assumptions in sociocultural, economic, and even ecclesial spheres.[13] The originators of ToP were not seeking to canonize any particular cultural vision nor to romanticize the poor, but were instead pressing toward a renewal that was subsequently described in CELAM's Aparecida document:

> The Church's ministry cannot ignore the historic context in which its members live. Its life takes place in very specific sociocultural contexts. These social and cultural transformations naturally represent new challenges to the Church in its mission of building the Kingdom of God. Hence the need, in fidelity to the Holy Spirit who leads it, for an ecclesial renewal that entails spiritual, pastoral, and also institutional reforms.[14]

The confidence placed in the work of the Holy Spirit through the lives of the people and particularly the poor and marginalized is not based on a desire to adopt any cultural norms uncritically, but rather on the invitation to carefully seek the marks of the Spirit's presence, and shape responses accordingly. This is done in the gospel conviction that God does not abandon his people. It is assured that this search, diligently and unstintingly pursued, will also reshape the Church, from its local to its universal manifestations. Tello is succinct on this point: "This needs to be taken very seriously, that not only does the faith influence the culture, but also the culture greatly and *decisively* influences Christian life."[15]

WHO ARE "THE PEOPLE," THOUGH?

Rafael Luciani, theology professor at Boston College, identifies three distinct uses of the term *the people* in the writings of Pope Francis (heavily influenced by theologians already cited here and a variety of other places).[16] There is a *social* sense ("the people" as the poor and marginalized), a cultural and political sense ("the people" as an entire *nation*), and a *spiritual* sense ("the people" as "the faithful"). For his own part, Francis leans very heavily (not surprisingly) on the spiritual sense while blending all three perspectives into one deeply moving explanation of "the people." It is a "mythical concept," he claims, "a particular story that makes a universal truth tangible and visible." This story draws "above all" on "a collective wisdom and memory."[17] "At the beginning of the story of every people," Francis writes, "is a quest for dignity and freedom, a history of solidarity and struggle."[18] He continues,

> The people is always the fruit of a synthesis, of an encounter, of a fusion of disparate elements that generates a whole which is greater than its parts. A people may have profound disagreements and differences, but they can walk together inspired by shared goals, and so create future....It shares experiences and hopes, and it hears the call of a common destiny.[19]

Francis goes so far as to say that "the people" is "a living reality" and "has a soul."[20] Ultimately, a people's awareness of its own dignity can only come from "God's love and closeness,"[21] not from its peculiar characteristics or any logical concepts. For this reason, a people "can really only be approached through intuition, by entering into its spirit, its heart, its history and traditions."[22]

The idea of "the people" has always, of course, figured heavily in the Church's understanding of itself (*ecclesiology*), based on the analogy between ancient Israel and the Church (i.e., those whose faith is in Jesus Christ). The First Letter of Peter, 2:9–10, to which the pope also refers,[23] alludes to at least five different passages in the Hebrew Bible:

> But you are a chosen race [cf. Isa 43:20–21], a royal priesthood, a holy nation [cf. Exod 19:6], God's own people [cf. Mal 3:17], in order that you may proclaim the mighty acts of him who called you out of darkness into his wonderful light.
>
> Once you were not a people
>   but now you are God's people;
> once you had not received mercy
>   but now you have received mercy [cf. Hos 1:9 and 2:25].

This perspective was revived by Vatican II in *Lumen Gentium* in which, after being first described as *mystery*, the Church is next presented as "The People of God" (*LG* 9–17). *Lumen Gentium* insists that "God...does not make [human beings] holy and save them merely as individuals," but rather has created "a people which acknowledges Him in truth and serves Him in holiness" (*LG* 9). The Council then goes on to discuss the call of the *entire* people of God to participation, by the work of the Holy Spirit, in Christ's threefold office of priest (holiness), prophet (justice and truth), and king (unity).[24] This notion of a Spirit-anointed people of God is the key concept Pope Francis has relied on in making his relentless call for a "synodal Church":

> A synodal Church is a Church which listens, which realizes that listening "is more than simply hearing." It is a mutual listening in which everyone has something to learn. The faithful people, the college of bishops, the Bishop of Rome: all listening to each other, and all listening to the Holy Spirit, the "Spirit of truth" (John 14:17), in order to know what he "says to the Churches" (Revelation 2:7).[25]

From this perspective, then, once again "the people" refers not merely to *recipients*—of the Church's mission, in this case—but to the *whole* Church as also the agents of that mission, those who collectively carry out God's will for his people. To understand itself in this way the Church must again rely on its trust that the Holy Spirit is at work within the faith that the whole people of God professes. This is the charism of *infallibility* (of which *papal* infallibility is but one manifestation) referred to in the Church's documents as "the sense of the faith" (*sensus fidei*).[26] The work that ToP has taken on is to emphasize the more hidden, but just as ancient, corollary to this doctrine, that to trust the Spirit's work in the Church is to seek it, lived out, in God's faithful people (*sensus fidelium*). This lived faith is what the most enduring doctrine and pastoral norms have always sought to articulate, although they can never thoroughly encompass or exhaust it. Clemens Sedmak, of King's College London, has written of this trust of the Spirit's work among the people from a distinctive point of view: Sedmak uses the term *epistemic mercy*, applying the basic ethical concept of mercy to questions of how and when the Church *learns* and comes to *know* something:

> Epistemic mercy is an aspect of the spiritual work of mercy of counseling and instructing, but also of the humility to accept counselling and instruction from unusual voices, especially people on the margins. Epistemic mercy is the willingness to allow the chaos of reality to shape one's thinking. It is an attitude that allows for transformative dialogue.[27]

Sedmak's mention of the marginalized brings us to a final crucial step in ToP's theological process, the highlighting of the "preferential option for the poor." There are always efforts to neutralize this challenging teaching with the suggestion that "the poor in spirit" (Matt 5:3) refers to everyone in one way or another (and therefore to no one in particular), or with a mistaken association of its more radical implications with Marxism and socialism (thereby making these implications suspect and even dismissible by many Christians).[28] Nonetheless, this doctrine is rooted in Scripture and presented in a variety of ways by modern popes as far back as Leo XIII.[29] Speaking in Bolivia, Pope Francis called this attitude the Church's "evangelical option for the poor, for the discarded, for the excluded," recalling that "the living expression of the new commandment of Jesus" requires Christians to "work for the integral development of the person, as well as for the care and protection of those who are most vulnerable."[30] This preference provides the ultimate key to understanding how "the people"—the whole people of God in any given place—can animate the Church's overall mission. Later, during a visit to Peru and Chile, Francis was even more challenging about the implications of welcoming the marginalized:

> The problem is not feeding the poor, or clothing the naked or visiting the sick, but rather recognizing that the poor, the naked, the sick, prisoners and the homeless have the dignity to sit at our table, to feel "at home" among us, to feel part of a family. This is the sign that the kingdom of heaven is in our midst. This is the sign of a Church wounded by sin, shown mercy by the Lord, and made prophetic by his call.[31]

POPE FRANCIS AND "MISSIONARY DISCIPLESHIP"

Since his election in 2013, Pope Francis has been introducing the world Church to theology of the people (without necessarily using the term) through seemingly every aspect of his pastoral, synod-oriented ministry. It is joked that one of the few things Cardinal Bergoglio brought with him for the "short visit" from Argentina to the Roman conclave that elected him pope was the Final Document from CELAM's Fifth General Conference at Aparecida, Brazil, in 2007. In his capacity as chair of the conference committee that was charged with preparing that substantive statement, Bergoglio had a great deal of influence over its content. The official text does, indeed, present in their original Latin American context many insights that have found ample expression in Francis's papal homilies, speeches, and documents, beginning with his first independently authored apostolic exhortation, *Evangelii Gaudium* (2013).

Particularly notable in the Aparecida document is its detailed presentation of the Church as a collaboration by the "Disciples and Missionaries of Christ"[32] with "the holy action of its Lord" (Aparecida 5) in the world. Though easily read as a traditional hierarchy, each level of this description of the Church features a reference "downward" toward those more usually seen as subordinates. The Blessed Virgin "has been very close to us, has taken us in, [and] cared for us and our labors," just as specific Latin American patrons "have preceded us as disciples and missionaries in the Lord's vineyard" (Aparecida 1, 3). The pope (Benedict XVI had been present to open the conference on May 13, 2007) is described as "Head of the College of Bishops" and the "rich magisterium" of the popes as having been "very present in our work" (Aparecida 2). The bishops themselves—gathered to give pastoral direction to this huge and crucially important region of the world Church—look to the faithful, especially "the multitude of pilgrims to the shrine from all of Brazil and other countries of the Americas, who edified and evangelized us" (Aparecida 3).

This way of imagining the Church and its work of evangelization sets the scene for the bishops' recognition of the ordinary lives and culture of the people as places for encountering God's revelation. Acknowledging that the "'Seeds of the Word' [were] present in the native cultures [during the initial evangelization of the Americas],"[33] they go on to write,

> We accept the entire reality of our continent as gift: the beauty and fertility of its lands, the richness of humanity expressed in the individuals, families, peoples, and cultures of the continent. (Aparecida 6)

Specifically Christian expressions of this richness are found both "in the mature faith of many of the baptized and in popular piety," which demonstrate a "consciousness of the dignity of the person, wisdom about life, passion for justice, hope against all hope, and the joy of living even under many difficult conditions that move the hearts of our peoples" (Aparecida 7). "What is required" of the Church, the bishops declare, "is confirming, renewing, and revitalizing the newness of the Gospel rooted in our history, out of a personal and community encounter with Jesus Christ that raises up disciples and missionaries" (Aparecida 11).

It is not difficult, certainly, to recognize the work of the bishops at Aparecida in Francis's priorities for his papacy. "How I would like a church that is poor and for the poor," he told an audience of journalists immediately after his election to the papacy.[34] In *Evangelii Gaudium* he specified this further, first with his now-famous image of evangelizers taking on "the smell of the sheep" (*EG* 24) and later in the exhortation with this call to mutual discipleship:

> All the baptized, whatever their position in the Church or their level of instruction in the faith, are agents of evangelization, and it would be insufficient to envisage a plan of evangelization to be carried out by professionals while the rest of the faithful would simply be passive recipients. The new evangelization calls for personal involvement on the part of each of the baptized.[35]

Francis goes on to use the example of popular piety and devotions to underscore the idea of "evangelization as inculturation." Quoting both Puebla and Aparecida, he reminds his readers that "a people continuously evangelizes itself" (*EG* 122). His complete trust in this principle is echoed, nearly seven years later, in his apostolic exhortation *Querida Amazonia*. There, in the context of one specific people—the people of the Amazon—Francis's "dreams" of human "dignity advanced," the preservation of "distinctive cultural riches" and "natural beauty," and the appearance of "new faces with Amazonian features" in the Church,[36] suggest criteria that can shape the first local steps toward a synodal Church within parish communities of missionary disciples.

PARISH CLOSURE: A COUNTEREXAMPLE

It may be useful at this point to pause and recall one of the most notorious examples (apart from the sex abuse scandal itself) of just how far away from "synodality" the pastoral practice of the Church regarding parishes has sometimes been. In the Archdiocese of Boston, in 2004—with huge liability payments looming as a result of the abuse scandal, the previous archbishop having resigned, and an unpopular interim replacement having just turned over the reins to a new archbishop—stunningly broad parish closures were announced. In the end, more than seventy parishes were shuttered or merged (and more have followed in less spectacular fashion), reducing the overall number by over one-fifth.[37] Community life in many of the remaining parishes was disrupted in significant and lasting ways by the need to "welcome in" significant numbers of parishioners displaced from other communities (most often undertaken without sufficient preparation of the "welcoming community" itself). Coming so close to the explosion of the scandal (which also first broke into public consciousness in Boston), this "parish reconfiguration process" was almost immediately linked in the popular imagination with the legal expenses incurred because of clerical mismanagement, dishonesty, and lack of accountability.

The preparation for this ecclesiastical earthquake had consisted of local meetings of usually hand-picked parishioners, professional staff, and clergy from clusters of parishes that had been defined by the staff at the archdiocesan chancery. Initially, those meetings were asked to consider two questions: First, if *one* parish in this cluster had to close, which one should it be? Second, if *two* parishes had to close, which ones should be chosen?[38] At this early stage of what has become a painfully familiar ritual across the United States and in other parts of the Western world, there was little knowledge among the people, and no discussion, about what "closure" of a parish would really mean. Especially since the parishes that would eventually be shuttered had not yet been determined, of course, very few of the ordinary parishioners (and not many of the professionals and clergy either) could imagine how *any* possible response might affect them and their communities. Predictably, therefore, these discussions often degenerated into embattled camps, everyone doing everything possible to keep their own parish off the "potential closure" list.

From the perspective of the people (including most parish clergy and professional staff), the conclusion of the process was also unpredictable. They were told that their input would be weighed by a central committee with representatives from all over the archdiocese. In addition to the local input, the committee would also apply something called a "sacramental index" that purported to be able to calculate a community's vitality by using, according to a preestablished and rather complex formula, recent figures for the numbers of people attending various services and receiving various sacraments. Many parishioners were deeply offended, though often not terribly surprised, to find that whatever they had argued for in the local meetings seemed to have had little impact on the ultimately approved closure list. The final blow to parishioners' confidence came in the way the decisions were conveyed to the whole archdiocese. On a single day—May 25, 2004—every parish in the archdiocese received a Fed Ex'd letter from the archbishop. That letter contained the decision of whether the parish would be closed (and if so, when), or merged with another (and if so, which other), or allowed to remain open as it was. The stories of the reactions of the hundreds of little gatherings of parishioners, clergy, and staff receiving the terrible (or confusing, or relieving) communiqué were fodder for local news organizations for months and years thereafter.[39]

One of the clusters in a large suburb of Boston had been composed of four parishes that were contiguous to one another, similar in some ways, but also quite distinct.[40] All four parishes (for which I will use pseudonyms) served stable middle-class communities in neighborhoods that were primarily residential. They had continued to function well even as many parishes of the archdiocese were beginning to encounter early signs of emerging difficulties. Attendance was not in serious decline, the surrounding neighborhoods remained vibrant, and whatever parish debt may have existed was manageable within the means of the regular contributors. Each parish had had a regular succession of pastors.

Their distinct characters arose from the ways in which the communities attempted to live their faith. St. Catherine's was a standard "full service" parish, with a church-rectory-school complex on a busy commercial road but also very close to the pleasant residential areas where parishioners lived. Parish life was marked by familiar patterns of Sunday Mass, various parish groups, religious education, sacramental preparation, annual reception of first holy communion and confirmation, and special events for fundraising and community building. The former parochial school was no longer functioning, and the building had been leased to a nonreligious private school, but this was not unusual among similar parishes in the archdiocese. The dedicated volunteers who kept the religious education programs going were very proud of the cooperation they had worked out with a larger parish nearby for a joint youth program that was getting good reviews among many of the teens from both parishes.

Another of the cluster parishes, St. Martha's, was like St. Catherine's in many ways, but had experienced a more serious dip in attendance at an earlier phase in its recent history. The pastor who was credited with "turning the parish around" had strongly emphasized a more progressive program of parish renewal, so that St. Martha's parishioners came to think of themselves as representatives of "the Vatican II Church." The community grew by attracting like-minded Catholics from nearby as well as from neighborhoods and towns outside the canonical boundaries of the parish. A similar spirit prevailed at Blessed Sacrament, a smaller member of the cluster that had embraced the idea of "parish covenant"[41] in the decade prior to the reconfiguration. Parishioners there had participated in a process that encouraged them to discern together the mission goals of the community and the clearly defined roles and responsibilities that each was able to fulfill. The active members had for some years been working together with the pastor in this way to build up and maintain a deeply engaged parish community. The last of the four parishes, St. Martin's, was a small congregation in an appropriately compact building tucked into a quiet neighborhood, but its dedicated membership of professionals and their families provided well for the traditional parish ministry that was offered there.

The story of what became of these parish communities when they entered the vortex of Boston's parish reconfiguration is longer and more complex than can be recounted here. It is by turns a tale of bureaucratic decision-making, stubborn refusal by many parishioners to accept the first results of the flawed process, dramatic protest, and reversal. In the end, though, it remains a story of functioning communities of faith dismantled and remade according to a process remote from the faithful people themselves, the institution taking the role of a kind of service provider to clients, which could one day withdraw that service and urge the clients to meet their needs elsewhere.

On the fateful day in 2004, it was announced that St. Catherine's and St. Martha's would be closed, and their parishioners would join Blessed Sacrament (in the case of St. Catherine's) and St. Martin's (in the case of St. Martha's). Some parishioners at St. Martha's, however, balked when it was discovered that one of the committee members was an influential parishioner at St. Martin's. Involved parishioners at St. Catherine's also began to speculate that, given the comparison of their physical facilities to those at Blessed Sacrament, the only explanation for the decision to close St. Catherine's was the superior value of the property. When it was rumored that the archdiocese would sell the whole parish complex to housing developers, a group of well-connected members went to work on the eventually successful passage of a zoning ordinance in the city council that prohibited development of multiunit housing on the property. In the meantime, just prior to what would have been the date of the final closing of the church, another group occupied the building and organized a 24/7 "vigil" inside that continued for several months, adopting tactics used in other parishes, some of which continued their occupations for over a decade.

The resistance put up by parishioners across the archdiocese against the reconfiguration decisions didn't ultimately alter the overall picture very much. Yet the archbishop was sufficiently embarrassed by the public demonstration of disunity that he appointed a new archdiocesan commission in October 2004 that reviewed the most highly contested closures and reversed a few of them.[42] In a rare victory for this type of protest, St. Catherine's was allowed to stay open. That change, though, shifted the archdiocesan calculus and caused a series of new decisions to be made. Blessed Sacrament was merged with St. Catherine's under one pastor. Ultimately, it was the Blessed Sacrament community that had to give up its building (which eventually become a parish for Korean Catholics) and its distinctive approach to parish engagement. St. Martha's also received a reprieve—their much larger church was designated to receive the parishioners of St. Martin's, instead of the other way around. But St. Martha's, whose parishioners had so prided themselves on "Vatican II worship," was also made the "receiving parish" for members of an uprooted community that favored the Tridentine Mass (the traditional Latin Mass, now called the "Extraordinary Form"). What was more, the pastor of the traditionalist group now became the pastor at St. Martha's, and the character of the parish made a ninety-degree turn.

There is no doubt that the Archdiocese of Boston was faced with almost unimaginably difficult circumstances in 2004. The disaster of the abuse scandals had hit just at the time when deteriorating infrastructure, dwindling numbers of priests, shrinking income, and aging congregations all started to become impossible to ignore. With the sudden death of Catholics' confidence in their own leadership, the Church's affairs could not possibly have continued as they had before. Strong leadership was necessary to make and execute crucial decisions. What makes this period remarkable as a counterexample of the synodal Church is not the tough choices that had to be made or the highly visible physical symbols of Church presence that had to be relinquished. Nor was it a case of universally incompetent or venal clerics in charge. Instead, the real scandal of this episode was that the culture of the Church still leaned so heavily toward deference to the clergy, and that so little concern was shown for the experience of the people, despite the lessons that many were beginning to draw from the way abusive priests had escaped real scrutiny for so long.

The decisions to quietly move abusers from one parish to another had taken no heed of the real and present danger to parish communities. In the same way, parish reconfiguration processes spared little concern initially for the depth of the disruptions that would occur in local communities. Even more crucially, the possibility had been ignored of learning from the experience and local cultures of those communities before making irreversible decisions from a "safe" distance. Most parishioners themselves did not yet realize the latent authority that they held as baptized and active members of the Body of Christ. Some woke up dramatically to fight hard for their communities during the reconfiguration but were successful in only a few instances out of hundreds. Most carried on seeking personal nourishment in a parish setting that was just a bit more unfamiliar than it had been before. Others set off in search of a "new spiritual home," either in another parish or outside of the Catholic community altogether. Many just quietly absented themselves from any public religious observance.

WHAT, THEN, IS A "PARISH OF THE PEOPLE"?

In describing a synodal Church, Pope Francis turns in a very different direction from this kind of institutionalized decision-making. He invites the whole body of believers to a new, more sustained, and more reverent look at the cultures that shape us as Catholic Christian peoples. As he said to a Latin American conference on religious life in August 2021,

> Let us not forget that a faith that is not inculturated is not authentic....Enter into the life of the people of faith; enter with respect for their customs, their traditions, seeking to carry out the mission of inculturating the faith and of evangelizing the culture. It is a pairing, to inculturate the faith and to evangelize the culture. Appreciate what the Holy Spirit has sown in the peoples, which is a gift for us as well.[43]

The pope's extensive use of the major themes of theology of the people in many statements of this sort demonstrate ToP's relevance (both when it is applied and when it is ignored) for the whole Church throughout the world. This relevance sustains the hope that attention to the concrete, face-to-face realities of Catholic's lives will guide local interpretation, application, and adaptation of the Church's tradition far into the future.

In concluding this chapter, I will sketch some of the implications of this hope for the life of the parish as a local church community. The point is neither legal nor sociological: I do not mean this discussion of various characteristics either as an immediate *prescription* for or an objective *description* of particular parish communities existing in the Church today. Rather, I offer brief concluding reflections upon a set of goals that we might extract from both the current conversation about ToP and the combined experience of parishes all over the world. Such ideals can provide a certain orientation for understanding the role and identity of the parish and for growing and developing its contributions to the mission of the universal Church.

A Community of Believers. As we have already seen, from the very beginning the local church community was not conceived merely as an ecclesiastical structure, but rather as a gathering of Christian believers, a *paroikía*, a community of "alien sojourners." As such, it was set apart and made distinct from the people around it by its faith, origins, values, and expectations—the very characteristics that ToP refers to as a people's *culture*. To this day, such a local community is also called "the Church living *in the midst*" of a larger people. This tension between being "set apart" and "living amid" (as we will see in greater detail in chapter 3) is not a contradiction but has been part of the very essence of Christian community since New Testament times. The *paroikía* is thus called to be both a model of the distinctiveness of Christian living and a community of proclamation rather than aloofness. In such a community, the love of God is lived and made known both to its members and to all of those in whose midst the parish exists as a community of *missionary disciples*. The work of building authentic Christian communal life unfolds within a network of persons, communities, authorities, and traditions that mutually influence one another. It is the ordinary process of human life, which can be relied on to the extent that Christians remain open to one another, to the living tradition of the Church, to surrounding communities, and to the Holy Spirit at work in all these sources of life. A parish of the people will consecrate its time to creating encounters that further this openness toward God, the Christian story, and the whole human community.

A Place for "Living Theology." It is because its mission is ongoing in a constantly changing world that a parish of the people cannot be satisfied with "fidelity" to some static way of preaching and interpreting the gospel. As noted in the previous chapter, Pope Francis writes that the parish has value to the universal Church today "precisely because it possesses great flexibility" and can draw on "the openness and missionary creativity of the pastor and the community" (*EG* 24). If the parish is the Church in their midst, the community's collective way of speaking and living the Church's faith ought to *grasp* and *challenge* its members and shape the message they share with the larger Church and offer to the world around them. In this way, theology—a way of "speaking about God"—comes to be recognized as an essential characteristic of parish life and far from being useless verbiage. The relationship of the two marks the transformation of both "parish" and "theology" into a "parish theology" that is available and understandable to the people. This theology is spoken, lived, and developed by them, even as it demands that they be pilgrims en route to the reign of God. Their theology is, all at once, their proclamation of that reign, their self-understanding as missionary disciples of Christ, and their dialogue about the ongoing struggle with the practical challenges of faith. A parish of the people will insist on its own ability and need to reflect upon, articulate, and share what they have come to know about Christ as he is embodied in their lives of faith together.

A Community that Reads the Signs of the Times. Attending to their own conversation about God allows the people to see that reverence toward the Church's *tradition* does not demand an intransigent tradition*alism* (i.e., an idolization of one particular set of expressions). Instead, tradition names the very process of carefully receiving, living, and passing on what the Spirit has given (*sensus fidei*) while also attentively heeding "the signs of the times" so as to grasp the practical meaning and application of the Spirit's continued work within their own particular circumstances (*sensus fidelium*).

To continue in this mission day to day, the parish must become a "community of communities" (*EG* 24), bringing smaller groups of shared prayer, reflection, and action together into the coordinated practice of the parish, and into communication and cooperation with the many overlapping communities within which the people live their lives.

In these mutual relationships, today's parish can be neither "subordinate" to the social world around it (degenerating into a sort of uncritical "chaplaincy" to some popular ideology), nor "dominant" (returning to clerical or colonial assumptions that can no longer be supported), nor "escapist" (becoming no more than a provider of opportunities for "personal spirituality" without communion or mission). With these principles in mind, the parish can seek to become a *point of contact* where the Christian identities of its members meet the realities of the secular world in which they must live.

None of this, of course, is possible if there is any systematic exclusion from this whole ongoing process of participation—either by intention or by neglect—of any category of person. The *whole* people must be heard within the church community, just as in the ongoing sharing of daily experience the faith of the whole Church must be present for the parish's evangelizing mission to be accomplished. That evangelization will grow from faith enlightening every aspect of human life, from Christ's presence found in the people and in the world, and from the building up of strength in the community to challenge what might obscure Christ's presence. Taken together, all these aspects form a continual interaction within the community of listening, self-emptying (*kenosis*, traditionally applied to Christ in passages such as Phil 2:5–11), and empowerment. This interaction, in turn, requires a mutual interchange between traditional "institutional agents" (the clergy and professionally trained lay ecclesial ministers) and those traditionally "without voice." In the parish of the people, they all become agents of each others' growth as they share their faith lives with one another and become increasingly accustomed to doing so.

A Community Shaped by the Poor. As a community of missionary disciples, a parish of the people would have to move beyond a traditional sense of "being charitable," in a concerted effort to see the world and the Church through new lenses provided by Christ. The Lord tells his disciples that the reign of God belongs to *the poor* (Luke 6:20), that the *meek* inherit the land (Matt 5:5), that "you also ought to wash one another's feet" (John 13:14), that "whoever wants to be first must be the last of all and *servant* of all" (Mark 9:35). Whether or not a specific kind of *material* poverty is the most pressing issue within the local context of a particular community, the call is for an attitude of humility and a strategy of accompaniment. Such an attitude will not fail to notice whoever is most likely to be left behind among those touched by the community's network of relationships.

It is in response to these teachings of Christ that specific Catholic doctrine on social justice has been articulated in papal documents since 1891. Emerging from a variety of attempts to condense the many relevant documents into a series of "Catholic Social Principles" is this list of four: *human dignity*, the *common good*, *solidarity*, and *subsidiarity*.[44] As well-established as the list has become, these basic principles remain revolutionary when taken with utter seriousness. Their potential impact on understanding the life and work of the parish community can hardly be over-estimated. Recognition of human dignity requires that the community both receive and hear *every* member and potential member—especially those already marginalized by the society at large, as well as those traditionally marginalized within the Church itself.[45] The principle of the common good requires the faithful to measure their much-vaunted Christian "love" and concern for "justice" according to the places occupied by the *weakest* in society. Solidarity defines a common ministry of *accompaniment* with these weak and marginalized persons. A local church community making efforts to define itself by its outreach, its listening, and its accompaniment is already an expression of the principle of subsidiarity. Going further, though, subsidiarity implies the community's recognition and claim of its own *particular authority* within the whole Church, the authority it bears by virtue of its authentic missionary discipleship marked also by its vibrant sacramental life.[46] In parishes of the people, opportunities would be created to move these social principles from vaguely relevant ideals to *constitutive* characteristics that produce concrete practices and dynamic dialogs.

The Pilgrim Church. In the United States as elsewhere, the traditional parish has often embodied the more general description of the Church as the "rock of faith." Particularly within immigrant communities, the parish has been seen as a steady and unmoving foothold in the world for those whose faith is being severely tried by the world's ways. Theology of the people, however, suggests emphasis of another traditional image, one that is also becoming more and more understandable and relevant amid the signs of our own time: the "pilgrim people," the "Church that goes out," the community of missionary disciples. A people "on the Way" gathers its strength from the faith that empowers the mission, and from the "reason for the hope"[47] that all followers of

Christ can share, speak, and live. The metaphor is beautifully developed in Psalm 84:5–7:

> Happy are those whose strength is in you,
>   in whose hearts are the highways to Zion.
> As they go through the valley of Baca,
>   they make it a place of springs....
> They go from strength to strength;
>   the God of gods will be seen in Zion.

The way of a pilgrim community is self-sustaining—not because the community is autonomous but because it is formed by and remains in the hands of God like all the rest of the Church. Yet, because it is a functioning, cooperating member of the Body of Christ, it may no longer be treated as the possession of some "higher" level of the Church. Pope Francis's desired "poor Church for the poor" could not try to *possess* its members, but rather to *empower* them. Within the Church renewed by this vision, the parish would no longer be a mere "administrative unit," and no longer "parochial" in that dreaded pejorative sense of "narrowly focused on its own local perspective." The parish of the people would be "on the move," not with social restlessness and the desire to "keep up" with the times, but rather with the power of the Spirit, accompanying one another and whomever they encounter as missionary disciples of Christ. This will require the same openness to both the need and the gift of those whom they accompany—the willingness to be transformed just as they seek to help others be transformed by the Spirit of God.

Chapter 3

THE PARISH AND THE MISSION OF THE CHURCH

How very good and pleasant it is
  when kindred live together in unity!...
For there, the LORD ordained his blessing,
  life forevermore.

Psalm 133

A COMMUNITY BROUGHT TOGETHER BY NECESSITY, WISDOM, AND CHARITY

Corpus Christi Parish[1] *is located in a small city on the edge of a major metropolitan area within the traditional Northeastern/Midwestern "powerhouse" of U.S. Catholicism. It has a particularly interesting history, of the sort that is becoming more familiar as parishes as much as 150 years old are closed, clustered, or merged in various ways. Before the 1990s, its territory had been served by up to six different parishes, founded between the 1840s and the early twentieth century. Originally, these parishes served Irish, German, and eastern European immigrant groups that arrived in the United States throughout that period. Changing demographics, material resources, and leadership led to a series of mergers from 1991 through the first decade of the twenty-first century, and gradually all six parishes were gathered into one. By that time, the great majority of Catholics in the area were recently arrived Latinx immigrants.*

Prior to the mergers, as the population had begun to change, one archdi-

ocesan priest had been given a city-wide assignment to work with these newly arrived Catholics to build a network of "small Christian communities," inspired by the comunidades de base[2] *still found in many areas of Latin America. The response was very enthusiastic, and considerable numbers of people began meeting for prayer and discussion in their homes as well as in meeting rooms of some of the parishes. Soon, these meetings quite naturally turned their attention to the serious material and social needs of some of their own members and others just arriving. A partnership emerged with one of the pastors who was then engaged in an early merger within the cluster. Some small efforts at assistance began to grow into much larger projects—legal aid and English classes for new immigrants, food pantries and clothing closets, parish participation in running an overnight shelter and, eventually, a shelter for abused women.*

In the meantime, the diminishing remnants of the original ethnic communities had gradually come to understand not only the social, cultural, and economic transitions their city had undergone, but also their parishes' new role amid all the changes. In the approximately eighteen years that it took for the whole merging process to be completed, multiple communities that might otherwise have been splintered and struggling for relevance were built, step by step, into a single new multifaceted community, set on the foundations of group identity, faith, and charity that both the old and new immigrants had brought with them. What it had taken was a lot of listening, dynamic and partnered leadership from both clergy and laity—work that was fueled by a determination not simply to provide for but to empower the people of the emerging Corpus Christi Parish. On one crucial day, a new church building—actually, a "campus" recently purchased from its original Protestant congregation—became the destination of two processions of parishioners, leaving behind their old parish buildings but carrying their treasured images and other symbols of their community identities. They converged on the new church and quickly made it a dynamic hub of parish activity. The older buildings, in the meantime, became a social service location and the first home of a Catholic high school for underserved students in the "cooperative education" model. Eventually, after the incorporation of yet another earlier community, the one merged parish retained three separate worship sites, one grade school, and several of the direct charitable services.

The story of Corpus Christi suggests a strong link between the vitality of a parish and its sense of calling. This link is not merely a matter of organization and function. At Corpus Christi, the crucial factors included a combination of forward-looking yet patient leadership, careful processes of listening to many voices, action on smaller goals leading to larger projects, and openness to an emerging vision. Overall, this parish benefitted from a deep and growing desire, on the part of many of its members and leaders, to be active and effective Christians. As Church of England pastor Fr. Bruce Saunders writes, "Whether [the parish system] lives or dies is not a structural matter: rather it depends on whether parishes can regain a sense of missionary purpose."[3]

IN CENTURIES PAST, Catholics in Europe and North America were accustomed to thinking of "mission" as something far away, strange, and heroic. In the twenty-first–century United States, at least, we have now grown used to seeing the word in much more mundane contexts. From the front pages of commercial websites to the lobbies of hospitals to the registration desks of hotels, every endeavor announces its "mission." For local communities of Christians today, however, much more is required. For Christians, the concept of mission needs to regain both its literal meaning—that of being *sent by* someone—and its *sacredness*. These encompass both the *urgency* of being compelled by the Spirit of God and the *reverence* owed to the divine purpose. To speak of the parish's *mission*, in short, needs to remind us of the first disciples of Jesus and of those very early Christians with whom they shared their message. From those who still, today, long to gather and to claim the Christian faith by their words and gestures, mission requires even more than being reminded of these origins. It demands that parishioners take up *as their own* that same reverence, that same urgency. Long before he became Pope Francis, Archbishop Jorge Bergoglio indicated all these connections in an address to teachers and students at Catholic secondary schools:

> Every encounter with Jesus makes us missionaries, because it founds us on stone [*Piedra*], not on the sand of ideologies....Our faith is revolutionary...[yet its] liberating potential comes not from ideologies but precisely from its contact with the holy.[4]

PARISH MISSION: "ROOTED AND GROUNDED IN LOVE"

The earliest generations of Christians had a deeply hope-filled vision for the people of God, despite the hardships they faced. A moving expression of that hope can be found in the Letter to the Ephesians (3:14–21), in the form of a prayer for the flourishing of the Church:

> For this reason I bow my knees before the Father, from whom every family in heaven and on earth takes its name. I pray that, according to the riches of his glory, he may grant that you may be strengthened in your inner being with power through his Spirit, and that Christ may dwell in your hearts through faith, as you are being rooted and grounded in love. I pray that you may have the power to comprehend, with all the saints, what is the breadth and length and height and depth, and to know the love of Christ that surpasses knowledge, so that you may be filled with all the fullness of God.
>
> Now to him who by the power at work within us is able to accomplish abundantly far more than all we can ask or imagine, to him be glory in the church and in Christ Jesus to all generations, forever and ever. Amen.

This blessing prayer claims that the community that receives this letter should bear God's name the way that a family bears its ancestral name. Further, because to bear God's name means also to bear the name of the risen Christ, they are to become the very *home* of Christ, and to act with the power and strength of Christ's living Spirit. In this trinitarian identity, they will be "rooted and grounded in love." We might say that God's love is to be the principle of both the Church's *growth* (the roots that nourish) and its *endurance* (the ground, the foundation, that holds steady). This love is the way the community will be able to join the entire Church and the heavenly host ("all the saints") in intimate knowledge of Christ's love and in being "filled with all the fullness of God." Through that relationship and the divine power within it, it is *God* who will "accomplish abundantly far more than all we can ask or imagine."

In some ways, the Letter to the Ephesians is an odd choice as source for a foundational text on parish mission. Scripture scholarship raises complex questions about the authorship, purpose, and intended audience of this letter. Most scholars agree that it was almost certainly *not* written directly by the Apostle Paul. There are further hesitations about whether it was indeed originally intended for the Christians at Ephesus, and some even wonder whether it was actually a "letter" at all. The use of the word *church* in this document goes well beyond the focus on individual local assemblies that we see in most of Paul's other letters. Here *church* seems to refer almost exclusively to the universal Body of believers. Despite the doubts of some, however, many scholars still take for granted that it was at least written to be read within local community settings (as was the Letter to the Colossians, with which it is strongly linked).[5] Those communities, moreover, were exhorted to *love*, in ways that bring the cosmic and eternal dimensions of the mission into view—just as the Apostle exhorted the communities addressed in each of his undisputed letters, albeit in strikingly down-to-earth ways.[6] In the end, the relevance to parish communities of this beautiful blessing rests most fully on the fact that the Letter to the Ephesians has been regarded—by all Christians for nearly two millennia—as Sacred Scripture. Its words are addressed to *all* Christian communities, and they help to connect these communities across space and time in fundamental ways. As "the Body of Christ" (see Eph 4:15–16), each community is the mission's *enfleshed reality* in its own time and place, and the prayer's potential is not restricted to its first hearers (whoever they were!), nor is it fully realized even to this day.

IMPLICATIONS OF THE MISSION

One of the virtues of the Ephesians text is that its broader vision allows us to see that the *mission*—what might be called the "business" of the Church—has as much to do with who Christians *are* (by God's grace) as with what they might *do* (by the power of that grace "at work within us").[7] This emphasis on the *character* of local Christian communities rather than their *function* is also carried by the ancient term *paroikía* discussed earlier.[8] The communities described as *paroikoi* in the New Testament contained or were directly connected to everything that the early Church was or struggled to become. They were not at all "stable" in the institutional sense; they had no templates for leadership and ministry other than the movement of the Holy Spirit and the teaching and example of the missionary apostles[9] who had founded them. Nonetheless, they were led in the sharing of word and sacrament by "the elders" (*presbyteroi*, from where we get the English word *priests*), assisted in their physical needs by members who would eventually be called deacons (*diakonoi*, servants), graced with prophets and healers, urged to live their ordinary first-century lives in visible faith and love.[10]

These early disciples became "alien sojourners" in their own home places—but even this way of naming themselves carried both the idea of "passing through" *and* the idea of being "the neighbors." They carried with them their languages and cultures, even as they distanced themselves from the usual worldly aspirations and beliefs of the societies from which they came. They had no idea how long they would need to organize their community life; they were awaiting "new heavens and a new earth" in the coming reign of God (see 2 Pet 3:13). They were communities with a shared identity that found stability not first in worldly *structure* or *status*, but in their *being* as the people of God. For twenty centuries, local church communities have in various ways kept asking, "Are we mostly *pilgrims*, with our eyes on our heavenly destination; or are we mostly *neighbors*, reaching out to *all* of God's beloved creation as we find it all around us? Or must we always be trying to be, more and more fully, *both* of these?"

From a modern administrative point of view, much of the "sojourning" dimension of this description might still suggest a kind of "accidental" and temporary structure, rather than something belonging to the essence of the Church.[11] On the other hand, given what has transpired over its long history, the parish might now be understood as having *become* an indispensable administrative structure. Once they had become the *parochiae* of the Latin-speaking world, a few centuries after Paul, parishes were erected (this word itself shows the significant shift in metaphor) as much with reference to their location and buildings as to their people. By then, the Church had been established as an integral part of the social and legal fabric, first of the Roman Empire and then of the complex feudal structures that succeeded the Empire in Western Europe. With that shift, the Christian people as such was taken more and more for granted in the parishes, rather than as the very reason for the parishes' existence. The need of the time was for order and control, and that function swallowed the original "pilgrim" character of the *paroikía*.[12]

In the story of these developments, we encounter some of the serious *tension* into which the Church as a whole, and its local communities in particular, have always been called: the tension within the Christian hope for the reign of God, so often described as "the *already* and the *not yet*." In looking at the alien sojourner from the two perspectives of the neighbor and of the pilgrim, we get a sense of how this tension is built into the mission to live "rooted and grounded" in the love of Christ.

Local Christian communities know the tug toward shallow congeniality with those around them, as well as the opposite temptation toward fearful isolation from what remains outside. Both threaten the strong, quiet evangelism recommended in 1 Peter 3:15–16: "Always be ready to make your defense to anyone who demands from you an accounting for the hope that is in you; yet do it with gentleness and reverence. Keep your conscience clear." The Church can no longer take for granted the recognition and privileges once given in large parts of the world by a surrounding society shaped by Christian ideals. Yet, for that very reason, the parish is poised to rediscover one of the most crucial aspects of its original character—its sense of being a missionary community, by the plain fact of its continued existence.

Yet, if the first focus is on *being*, if *doing* is seen primarily as an outflowing of what the community *is*, what could this call to "mission" mean, when it sounds so much like a *task* or *function*? At the dawn of the Second Vatican Council, Yves Congar, the great French Dominican theologian, contributed toward an answer. He imagined "a Church poor and servant-like," leading toward "a humanity in communion" that is unwilling to "destroy others in order to maintain our own lives," a Church following "the way of humble, loving service."[13] Shortly after he wrote these words, Vatican II's adoption of the "Pastoral Constitution on the Church in the Modern World" justified his insight. *Gaudium et Spes*—"Joy and Hope" (to which Congar himself devoted much time and effort), set the whole Church's *being* into the context of discipleship that embraces availability, service, and confident proclamation alike:

> It will be increasingly clear that the People of God and the human race in whose midst it lives render service to each other. Thus the mission of the Church will show its religious, and by that very fact, its supremely human character. (*GS* 11)

> Since they have an active role to play in the whole life of the Church, laymen are not only bound to penetrate the world with a Christian spirit, but are also called to be witnesses to Christ in all things in the midst of human society. (*GS* 43)

For Christians to engage so fully in the world in which we live—losing neither the urgency of the task nor the clarity of the authority that sends them—requires a connection to the Body of Christ that is just as clear and immediate as the mission it supports. Everything that the parish *does* thus flows from and is in service to what it *is*: its celebration of the sacraments that nourish its life of faith in Christ, its orientation to the reign of God that Christ brings about, and its reaching out in love and hope—as concretely and cooperatively as it can—to the world as it is here and now.

THE "ARK," THE "SERVICE STATION," AND THE "DYNAMIC COMMUNITY"

An old anniversary souvenir book from St. Joseph's Parish in Biddeford, Maine, gives this description of the parish's purpose, written in the French language of its immigrant founders, who came from Québec to New England in the 1850s and '60s:

> When we count fifty years of parish life, we count as many years of generous sacrifices for God and his Holy Church. The virtues of justice, of probity and order which make for honest citizens and happy people originate in the life of the parish. For it is the holy ark where pious traditions are conserved; it is the cornerstone of family life; it is the buttress assuring the solidity of world government.[14]

The image of the parish as an *ark* demonstrates the attitude of defensiveness toward the modern world that was already centuries old when these sentences were written. It is an understanding of parish that connects directly to the *apartness* of the "sojourner" aspect of the ancient ideal. In this quite typical case of a U.S. immigrant parish, the attitude was encouraged by decades of often bitter experience among Franco-Canadian Americans. Though they eventually flourished in their adopted city (and many others), they also endured treatment as second-class citizens, long-term relegation to menial jobs, and discrimination against their language even within the Catholic community (dominated at this time by earlier Irish immigrants). Given this context, the defensiveness of the ark metaphor is understandable. It is fascinating to note, however, that by this fiftieth anniversary, the perception of the parish's protective purpose had already become more complex. It continued to guard Franco-American parishioners from the Protestant Anglophone culture that they still regarded with great suspicion. (Hence the continued exclusive use of the French language; the adage *Qui perd la langue perd la foi*—"Who loses the [French] language loses the faith"—would remain popular for many more years to come.) Yet the centerpiece of this vision of the parish is the *civic good* that it brings to the entire society in which it is located.

By contrast, at its one-hundredth anniversary in the early 1970s, St. Joseph's was struggling to put a brave face on the end of an era, as were very many of its sister parishes around the United States. The French language was becoming more symbolic than practical for younger generations of parishioners. The parochial high school had just been closed. Renovations to the worship space had replaced marble and the high altar with wall-to-wall carpeting and an oak altar and ambo. What was just beginning to emerge was what has since often been called the "*service station* model." Parishes were exchanging their protective ark function for the feel of "quick stops" for social, sacramental, or spiritual "fill-ups" as parishioners rushed on with their busy lives in the world. In the United States, such communities, often without fully realizing it, have lived off the social capital[15] that was accumulated over decades by highly successful ark parishes that had remained carefully shielded from the outside world, very strong in their distinct identities, and protective of the tradition as handed on by the immigrants. Service station parishes often successfully served the evolving religious needs of communities made up mostly of younger generations of assimilating immigrant communities. By the turn of the twenty-first century, however, their propensity to dissipate a community's consciously Catholic quality had become better understood.[16]

At the same time, it also became obvious to many that a return to the days of closed, self-sufficient Catholic communities had become impossible, even if it were desirable. It is true that the use of what are canonically called "personal parishes," legally defined by their membership or purpose rather than by a territory, has been growing in the United States.[17] These, however, remain an often-controversial solution to local challenges and a tiny percentage of the overall number of communities. Much more common is the also-emerging phenomenon of the "shared parish,"[18] where two or more quite separate groups use the same church facilities and usually have the same official pastor but retain group identities that may be distinct culturally, linguistically, liturgically, or combinations of all these aspects and others. What may in the end make this approach more desirable from the point of view of parish mission is that the "sharing" itself challenges the insularity of the separate groups and the tendency among the "original parishioners" (in the United States, usually the descendants of earlier immigrants) to take the parish for granted. Instead, having to share in very practical ways requires discussion and cooperation and so at least points toward openness and discernment among parishioners, even when strong social forces pull in the opposite direction.

In place of both ark and service station models, many Roman Catholics and other Christians have been longing for a renewed approach to parish mission and so welcome such opportunities as the *shared* parish may present. The ark parish can only truly safeguard and protect its community's Christian character when that community is eventually sent out, like Noah's dove (see Gen 8:8–12), into the world. The very tradition that the ark protects must be presented to the transforming give-and-take of the living church community in both its internal and external relationships. The service station parishes have sometimes claimed this approach, but without sufficient reflection on the tolls that contemporary life exacts on communal faith. A better negotiation of the parish's place in the contemporary world could be called "the parish as *dynamic community*."[19] In this model, the parish seeks to remain attentive to God's love, to itself as a vital community, and also to the broad social contexts within which it is immersed. If the parish community remains "rooted and grounded in love" before all else, it will be able to draw on the best of both sides of its ancient identity as *paroikía*, being "neighbor" as well as "pilgrim."

The practical goal of this underlying vision is well expressed by Bruce Saunders as he presents an ideal for parishes in the Church of England:

> It is God's own commitment to relationship-building, to communion in all its many forms and faces, personal, political, social, spiritual, that is entrusted to the Church as its mission.[20]

It is the placing of this mission of "relationship-building" within the context of "God's own commitment"—the God who is "in Christ... reconciling the world to himself" (2 Cor 5:19)—that marks this vision of parish not only as *social*, but as firmly *evangelical.* Such a parish aspires to become a living proclamation of the gospel in the context of a local church community enmeshed in a genuine and vibrant network of relationships among its own members, a network that extends outward into all dimensions of the world around it, whether welcoming or resistant to the gospel. The need for discernment and flexibility in this situation is the point of the descriptor *dynamic* that names this model. As Greek Orthodox theologian John Zizioulas points out,

> During her historical existence, the Church strives to model herself on the pattern of the Kingdom, and should never cease to do so. But the achievement of full and perfect communion in history is a matter of constant struggle with the powers that threaten it. Any complacency concerning this struggle for communion can be destructive for the identity of the Church.[21]

The dynamic community model, rather than *removing* the inherent tension preserved in the term *paroikía*, seeks to "lean into" the tension. The mission to *be* communion, to live rooted and grounded in divine love, is a constantly developing call, a self-understanding that requires the close relationship of the community with the Spirit of God, who therefore binds together all of the members.

IN SEARCH OF WAYS TO LIVE THE MISSION

"Fresh Expressions of Church" in England. Naturally, the results of the dynamic community approach differ and are more or less satisfying depending on the cultural situation involved. In the Church of England, in which Bruce Saunders serves, the parish church has long been preserved as a symbol of a united community rooted in a particular place. The idea (more consciously held than is often true of a similar principle in Roman Catholicism) is that *all* residents of the territory are somehow "members" of its official parish and of the Church as a whole. While this description may seem to honor both the "fixed" and the "mobile" poles of the ancient ideal, many Anglicans now disagree. As noted previously, a new pastoral movement calling for "Fresh Expressions of Church"[22] has arisen in recent years, arguing that the traditional parish actually provides a loud proclamation of the immobility, segregation, lack of diversity—indeed, the *parochialism*—of the Church.

Some of the "fresh expressions" that the movement offers seem to let go of the parish model altogether, in favor of more mobile approaches with less implied commitment. Saunders and others, however, look more attentively for ways to bring that kind of accessibility back into relationship with a stable traditional parish. Their effort is to keep alive both the *communal* and the *evangelical* aspects of the mission. Both Corpus Christi parish, described at the beginning of this chapter, and Patriarca San José, presented in chapter 2, provide similar examples within Roman Catholicism of the social contexts of parishioners being allowed and encouraged to shape the evangelical mission of the parish.

German Initiatives after Parish Mergers. In the Diocese of Essen, in the Ruhr valley of northwestern Germany, a serious decline in both the Catholic population (with serious financial implications) and the number of priests serving parishes led to rather sudden and massive restructuring in the second decade of the twenty-first century. Over three hundred parishes were combined into only forty-two. One of the amalgamated parishes in the city of Bochum, for example, now comprises the territory, and most of the buildings, of seven former parishes, and has an overall membership of thirty-four thousand. (In Germany, such parishes are called, with a sort of grim humor, "XL" parishes.) This approach centralizes planning and financial decisions and facilitates cooperation and resource sharing among the various communities. However, it has also left many parishioners feeling bereft of their familiar churches and pastors and abandoned by the diocese. It is not surprising that opposition and resistance, both passive and open, arose almost immediately and have continued in various forms. Even after more than a decade, the diocesan reorganization seems to have created enormously heavy administrative burdens for both parish priests and their professional collaborators, while still failing to bring about a new vision for the continuation of the Church's mission at the local level in twenty-first–century German society.[23]

That very question of a renewed vision of parish and its mission, however, has generated some exemplary discussion, creative thinking, and experimentation toward expanding church outreach and enlivening participation in the years since the restructuring began. For example, some of the former parish churches that are no longer being used in the traditional way by the new XL parishes have found creative new uses—as centers for the arts or other civic activities (with a continuing nod to the Church's presence), or for more directly religious purposes such as centers for youth ministry. Some of the new parishes have had some success with adapting the concept of parish stewardship used in some American dioceses.

In 2012, members and students of the Catholic theological faculty at the state-funded Ruhr University at Bochum established the Zentrum für angewandte Pastoralforschung (Center for Applied Pastoral Research, advisedly nicknamed *ZAP*) to offer "support for all concrete plans that promote a better organized presence of Christianity in our society," with specific reference to "the widely discussed concept of 'local church development.'"[24] Working with dioceses all over Germany and in connection with the "Citychurch Project" network, the ZAP has been in the forefront of some of the efforts (similar to those of Fresh Expressions) to reach into sectors of city populations that are no longer affected at all by the life of traditional parish communities.

Pastoral Restructuring in Germany and France. A rather different social situation suggests another approach in a separate German diocese—Hildesheim, in heavily Lutheran Lower Saxony, where only about 5 or 6 percent of the people identify as Roman Catholics. There, the term *mission* has often had its more traditional ring, with a focus on evangelization and on maintaining the faith within the small Catholic community, nurturing it to become both more visible and more "livable," in the sense of its interaction with contemporary social realities.[25] Despite the perception that a diocese in such a situation "cannot spend too much time fussing with structure,"[26] great progress has been made with inspiration from two quite disparate sources. On the other side of the world, in certain parts of the Philippines, a variation on the "base communities" found in Latin America has flourished, with an emphasis on ongoing formation of community members to develop and support each other's faith and practice, in cooperation with ordained leaders (who are spread too thin for traditional parishes). Much closer to Hildesheim, the Archdiocese of Poitiers in France entered a different sort of restructuring project, involving community-level lay pastoral teams, just at the turn of the new century. News of the success of both these pastoral experiments was received with interest and initiative in the Diocese of Hildesheim. Overall, the effort there has been to find ways to encourage a sense of *ownership* and *participation in mission*, genuine stake-holding among those who might otherwise have considered themselves mere "ordinary parishioners."[27]

In the Poitiers example, the archdiocese began in the 1990s to restructure its local communities in large "pastoral sectors" rather than realigning the old parishes. The new sectors were each under priestly leadership and had their own finance and pastoral councils. However, urban neighborhoods and suburban and rural villages with enough engaged parishioners could still be acknowledged as functioning local church communities within the pastoral sectors. These small communities may or may not have formed around a previously built parish church; they could meet anywhere that was practical for them. What they needed was enough engagement from their members to form a carefully conceived lay "pastoral team," consisting of five officers with strict term limits: coordinator, treasurer, and leaders of worship, catechesis, and charitable outreach. Any self-organized community able to meet the requirement could apply to the overall sector to have their community formally recognized and their team commissioned by the archbishop.[28]

Pastoral Listening. Crucial to all such attempts to allow local church communities to effectively engage the Church's mission is the attitude of listening to which I have already referred frequently. Although it involves attentiveness to others both inside and around the community, and to the "signs of the times," it is specially shaped by its evangelical purpose. The goal of pastoral listening is never mere "information gathering"—even less of the sort that gives rise to gossip, rumors, and judgments—or "mission by survey," constantly "taking the pulse of the community," perhaps even in preference to responding to it. Rather, the goal is an ongoing prayerful encounter of the *people* of God with the *Spirit* of God who is in its midst. This encounter is the very definition of being rooted and grounded in love. Moreover, such an encounter is the foundation of habits of spiritual discernment that can confront defensive and fearful parochialism and turn it into the prayerful *agility* of the pilgrim, with the missionary goal always prioritized over the mere maintenance of custom.

Here again is the tension of the alien sojourner. On one end of an apparent spectrum lies dedication to the *unique value* of the gospel message—but also the temptation to turn protectively inward to the community that already accepts the message. On the other end lie attitudes that give the community freer access to "the world," but could also legitimately be seen as minimizing the *evangelical reason* for desiring that access. The contemporary mission requires the community to hold both ends in a delicate balance—both a respectful and attentive approach to fellow human beings (i.e., *genuine love* for them) and a deep commitment to and enthusiasm for the proclamation (i.e., genuine *surrender* to the gospel and *relationship* with Christ in the Spirit). Such a balance reveals some of the true depth of St. John Paul II's simple statement, in his apostolic exhortation *Christifideles Laici*, that "the parish is founded on a theological reality, because it is a *Eucharistic community*" (*CL* 26). The parish is the Church's primary venue for celebrating the sacrament and the permanent relationship between God and humanity that it embodies. For this reason, it is also one of the Church's most potent means of evangelization.

PARISH AS "LIVING THE GOSPEL"

"The parish is not principally a structure, a territory, or a building," John Paul II also insisted, "but rather, 'the family of God, a fellowship afire with a unifying spirit,' 'a familial and welcoming home,' the 'community of the faithful.'"[29] This way of speaking relies on the Church's understanding of salvation as the most basic human need, and of Christians as brothers and sisters of all humanity—the same idea invoked by Vatican II's *Gaudium et Spes*. Bringing these images together underscores a familiar hominess of "parish as neighbor" and marks its character for its own members *and* its surrounding community. As neighbor, it is simply the parish's nature to offer, as Bruce Saunders puts it, "ways of telling the God-story" and "opportunities for relationship"[30] to any and all who approach, to whatever intensity or degree of commitment one is able to respond.

Parishioners live "normal" lives, which are affirmed and supported by the relationships they form within the community, and by the works of the community at large. Their specifically Christian outreach may occur within family, friendships, or work relationships that reach far beyond the visible parish network, or in those situations that I have referred to as "touch and go" ministry. The emphasis throughout is on being "in the midst" of the social world in which the community is embedded. For his part, Pope Francis has been particularly eager for the whole Church to recall that this embeddedness remains at the service of the gospel, that parishioners are also "missionary disciples" (*EG* 120), that they are called to be "a Church which goes forth" (*EG* 19). Commenting on Francis's *Evangelii Gaudium* 25, Argentine bishop Enrique Seguí remarks, "Evangelization does not consist in administering pastoral programs, but in the living testimony of faith in Christ that is spread from person to person."[31]

In effect, even as it exercises its neighborly character by reaching beyond itself, the community is reminded that its members are equally alien sojourners, on their way to the fulness of the reign of God. Their outreach to others is about more than companionship in shared circumstances; it is an invitation to the shared journey. Here, the Church's recognition of salvation as a *gift from a loving God* is brought to the fore. The parish gathers, before all else, to worship this loving God, to seek *communion* with God, to find its fullness in being united to Christ as a eucharistic community. If this seems at first like a turning inward rather than a "going forth," a negation of the neighborliness of the first perspective, or the origin of the impulse toward "the ark," Saunders reminds us that parishioners are always to be the same "embedded Christians" we have been discussing:

> [The activity of the parish] is not only about teaching, but about supporting the missionary lives of the congregation with prayer, and making their work and the lives they lead outside church all part of the spiritual and sacramental offering of praise and thanksgiving to God.[32]

If this is to be the description of the parish, however, the *flexibility* of the institution that Pope Francis also highlights in *Evangelii Gaudium* needs to be taken seriously and carefully explored. Likewise, the *distinctiveness* that both arises from and serves that flexibility must be honored in the various types of evangelical ministry expected of and fostered by each parish. For example, some communities will be better situated for touch and go urban ministry, just as others will have the right circumstances to flourish as primary social hubs. At the same time, each parish will be called on to mirror the diversity—the *universality*—of the Church as a whole. Here, then, is yet another fundamental tension that resides not just within the overall Church—"the local and the universal"—but also within the parish community per se—"commonality and difference."

The notion of basing the parish's flexibility on the *personal experience* of the tension of commonality and difference is very attractive. The pastoral experiments in Hildesheim, mentioned above, those that inspired them from the Archdiocese of Poitiers and those comparable efforts such as *comunidades de base* in Latin America and their counterparts in the Philippines and many other places, show some of the ways in which individual gifts and talents can become foundational for a flexible parish. Yet, without structures of *unity*, communities of missionary disciples whose strength is in "going out" may perhaps have difficulty "finding their way back." This is where we encounter, as part of a parish's response to mission, the continuing relevance of the diocese and ordained ministry, as well as the concept of the parish as a community of communities, all of which will be discussed in upcoming chapters.

THE MISSION-ORIENTED PARISH

In the opening of *Querida Amazonia*, his apostolic exhortation following the tumultuous Synod on the Amazon in 2019, Pope Francis expressed a series of "dreams" for that local church that are really a specific articulation of the Church's mission everywhere:

> I dream of an Amazon region that fights for the rights of the poor, the original peoples and the least of our brothers and sisters, where their voices can be heard and their dignity advanced. I dream of an Amazon region that can preserve its distinctive cultural riches, where the beauty of our humanity shines forth in so many varied ways. I dream of an Amazon region that can jealously preserve its overwhelming natural beauty and the superabundant life teeming in its rivers and forests. I dream of Christian communities capable of generous commitment, incarnate in the Amazon region, and giving the Church new faces with Amazonian features.[33]

The pope's dream for *this* people returns us to the heart of theology of the people and its attention to the concrete reality of *each people* who encounter the gospel. It provides us with an opportunity to summarize and concretize the call to participation in the Church's mission that must shape the reality of parishes in the twenty-first century.

A Community of Believers Becoming Missionary Disciples. The members of the missionary parish will seek every opportunity to call each other to greater attention and commitment to their own community and to the larger community around them. As I will discuss in the next chapter, human community is not created "from nothing" by a parish church. Rather, as an essential and inevitable feature of the humanity that *God* creates, community is encountered and embraced by the parish. In this way, the *Christian* community may support human community more generally and contribute to developing it toward the reign of God.[34] This understanding of parish *community* opens into the understanding of parish *mission* that I have been presenting: it is conferred by the Spirit of Christ, not by the parish alone nor by the hierarchy. (This is *not* to suggest that the parish is beyond hierarchical authority but rather that mission, at this most foundational level, is integral to Christ's call to every Christian.) This mission is always some variation of being "rooted and grounded in love," shaped by the actual contexts of the community itself. It will point the parish community away from the kind of "belonging" that excludes instead of welcoming, maturing away from a central focus on issues such as iconic markers of parish identity or distinctive liturgical styles. The community will move instead toward discernment of where and how Christ is to be encountered and proclaimed in the world around it. Saunders speaks of this sort of maturing as the discovery of "a sense of purpose that is first theological [attending to who God is and calls humanity to be], then strategic."[35] Many parishes, he suggests, may find their most important connection to "the Church's mission task" in the *preparation*, the very process of *becoming* missionary disciples. "A Church which signs up to this understanding of itself will itself become generous and self-giving, not just 'friendly and welcoming' but pouring itself out in love."[36]

A Community Shaped by the Disempowered and the Poor. As essential as *culture* is to this whole approach to parish, the respectful listening that a local church community requires must be extended to everyone, so that the peripheries of the community are always being invited "into the midst," closer to the center of community life.[37] This can happen, of course, only when those already perceived as at the center look for and act on opportunities to move out toward the periphery. It is interesting to note from the example of Corpus Christi parish at the beginning of this chapter that new arrivals, and others who are thought of as "outsiders" by many parishioners, may well end up embracing the role of missionary disciples even more readily. They have the potential for building relationships without taking for granted a certain status for themselves, and they do not have so much at stake in "the way we've always done it." The recognition of people on the margins of the community (however long they may have been there) may signal the arrival of a true renewal in a parish community—just as the energy of the *original* parishes that became Corpus Christi was provided by waves of newly arrived immigrants a century or more ago.

A Community of Prayer, Sacrament, and Shared Faith. Missionary disciples steeped in the urgency and sacredness of their task are trained to listen—both formally (as the community develops its educational capabilities) and by the very process of becoming disciples, deepening their prayer, and being sent. They learn to listen to the living word of God, to its articulation guided by the Holy Spirit in the process of the Church's tradition, and to the Spirit alive in each other and continually nourished in the community's sacramental life. In the context of a "parish of the people," these disciples are also formed as people who *are listened to*, by both laity and clergy, in the context of community discernment and shared Christian life. This mutual listening fosters the *widening* of the horizon and the concerns of the parishioners already assumed by the call to welcome the marginalized. In this way the traditional shared life of prayer and sacraments continues as in every parish, yet now lifts the community out of any defensive "trenches" it may be tempted to dig, and sends its people *out*, toward the rest of the world. As Saunders puts it,

> The Church is called not merely to be a signpost towards some far-distant fulfilment of God's reconciling purpose. Through the mystery of the Church's sacramental now-and-not-yet, here-and-hereafter nature, we are also called to be the here and now household of God.[38]

A Community of Deepening Reflection and Discernment. This experience of *widening* the context and meaning of the parish's shared spiritual life can also be an invitation to *deepening* the reflection—the personal and communal "dwelling" in the insights and experiences to which prayer leads. Greater depth aims at ensuring that the parish's contribution to the "Church that goes forth" is not naïve, irrelevant, or counterproductive. A community of missionary disciples is always coming to understand the faith and practices that bind its members together, despite their diversity. From that vantage point, the community becomes ever more sensitive to the physical, social, and spiritual needs of *all* its members and their families. That sensitivity then returns the community to the *widening* just described, putting it in touch with the networks of friends, neighbors, and systems that shape its members lives and that always invite deeper attention, more alert accompaniment.

A Sojourning Community. So, the missionary community continues its sojourning, its pilgrimage. It encounters and carefully makes a series of choices to *let go* of old "anchors" (often things such as particular buildings, vestiges of once-dominant languages, and so forth) that were once important responses to "the times" but have more recently been functioning as excuses *not* to "move on." Such "letting go," though it may be *ordered* by exigencies out of a community's control, needs to be done with the greatest possible sensitivity. Even in our example of Corpus Christi parish, material needs, resources, and politics have continued to shape this community. Its mission now is understood, by its leadership and many of its members, in a less "temporal" mode than it was a few years ago, yet the values that led to the establishment of the social services continue to motivate those who have been touched and in turn have touched others.

Proclaiming the "Good News." The New Testament preserves a variety of ways of expressing what the gospel, the good news, actually *is*. Its central feature, though, is always *the love of God demonstrated in the resurrection of Jesus from the dead*, and the call to us to share in that relationship of love here and now as well as eternally. It should be clear at this point that the concepts of mission and proclamation cannot be understood to suggest the "replacement" of one community's cultural values and authorities for those of another community. The Christian community proclaims Christ's love authoritatively by living it authentically, and it can only do this by transforming its *own* culture through its incorporation of the Christian story. It is an unending process that, fully embraced, rules out racial hatred and other bigotry and rejects ideologies and practices of domination on principle, and insists that every Christian community by right has its own space for authentic development. Proclamation of the gospel is most believably made amid the attitudes and deeds that characterize a parish community and give credibility to its preaching.

In many of the parish stories and examples I have been drawing on, such proclamation is heard in the life-amid-struggle that local communities lead: the welcome and provision of material and social needs to recent immigrants; the solid foundation needed by those unsure of a new identity or seeking to build on a very old one; signs of hope and life in the midst of social decline; suggestions of purpose in a faceless urban landscape. Since the beginning of the Church's history, the Spirit of God has been manifested and proclaimed both silently and in loud witness by face-to-face communities that have provided spiritual companionship for alien sojourners amid the fears and challenges of life. In a time of complex crises such as humanity is experiencing in the twenty-first century, parish communities are in critical need of reexamining and understanding their mission. They must find the models, old and new, that will help them to *live toward justice*: to discover and live within the mind and heart of God, once again "rooted and grounded in love."

Chapter 4

THE PARISH AS COMMUNITY

If then there is any encouragement in Christ, any consolation from love, any sharing in the Spirit, any compassion and sympathy, make my joy complete: be of the same mind, having the same love, being in full accord and of one mind. Do nothing from selfish ambition or conceit, but in humility regard others as better than yourselves. Let each of you look not to your own interests, but to the interests of others. Let the same mind be in you that was in Christ Jesus.

St. Paul to the Philippians (2:1–5)

THE "WESTERN MISSION"

West Wyalong, Australia—a town of about three thousand people in the middle of a vast, arid plain—is the service hub for a scattering of tiny farming communities spread over thousands of square kilometers in a remote area of New South Wales, about five hundred kilometers from Sydney. In May of 2009, I had the opportunity to assist the pastor of St. Mary's Parish there for about a month. Although several of the small villages also had parish churches, the Archdiocese of Canberra and Goulburn (headquartered about three hundred kilometers away) did not have enough priests to send resident pastors to all of them. The whole territory was participating in an experimental pastoral arrangement that involved one parish priest serving multiple canonically separate parishes. On alternate Sundays, in addition to his schedule at his "home parish" of St. Mary's, he would drive circuits of about 250 and 350 kilometers, respectively, to preside at Mass in three or four locations each week. Various special sacramental services or social functions might call him back to one or another of the small churches during the week as well. At the time I visited, the experiment was called "the Western Mission" (referring to its position relative to the whole archdiocese). Later, when the experiment was ended, the group of parishes was reorganized yet again into a deanery (a standard administrative unit within a diocese).

On a day-to-day basis, these little church communities were held together by the efforts of their most energetic parishioners, in some cases with the guidance of a religious sister as resident pastoral associate. The parish life sustained in this way was remarkable for embracing a full generational spectrum, struggling on to keep religious education and sacramental preparation going, and providing celebrations, reflective gatherings, companionship, and a lot of personal and family support within a harsh natural and social environment. All this activity was understood—by Catholics and non-Catholics alike—as truly vital "glue" for the little villages where the churches stood. The long-suffering, emotionally controlled, salt-of-the-earth farmers and their families, regardless of what church they belonged to, all shared both the joys and the burdens of their agricultural lifestyle. In that part of Australia, the recurrence of drought is a near-constant concern; planting is generally done using seed drills without plowing, to preserve what little moisture there is in the soil. As is so common in agricultural economies all over the capitalist world, the market forces the owners of small farms into selloffs whenever precarious conditions get a little worse. Consolidations of family farms follow, and agricultural conglomerates look for bargains. The younger generations feel the pull of faraway cities as they plan their futures, and the most desperate situations have fueled a rise in the rate of suicide.[1] Here, the importance of community support has less to do with material poverty and much more to do with the growing threat of social isolation. Amid a palpable anxiety about the future of these communities, Catholic parishes were one important part of a proud but fragile system.

Beyond their individual villages, the parishes contributed to a network of social institutions that connected these scattered people. Parishioners in the more outlying communities felt a bond to the larger parish, St. Mary's, in West Wyalong. This was in part because of their own familiarity with the shire town that they needed to visit for shopping, business, and recreation, but also because their pastor, whom all the communities shared, was in residence there. St. Mary's fulfilled its social role in town not only with the expected sacramental, instructional, and celebratory gatherings, but also by sponsoring and giving pastoral support to a well-respected Catholic primary school that drew students and faculty from some of the nearer towns. St. Mary's War Memorial School still describes itself as a place where "students are given the opportunity to develop Christian values by firstly knowing that they are loved by God and others and then following Jesus Christ's example of loving others."[2] In 2009, there was good evidence that this description was being sent into a receptive milieu. That receptivity was on display during Eastertime, on large banners suspended across the main street of West Wyalong proclaiming, "Jesus Is Risen!"

WHAT IS A "CHRISTIAN COMMUNITY"?

THE IDEA OF "local church community" has been assumed throughout this book so far, given the roots of *paroikía* in the idea of a "household," and the canonical definition of *parish* as a "certain community of the Christian faithful." But what really *is* a Christian community, and what is its relationship to the institutional structure of a parish?

To answer the question, the description of these remote but interlinked Australian parishes needs to be reflected upon together with that of the huge urban parishes of Buenos Aires described in chapter 2. In light of these examples and the opposite extremes they seem to mark, it is appropriate to begin a discussion of the parish and community by recalling the Christian faith's reliance on *incarnation* as a basic principle. This, like the very existence of Christian community, has been assumed throughout this text. Not only do Christians believe that God "took flesh" in Jesus Christ, but that by the work of the Holy Spirit, God remains incarnate among us, in the sacramental community that is the Church. This means that Christ is present in every moment of daily life for those who are "members of Christ's body." Local Christian community is a face-to-face living out of that conviction. But this firm belief that Christ enters into human community in the incarnation requires a crucial nuance in the common idea of "parish as community," which was already underscored in the discussion of parish and mission in chapter 3. The nuance is this: the existence of the human community in a given place, with its distinctive shape and purposes, with its particular "joys, hopes, griefs and anxieties" (*LG* 1)—in other words, its *culture—precedes* the foundation of the *parish* community in that same place. This larger human community provides the context for the parish even where there are numerous and serious points of tension between "secular" and "sacred" understandings of the world. Inevitably, the local Christian community is formed from the real flesh-and-blood human beings who become its members, with all their personal and communal stories and ties and commitments.

The ambiguity involved here (Where does human community end and Christian community begin? Does such a distinction even make sense?) is proper to the relationship between the *host* community and the *alien sojourner* in the central concept of *paroikía*. The same ambiguity also underlies the other tensions that we have been encountering—"sojourner" versus "neighbor," "gospel" versus "culture," "local" versus "universal," "commonality" versus "diversity." In each instance, an element of the distinctive Christian character of the parish is apparently at odds with a reality that seems to call the church community "out of itself." Yet, the severing of the community's relationship with these realities is already unimaginable. A striking example is found in the letters of St. Paul, as he tries to explain to the Christians at Corinth his policy regarding what is still called "shunning" in some Christian traditions, and what came to be known as "excommunication" among others (including Catholicism):

> I wrote you in my letter not to associate with sexually immoral persons—not at all meaning the immoral of this world, or the greedy and robbers, or idolaters, since you would then need to go out of the world. (1 Cor 5:9–10)

Local communities are like the Church as a whole, which has always understood that it retains both a kind of relationship with and responsibility and accountability toward even those whose place in the body of believers is somehow compromised. Embedded in the human community, parishes cannot simply "opt out" of the cultures that surround them, regardless of the peculiar sins of those cultures or the difficult social circumstances that stretch or threaten to break the parish's structures and functions.

As clear, inevitable, and deeply relevant as this human bond is, and basic to everything else that builds upon it, the understanding of community that is most *specific* to the parish as a Christian community is, on the other hand, a profoundly theological one. It begins in the series of interrelationships that Jesus sets before the apostles in the Last Supper Discourses in the Gospel of John, by which he invites them into the very bond that unites the Son with the Father: "On that day you will know that I am in my Father, and you in me, and I in you" (John 14:20). But this is not merely as a future pledge; the bond with Christ is given to the community of disciples here and now: "I will not leave you orphaned; I am coming to you. In a little while the world will no longer see me, but you will see me; because I live, you also will live" (John 14:18–19). The presence of Christ's life within and among his disciples in this world is what will eventually allow the Church to recognize and name the Holy Trinity, for Jesus says to them,

> I will ask the Father, and he will give you another Advocate, to be with you forever. This is the Spirit of truth, whom the world cannot receive, because it neither sees him nor knows him. You know him, because he abides with you, and he will be in you. (John 14:16–17)

This divine community has already entered our discussion of parish through the Greek word *koinonia*, "that which is held in common" (introduced in chapter 1). In its Christian sense, *koinonia* (*communio* in Latin) is integral to evangelization, the proclamation of the good news, in that it speaks first of the communion that Christ has with the Father, then of his sharing that profound relationship with humanity, and finally of the communion that Christians enjoy with one another through their bond in Christ. As Orthodox theologian John Zizioulas reminds us,

> *Koinonia* derives not from sociological experience, nor from ethics, but from *faith*. We are not called to *koinonia* because it is "good" for us and for the Church, but because we believe in a God who is in His very being *Koinonia*.[3]

This *is* the gospel—God with us in Christ—and so *koinonia* is also integral to the mission that was discussed in the previous chapter. Recall that the most basic approach to this mission is not through what a parish "accomplishes" so much as by what it *is*—a specific embodiment of the "family of God," living "rooted and grounded in love." This is why the parish community's proclamation of this identity in its celebration of the sacraments, and especially the Eucharist, is so central both to what it is *and* to what it does.

Yet, the full effect of this sacramental proclamation has not yet been embraced until the community begins to follow where that proclamation leads. As it emerged in the discussion of mission, this leading moves in two paradoxically opposite directions: inward, toward greater and stronger intimacy with Christ and therefore, necessarily, toward stronger bonds among all the members; and outward, toward more robust, courageous, and empathic encounters with the world at large. These directions do not present themselves as tasks, but rather as the dynamic presence of the Holy Spirit that moves within Christian *koinonia*—whether it shows itself in energetic enthusiasm for reaching out into the world or in the depths of heartfelt commitment to Christ within the community. This presence and what it enables or empowers is far more than *one* community (particularly as understood in the ordinary contemporary uses of the word) can contain. It is beyond any one parish to *be koinonia*, but it is entirely appropriate for the community to aspire to be its humble *icon*—a sacred image, a "sacramental" in traditional Catholic terminology, that guides those who encounter it toward a fuller embrace of genuine Christian communion.[4]

Zizioulas understands that the *fullness of koinonia* is found only in *God's own self*. This full revelation of communion relies on the intertwining of the roles of the three Divine Persons in the mission of Christ,[5] and in the Church's continuation of that mission as the Body of Christ.[6] As he puts it, "The Church must reflect in her very being the way God exists, i.e., the way of personal communion."[7] On the practical level it means, says Zizioulas,

> that the Church is *by definition incompatible with individualism*; her fabric is communion and personal relatedness. On the local level an ecclesiology of communion would mean that no Christian can exist as an individual exercising a direct communion with God. *Unus christianus nullus christianus* ["'One Christian' is 'no Christian'"], to recall an old Latin saying. The way to God passes through the 'neighbor,' who in this case is the fellow-member of the community. The Church is conceivable only as a structured local community.[8]

It might be said, then, that in situations like that of the Western Mission of the Archdiocese of Canberra, or the *villas* of Buenos Aires, parishes seek to preserve the Church's "fabric of communion" by working with the structures of "personal relatedness" where and how they find them, even when their own structures must be reshaped in the effort. (This is the work not only of local communities on their own, of course, but of whole dioceses, a crucial aspect of the context of parishes that will be taken up more fully in chapter 6.)

THE ORIGINS OF CHRISTIAN *KOINONIA*

To see the historical emergence of these essential qualities of "communion" and "personal relatedness," we might look once again to the New Testament stories of the intimate community among Jesus and his disciples. There are scriptural accounts of the social context that brings them all together, of course, and moving descriptions of the natural ties that develop among them. Yet, theirs is not a bond that begins merely in ordinary human friendship, but in Jesus's own understanding of his mission from the God he calls "Father." "You did not choose me but I chose you," he will tell them (John 15:16). In the Synoptic Gospels, the very call of the first disciples contains an overt reference to their share in the mission: "Follow me, and I will make you fish for people" (Mark 1:17). In the Gospel of John, depending on which moment is in focus, the disciples are pointed to, attracted by, or directly called to the unusual nature of Jesus's presence and preaching: "Look!" (John 1:36) or "Come and see" (John 1:39) or "Follow me" (John 1:43).

Right away, comparisons and contrasts are drawn between Rabbi Jesus with his followers and other master/disciple relationships familiar to the people. Jesus's disciples, though, quickly begin to witness the "signs and wonders" for which Jesus is becoming known, "and his disciples believed in him" (John 2:11). These initial encounters are charged with astounding *hope*: "We have found the Messiah" (John 1:41)! As Jesus's message unfolds, the call to the disciples to *live in love* for one another becomes louder and stronger: "Love your enemies" (Matt 5:44); "The greatest among you will be your servant" (Matt 23:11); "If I… have washed your feet, you also ought to wash one another's feet" (John 13:14).

We have seen that, ultimately, Jesus offers his friends deep identification with himself, as he is identified with the Father: "Those who love me will keep my word, and my Father will love them, and we will come to them and make our home with them" (John 14:23); "Abide in me as I abide in you" (John 15:4); "This is my commandment, that you love one another as I have loved you" (John 15:12). Throughout his ministry Jesus preached, showed, and lived this servant love with his disciples.

This love remains at the core of the *koinonia* he sealed with them in the Eucharist: "This is my body, which is given for you. Do this in remembrance of me.... This cup that is poured out for you is the new covenant in my blood" (Luke 22:19–20). It is in the parishes—where Eucharist is regularly offered to all the members of the Church—that this covenant seal is faithfully kept and reverently displayed. Christians and seekers alike have a right to look there for communities in which the *koinonia* is lived and regularly renewed in the hearts of believers.

Just how these "communities of the new covenant" would look and be organized started to emerge immediately after Jesus's resurrection. His body had been transformed, but he continued to present himself to his disciples in a series of beautifully intimate moments. These experiences of the risen Jesus revealed at an even greater depth the *koinonia* with God in Christ that the earlier community had only been able to hint at: "They came to him, took hold of his feet, and worshiped him" (Matt 28:9); "Were not our hearts burning within us while he was talking to us?" (Luke 24:32); "He had been made known to them in the breaking of the bread" (Luke 24:35); "Touch me and see; for a ghost does not have flesh and bones as you see that I have" (Luke 24:39); "Have you anything here to eat?" (Luke 24:41); "'Woman, why are you weeping? Whom are you looking for?'...Jesus said to her, 'Mary!' She turned and said to him in Hebrew, 'Rabbouni!'" (John 20:15–16); "He breathed on them and said to them, 'Receive the Holy Spirit'" (John 20:22); "Reach out your hand and put it into my side. Do not doubt but believe" (John 20:27); "Come and have breakfast" (John 21:12); "Do you love me?" (John 21:17). The richly sensuous character of these scenes, and the clear eucharistic overtones of most of them, have been powerful reminders for two millennia of the material, intimate, face-to-face origin of Christians' sacramental points of contact with the Lord and with each other. Once again, within the ordinary structures of the Church it is the parish that most clearly cherishes this sacramentality not only in sacred ritual but in all aspects of its communal life.

Structuring the communities that would carry forth the living communion with Christ was also about relationships with the larger world within which these communities would be embedded. Seen another way, these are relationships with the world through which the Church continually extends its invitation into communion with the Lord. During his public ministry, Jesus had established the expectation for this aspect, too. Not only the Twelve (Luke 9:1–2), but even "seventy [or seventy-two] others" (Luke 10:1), were sent out not with a mere verbal message but with works of power and authority embedded in a simple and peaceful determination to live *koinonia* in the name of Jesus. After Jesus returned to the Father and the outward mission expanded far beyond Galilee in all directions, those who responded to what the apostles identified as the Spirit of Jesus became the pilgrim communities, the *paroikía*, that we have been discussing.

The depth of the unity in Christ experienced by the original community of disciples, though, meant that the Church's development could not stop at this point. Gradually, one by one, across regions, throughout the Roman Empire and outside it as well, local Christian gatherings developed the structures of mutual communion and an ever-wider network of Christian relationships. This network was charged with the practical tasks of maintaining personal ties and a genuine unity of faith. Yet, it was also itself laden with deep religious meaning. The very character of "the churches" and "the Church" could tell faithful Christians who they were and what they were to do. Jesus himself had given his many disciples the leadership of the Twelve, reflective of the ancient heritage of Israel's twelve tribes. As the earliest generations began to pass, what the apostles had meant to them began to be expressed in evolving pastoral practices and institutional arrangements, and in a theology of communion capable of including even some of the most remote Christian communities that had been formed. Quite early in this history the bishop (*episkopos*, "overseer" of both the local elders and the whole community), as both a local pastor and a regional representative, came to embody that *koinonia*. Ignatius, the bishop of Antioch around 110 CE, writing to the Christian community at Ephesus, described this sacramental role in vivid terms: "I received, therefore, your whole multitude in the name of God, through Onesimus, a man of inexpressible love, and your bishop in the flesh, whom I pray you by Jesus Christ to love, and that you would all seek to be like him."[9]

In the Latin-speaking west of the empire, what came to be called *parochiae* had their own long and complicated history of development, often involving missionary and monastic founders who were not directly tied to a bishop or to what we would today call a "diocese." For some centuries, as a matter of fact, the words *diocesis* and *parochia* were interchangeably applied either to a local congregation or to a bishop's whole jurisdiction.[10] It has now been a very long time since *parochiae* first came to be understood as stable local communities with resident pastors, under the more remote authority of a bishop (who may or may not be generally familiar to the members of any one local community). Today's parishes, as local communities, have inherited key aspects of all this development. Some essential functions of the local church, which are still embodied in the office of the bishop, are delegated day-to-day to the parish. Centuries of practical experience and pastoral reflection have led to reliance on this face-to-face community as a kind of concentration of the local church into a single flesh-and-blood eucharistic assembly[11]—a place where believers can uphold one another in faith and love, and from which they are "sent out" still bound together in the *koinonia* nourished by the sacrament.

IS THE PARISH REALLY THE PROPER PLACE FOR *KOINONIA*?

Koinonia/communio is a deeply treasured concept for Roman Catholic and for Eastern Orthodox theologians alike. However, in the Catholic context, it does raise special legal and pastoral questions, owing to the much more centralized Roman understanding of church authority.[12] Here it is important to acknowledge what was written about *communio* in a letter by the Vatican's Congregation for the Doctrine of the Faith (CDF) issued in 1992, entitled "On Some Aspects of the Church Understood as Communion."[13] This document acknowledges a dimension of communion that binds all Christians to Christ and to one another—the *koinonia* described by Zizioulas. The letter stresses, however, the essential link between this aspect and the ecclesial communion made visible in the Church's hierarchy. The consequence of this approach to the question of the role of parishes in maintaining *koinonia* is made clear:

> Each member of the faithful, especially in the celebration of the Eucharist, is in *his or her* Church, in the Church of Christ, regardless of whether or not he or she belongs, according to canon law, to the diocese, parish or other particular community where the celebration takes place...since belonging to the *Communion*, like belonging to the Church, is never simply particular, but by its very nature is always universal.[14]

Here the Congregation reminds us that the Eucharist (also, of course, called "holy communion") that nourishes and sustains the faith community is given through the hierarchical order of the Church.

One might conclude, therefore, that while the parish certainly *benefits* from the gift of communion/*koinonia*, that quality is embodied in and pertains much more to the College of Bishops than to the parish. This interpretation also gives rise to a doubt about the description of the parish, in canon 515.1, as "a certain *community* of the faithful." Granted, the carefully considered word marked a change in perspective in the 1983 revision of the Code. But was this change really meant to occupy such an important place in the very definition of a parish? Couldn't undue emphasis on the word *community* be part of a potentially dangerous exaggeration of the significance of the parish?[15] The question is raised in particular by those especially concerned with perceived threats to the bishops' prerogatives in relation to parishes.

There is no question that the universal bond, through the hierarchy, that the CDF underscores by its letter is essential to the meaning of Christian *koinonia*. One Christ continues to be present in and with the one Church in all its members. The collegiality and authority of bishops, which embody the Church's universal dimension, cannot be placed at odds with the parish's face-to-face experience of *koinonia*, found in the specific expressions of relationship that transform the parish from a mere function into a genuine community. Vatican II never separates the people of God from its hierarchical leadership with the intention of giving some "advantage" to either dimension of the Church. The sacramental presence of Christ with the Church is visibly expressed in the hierarchy, as the CDF also argues,[16] but the very same bond can also be seen and embraced and lived in the life of a parish community that understands *koinonia* as tying it inseparably to the life of the universal Church. To argue otherwise risks suggesting that the members of Christ's Church have only indirect access to the divine life, which would seem to contradict the whole purpose of the CDF statement about communion (not to mention the bulk of Catholic tradition).

It is an interesting irony that this way of questioning the role of *koinonia* in the parish may give rise to another, from precisely the opposite direction. Today, the clericalism of key leaders and of the leadership culture of a given parish, diocese, or region can often become another reason for dismissing the concept of parish as community. Following the Protestant Reformation, the Church generally succeeded in its efforts to increase respect for, and the respectability of, its clergy. In the United States and elsewhere, this success provided Catholics with seemingly unimpeachable and utterly dedicated leaders through times of great trial and uncertainty. By the mid-twentieth century, however, as social change was undermining many traditional institutions and roles, the near-total reliance of the Church on clerical control was becoming more of an obstacle to necessary adaptation and broader participation than the advantage it had once been. Early in the twenty-first century, of course, the slow erosion of trust became a total collapse with the revelations of sexual abuse. For many former parishioners, the mention of "communion"—in any of its senses—without serious accounting for clerical abuses and for the many perceived inequalities in the structures of Church governance became empty, even offensive, rhetoric.

PARISH COMMUNITY AND LOCAL CULTURE

The disaster of the clerical abuse scandals brought to dramatic completion a cultural shift that had been underway for decades. Msgr. Philip Murnion—who was a priest-sociologist, advisor to the U.S. Bishops, and great advocate for American parish life in the last decades of the twentieth century—wrote in 1985,

> It has been a long time since we could assume that American Catholics would uncritically accept the teachings or the authority of the church....American Catholics have become part of other communities that have acquired significance for them, communities associated with their middle-class status and income level, with the neighborhoods in which they live, or with their vocational or avocational interests. The church is no longer needed as an enclosed, protective, and exclusive community.[17]

The comment brings several relevant points to light at once. It is first a reminder of a specific cultural development in the United States, pertaining especially to what I have called the ark model of parish. As such, it also exemplifies an aspect of the theology of the people that is more broadly applicable to the study of parishes everywhere: the conviction, discussed in chapter 2, that the Spirit of God is at work, ahead of the Church itself, in the cultural forces shaping "the people" who are the Church's members. Finally, Murnion's comment opens a larger question pertinent to this chapter's discussion: If the Spirit is at work in human cultures independently of the Church's actions or plans, should church communities be shaped to conform to those cultures (to be, in the term popularized after Vatican II, *inculturated*)? Or, on the contrary, should they learn to stand firm against the pressures raised by inevitable cultural blind spots, sin, and injustice—to act, that is, *counterculturally*? The question is pertinent not only to action or advocacy taken by parishioners in various capacities but, even more importantly, to the very form of the parish itself.

One hazard of the approach I have taken so far in this book, emphasizing parish *mission* ahead of *structures* and even ahead of *community*, is that it may suggest rather too strongly that the mission is simply revealed by the gospel, and that a general statement of it can take the place of a whole pastoral plan for a community of Christ's faithful. The crucial dimension missing from such a scenario would be the voice of the people themselves. That "voice" will almost invariably include particular voices speaking both from stable positions within the local culture and from more precarious positions on the margins. Listening to those voices is far more demanding than distributing a survey or holding an open parish meeting—especially when the question may be as foundational as the parish's structure or even its very existence.

A people's way of life, social ties, shared values, and beliefs that already shape them, have got to be acknowledged and *welcomed* within the parish community in some way. Otherwise, disillusionment or loss of relevance are likely to become the driving forces. In a later article, Murnion emphasized this point as well:

> Given the variety of levels, meanings, and commitments to community that parishioners have, and within which they find identity and values, parish leaders must recognize the voluntary character of commitment to each, discern the relative importance of each, and consider how much the life of the parish can and should relate to each if the church is to be inculturated.[18]

German pastoral theologian Matthias Sellmann, whose work I have noted more than once, has called such efforts "creative reception,"[19] part of his strategy for bringing about a "future-proof parish" with "an energetic metaphor that, as it were, attracts the future, motivates spiritually, convinces ecclesiologically, and works both culturally and operationally."[20]

Although from the point of view of evangelization this "reception" of the culture may seem strongly counterintuitive, it is actually unavoidable. Christians (even infants) or seekers who desire community do not arrive at a parish from nowhere but have already been, and will continue to be, profoundly shaped by their contexts apart from the parish. This remains true even when the tensions and contradictions between those contexts and the gospel of Christ may seem obvious. To "welcome" what is already ingrained is simply a resolution to accept people where and as they are, while the whole community continues its pilgrimage toward the reign of God. The hard work is to build and maintain, in specific places and circumstances, the structures and ways of living that encourage the growth of communities of faith whose members are willing to listen and make room for each other. Beyond that, it is to find paths to discernment that can openly affirm the gifts of God in all those cultural features that recognize and celebrate human dignity, promote human flourishing, and encourage solidarity across all boundaries that isolate people from each other.

The work of the inculturated community includes, by the same token, finding and activating effective challenges (within the community and outward into the broader culture) to any contradictions and temptations that lead to indifference, condescension, suspicion, hatred, and violence—among different socioeconomic classes, among races and ethnic groups, among genders and sexual orientations, among differing religions and religious communities. This is the community's work of continuing to witness to Christ living in their midst and moving in their cultural milieu.

CAN AN "INCULTURATED" COMMUNITY ALSO BE "COUNTERCULTURAL"?

Attempts to take such cultural acceptance and listening very seriously have in recent decades sometimes led to startling conclusions about the institution of parish. As I recounted in the first chapter, diocesan pastoral ministers in one of the German dioceses I visited told me bluntly, "The parish is dead." In this setting (in part for reasons particular to the recent history of the German church), there is a tendency to view "parish as community" as an old and failed ideal, a kind of romantic remnant of a distant past in which a church was at the center of every village or neighborhood. Instead, the signs of the times seem to urge a shift toward the urban pastoral movements that rely more on "touch and go" moments of contact than on the old-fashioned predictability of a more traditional time.

Matthias Sellmann takes a deeper look at this situation and sees a need for attention to a "meso-level," between the "systemic macro-level" of the Church's traditional hierarchical organization and the "interactive micro-level"[21] of individuals and distinct communities of believers. (A similarly defined term, *intermediate group*, has also been used in the literature.[22]) As Sellmann puts it, "One does not have to be a prophet to predict that the question whether parishes will be future-proof will be decided on this level."[23] The challenge for this meso-level is to face the macro-level rise of individual autonomy (which increases the importance of building the right decision-making context in parishes) and the increased importance of *market forces* because of this individualism.[24]

The meso-level, Sellmann observes, has already fostered enormous creativity in the task of reshaping Christian community to meet these challenges. "Examples are religious movements, pilgrimages, religious media contact, events, chaplaincy/ministry such as urban churches or migrant churches."[25] While many of these activities have existed in some form for centuries,

> more recent discussions about these initiatives have reassessed their pastoral significance. They are now considered "places of church," they sometimes even form their own community within the larger parish, and in any case, they are independent places of pastoral activity that are no longer regarded as fulfilling a bridge function towards the so-called "core community."[26]

The new "church places" exist, suggests Sellmann, in "a disposition of the 'occasion,'" rather than in the earlier "disposition of permanence" (which he identifies with a pre–Vatican II service-station mentality) and "disposition of proximity" (which he assigns to a post–Vatican II community model). In other words, the future may lie more in the "touch and go" model than in the parish model.

Here is where the challenge of cultural listening becomes clear. Sellmann's analysis, and others like it, can be appreciated. It is backed by sound sociological data and theory and is certainly not to be ignored. His enthusiastic description of the creative pastoral possibilities emerging from an entirely new understanding of local church is intriguing and inviting in many ways. Yet, the unanswered question is, where is all this pastoral activity generated? And how is it to be sustained if there is truly no "core community" that both nourishes and sends missionary disciples to be present at the proper "occasion"? In keeping with Sellmann's idea of religious autonomy (which is perhaps akin to the personal religions that sociologist Robert Bellah once called "Sheila-ism"[27]), we could imagine faithful persons following highly individualized patterns within the various meso-level movements, drawing spiritual support in one form or another from whomever they encounter, and sustaining each other in ways much less easily defined, even if no less real or personally significant, than a parish community. Yet, dispensing with the notion of an enduring *church community structure* may also mean dispensing with the most visible, accessible embodiment of Christ within the people of God (a *sacrament*, in the broader use of that term [*LG* 1, 9, 48]). What would it mean to invite this temporary alliance of religiously autonomous individuals, as they partake of the Eucharist, to "be members of the Body of Christ"?[28] Or is it more likely that the Eucharist, and the Church itself, would eventually become quite irrelevant as a "parishless" scenario unfolded?

This point could be spun out in many ways, but its essence is this: even when cultural trends seem to pull in another direction, a hallmark of the Church that embraces its call to *koinonia* must be a continual deepening of the habits of attentive presence to one another and to Christ in their midst. That kind of sacred listening is key to undertaking the demanding mission of being "rooted and grounded" in the love of Christ in our times—a mission that requires local communities that at least aspire to the spiritual unity and strength of genuine Christian communion. It is the work of discerning pathways that can lead both to openness to the Spirit's movement within a culture and to ready response—in small, habitual ways as much as in large, strategic ways—when the Spirit's call is to resistance and prophetic proclamation. Of course, there will be disagreement, tension, and struggle around this discernment. It is precisely amid such struggles that opportunities to grow and become stronger in love and faith will emerge. In the end, this conviction is not so different from one cited by Sellmann as a theological context for his work: "The Church realizes herself wherever she loses herself."[29]

Should a parish, seeking to strengthen Christian community, be *inculturated* or *countercultural*? The maddeningly paradoxical answer is, I believe, *both*.

THE PARISH COMMUNITY AS SOLIDARITY

Msgr. Philip Murnion, referred to above, addressed the problem of finding the right general concept of parish community capable of undertaking the demanding work of fostering communion in the Church. Ahead of his time in recognizing the serious challenges that were mounting, Murnion insisted on looking "beyond the rather romantic notion of community that so often is present in the Church,"[30] and with a sociologist's eye suggested several approaches that he observed in play around him in the mid-1980s, and that are still highly relevant today. He called these "the traditionalist response," "the sectarian response," "community as intimacy," "association," and "community as solidarity."[31] Each has its characteristic strengths and weaknesses. The traditionalists emphasize authority and clarity, but at the expense of mutuality and participation. The sectarians (whether of the "right" or the "left") promote deep personal conversion according to a very specific vision of Catholic faith but tend to leave behind those not ready for such intense commitment. Those emphasizing intimacy and emotional engagement tend not to stress action toward justice, especially not beyond the borders of the community itself. The association-style parish offers programs for seemingly every individual need but does not work so hard at the community bond.

Murnion's answer to the dilemmas suggested by these models—which encompass the problems of communion and culture I have been discussing—was a decided preference for the "solidarity" approach. He described such a parish as "an inclusive community...that sees its faith as a basis for action." The solidarity model values well-understood and strongly held tradition over-against a more sentimental kind of intimacy. It looks for the kind of commitment that can endure times of struggle and opposition. It seeks public expression of its faith in strong actions that in many ways can speak for themselves.[32] Comparing these qualities to the other approaches he outlined, Murnion continued:

> The alternatives, each in its own way, represent reductionism—a determination to minimize complexity and ambiguity. It is this more elusive and demanding approach that is more faithful to our tradition and pertinent to our situation. It calls for an adult church, where lay people, indeed all, are treated as adults.[33]

In light of the discussion of *koinonia*, one might say that the "adult church" is one in which each acknowledges the equal dignity of all in a relationship with God that flows to individual members through the community and returns to the community in the members' acts of love and dedication. Clearly, Murnion sees the parish as a reflection of the Spirit at work in the whole Church—as long as the idea of community employed, beyond mere "togetherness," invites a sense of mutual and enduring communion in the Spirit of Christ. Like mission, *koinonia* is much less about the *functions* of local church community, and much more about its *essence*.

A COMMUNITY OF COMMUNITIES

The encounter and engagement with culture, then, is both essential and deeply challenging. Sellmann's work demonstrates this in great detail. Despite the hesitations I have just expressed about some of its possible implications, his emphasis on the meso-level provides two insights that are key to moving forward with these realizations about culture. First, Sellman forces us to think about the role of sociocultural circumstances in shaping parish structures and rendering insufficient the simple definition of canon 515.1 (stable community, parish priest, bishop). Second, Sellmann's work offers us a way to reconceive the function of parishes vis à vis face-to-face communities. To borrow a phrase that he cites, we could think of parishes as "places of church,"[34] with specific responsibility for fostering, nurturing, and cooperating with a network of subcommunities in which parishioners more frequently experience *koinonia* as responsive to specific local conditions on the physical, face-to-face level.

I have throughout these chapters identified the parish itself as "the local church community," and this is indeed so on the level of permanent institutional structures. Nonetheless, in many instances parish communities are too large and varied to provide day-to-day the personal engagement and support that committed believers need. In vital and dynamic parishes, therefore, groups and subcommunities of all types are apt to multiply. This is generally viewed as a positive pastoral development, showing parishioners' desire to live their faith seriously. By the same token, leaders and engaged parishioners throughout the parish organization need to be attentive to the whole network of subgroups, for the sake of unity and mutual support. This overall phenomenon gives rise to the description of the parish as a "community of communities." The expression, which may have originated in Latin America, has been taken up throughout the Church and can be found in many episcopal and papal documents.[35] The parish per se, as an institutional entity, is seen as a "center," whether as a physical campus, a core membership, a leadership team, but *especially* as the full assembly of parishioners to which each member has real access. In whatever form, this center becomes a touchstone for the many more specific groupings of parishioners.

The parish community of communities has taken many different forms. In chapter 3, I mentioned the role that "Basic Ecclesial Communities" (BECs, also called "Small Christian Communities") played in the development of Corpus Christi Parish. Organization of a parish into these regular gatherings for prayer, study, and friendship is often precisely what is meant by "a community of communities." In many places, BECs have been organized as sectors of large parishes to promote social and spiritual concern for a group's particular area or network. They have been helpful in keeping parishioners of poor or over-extended parishes engaged in the healing and unifying aspects of the parish's mission.[36]

I alluded in chapter 3 to an interesting variation on such groupings that was created in the French archdiocese of Poitiers after a diocesan synod in the 1980s. The decision was made to rely on canon 516.2 (which allows the bishop, in matters of necessity, to provide for pastoral care of communities "in another way") to create not *parishes* but "pastoral sectors" in the diocese, each with its assigned priest-pastor and financial and pastoral councils. These sectors receive applications from various neighborhood and village communities within the sector to organize themselves with five-person "pastoral teams" according to a standard pattern, demonstrating long-term ability to provide for their own local worship, instruction, and charitable outreach, with effective leadership and financial management. This approach has transformed dying traditional parishes into centers of evangelization in broader areas than could ever have been reached by clergy working within traditional pastoral models.[37]

I observed a related strategy in the parish of San Jorge in Olanchito, Honduras, in 1991, which in addition to the population of its fairly large market town included the residents of scores of rural villages scattered in the mountains for many miles around. In order to allow their very poor residents to experience their oneness in Christ on a day-to-day basis, the Church acknowledged both the constraints and the gifts of their social situation. These tiny rural settlements (that a single pastor could only possibly visit once or twice a year because of their remoteness and their sheer number) were given a degree of ecclesial autonomy. Each village had one or two trained catechists, appointed to be the day-to-day leaders of prayer, study, and Christian living in their own communities. The catechists led weekly instruction and prayer services, were able to carry the Eucharist from the pastor to their own people, and were the regular liaisons between their villages and the pastor, meeting regularly with him or other parish leaders for ongoing training and support. It is interesting that, in a dramatically different cultural context, the Western Mission in rural Australia followed a similar model.

Even in parishes of a more convenient size and greater resources, where the ordained and professional staff remain able to provide traditional sacramental, pastoral, charitable, and instructional services, groups and subcommunities nonetheless form and attend to dimensions of *koinonia* that "professional service" alone cannot provide. They include an array of devotional and service groups (St. Vincent de Paul Society, Legion of Mary, Pax Christi, Christian Life Communities, etc.). They bring together certain "identity" or "interest" groups (women, men, married couples, elderly, youth and young adults, disabled parishioners and their advocates, LGBTQ parishioners, and many others). They acknowledge and dialogue with all the "human communities" of family, neighborhood, friendship, and other human ties that shape the lives of parishioners. The complex task of "bridging" and "gathering" these subcommunities—which clearly can be extremely diverse—cannot be ignored by the parish community or leadership in their efforts to be listening and responsive to their whole social network.

The recently identified phenomenon of the "shared parish" generally describes the existence of two or more different ethnic or language groups in the same parish. The serious challenge of bridging deep gaps of communication, assumption, and expectation, requires the skills of patience and mutual listening above all else. These parishes have much to teach *all* communities when it comes to acknowledging, embracing, and learning from their groups and subcommunities.[38] While the idea of parish community clearly needs some rethinking in the face of all these diverse conditions, the desire for *koinonia* offers disciples in every kind of situation a way to recognize and live the bond they share in Christ. Its social breadth takes in the whole world of cultures in which the Church is immersed. Its theological depth, seriously considered, points far beyond words and superficial accommodations into a shared spiritual richness at the very heart of the relationship between God and God's people.

THE WORK OF A "*KOINONIA* PARISH"

In the end, communion is *gift*, not a human accomplishment. John writes, "Beloved, we are God's children now; what we will be has not yet been revealed. What we do know is this: when he is revealed, we will be like him, for we will see him as he is" (1 John 3:2). Nonetheless, genuine Christian community, though firmly set on a vision of *koinonia* only fulfilled in the "New Jerusalem," must first be lived in our here and now material world, where human blindness and sin are constantly at work. In *Evangelii Gaudium*, Pope Francis describes the Church's greater interest in the building of strong and effective human communities this way:

> Becoming a people…is an ongoing process in which every new generation must take part: a slow and arduous effort calling for a desire for integration and a willingness to achieve this through the growth of a peaceful and multifaceted culture of encounter. (*EG* 220)

In parish communities, the Church as the people of God is gathered in face-to-face expressions of the communion that is God's gift. Here, a people has the opportunity to work toward its own "culture of encounter," in the hope of sharing it with the larger world. In a section of the exhortation, entitled "The Common Good and Peace in Society," Francis offers "four specific principles which can guide…the building of a people where differences are harmonized within a shared pursuit" (*EG* 221). It may be especially appropriate, then, to conclude this chapter by reflecting briefly on these principles as guides for those who seek to deepen Christian *koinonia*.

Slow, Steady Processes. "Time is greater than space," declares the pope (*EG* 222). He explains that "time" is about a process moving toward completion, whereas "space" is about fixing on a particular position or status. The principle is a reminder of the Church's continuing pilgrimage toward the fullness of communion with God and one another in Christ. Further, it is a call for communities to "hold lightly" their divisive concerns about property, status, and control in order to take the first steps toward a genuine "preferential option" in which *everyone* is called to the vulnerability of the poor and the humility of the "poor in spirit." In contributing their unique perspectives to such an undertaking, each segment of a diverse parish can see their gifts transformed from distinguishing features of a small group, perhaps jealously guarded, into strengthened and celebrated qualities of the whole community.

"The Profound Unity of Reality." "Unity prevails over conflict," Francis proclaims (*EG* 226). What is needed to bring this unity about "is the willingness to face conflict head on, to resolve it and to make it a link in the chain of a new process" (*EG* 227). In the life of the Church, the parish can play an important role in making this confrontation both real and fruitful. Superficial contact and avoidance of differences in politics, culture, and faith expression will almost always look easier and safer. The face-to-face community, though, is in a unique position to use the bonds of humanity and faith to work lovingly toward a unity that is both stronger and deeper. In parishes that may be too used to their own homogeneity, this principle calls for a sharper awareness, of both who is part of the community and whom the community is bypassing. It may call the members of more heterogenous parishes to careful bridge-building between previously aloof groups. In every parish, the unity principle will send members out into a world of diversity and conflict that too many may have been seeking to escape, a world where the Spirit of God is also at work. There, relying on their communion in Christ despite their own disagreements, parishioners may find among themselves the clarity, urgency, commitment, and hope to share that faith with the world.

Engagement in Ongoing Dialogue. "Realities are more important than ideas," writes Francis. "There has to be continuous dialogue between the two, lest ideas become detached from realities" (*EG* 231). Years earlier, as Archbishop Jorge Bergoglio, in a speech to Catholic teachers and students in Buenos Aires, he had already articulated the attitude with which such dialogue would have to be conducted:

> Another temptation is to privilege the values of the head over the values of the heart. It is not so. Only the heart unites and makes whole. Understanding without compassion tends to divide. The heart unites idea with reality, time with space, life with death and with eternity.[39]

This principle opens a pathway for the "slow unfolding" and the "honest confrontation" of the previous two principles. Among the elements of control that can be so hard for some members of a community to relinquish are the assumptions and perceptions—the fixed ideas—that begin as ways to sort out facts and experiences, but too easily end up as excuses to stop watching and listening to reality. Movement toward reconciliation of differences, greater unity, and true generosity toward the world at large requires *metanoia*, a change of mind and heart, a conversion. This cannot take place until any refusal of reality is relinquished. This is why true *koinonia* requires that the community maintain structures of *constant mutual listening* among all its members, seeking to ensure that there is no "silent majority," no "self righteous minority," no "sleeping dogs" left to lie, no place "where angels fear to tread." If realities are recognized as coming before ideas, no so-called community vision can be imposed by self-focused leaders or by an elite group. Truly encountering all the realities that the community faces precludes any authoritarian silencing of voices, dismantling of processes, or belittling of unfamiliar customs and practices. New facts, experiences, and observations are instead continually brought into the community's awareness and its prayerful discernment.

The "Polyhedron." A polyhedron is a multisided three-dimensional geometric figure, made up of flat surfaces of different dimensions joined along their edges so that the complete solid figure is irregular in shape. Pope Francis uses such a figure to illustrate what he means by the deceptively familiar principle, "The whole is greater than the part" (*EG* 234). The metaphor is a vivid way of discussing the interconnection of each community's particular contribution to the whole (diocese, Church, world), as well as each community's *need* for its relationship with the whole. Understanding the Church according to this metaphor calls for mutual respect between the *whole* and its *constituent parts*, and in all the parts among themselves. In keeping with the Christian understanding of *koinonia*, the Spirit of God can be said to be within the whole and, simultaneously, within all the parts—each member, every people, all their histories and cultures, each of their contributions to the tradition of the universal Church.

The Spirit is present, of course, as God's gift of grace—God's own presence for the building up the Church. But the grace comes with both responsibility and challenge. The peoples and communities of the Church need to maintain their bond with each other. Their histories must be told and heard *prophetically*, with their calls to fidelity and action along with the responses of both faithfulness and infidelity. The cultures of the various communities offer their transforming gifts to the *whole Church*. But the transformation depends vitally on the Church's embracing of *all* its members and contexts—a *continuing task*, rather than a set of reified features that will perpetually mark the Church's character. Extending the metaphor downward to every part of the whole, each member can be seen as a particular feature of the "face of the Church," contributing and inviting the community to see and hear. The whole Church can then be *formed* in some way by the reality of that person. Similarly, the believer who is "fitted into" the whole is also being transformed by taking up all the challenges and demands of communion in Christ.

So, the work of the parish community is not removal of all differences and distinctions, but rather of the barriers among members and groups that betray the concept of *koinonia*. In the parish that takes its communion in Christ seriously, where faces are seen and stories heard, shared experience and respect among all the varied members and groups is ever more carefully received. Knowledge and understanding, and companionship with even the most easily excluded, are built up in these local communities to be passed on to the Church at large. In its parishes, the Church as a whole can become more fully "a poor Church for the poor," and a living icon of Christian *koinonia*.

Chapter 5

THE PARISH AND SACRED PLACE

The LORD loves the gates of Zion
more than all the dwellings of Jacob.
Glorious things are spoken of you,
O city of God!

Psalm 87:2–3

A SLIVER OF ENGLISH CATHOLIC HISTORY

*In central London, tucked away on a corner of tiny Lamb's Passage, just north of the ancient enclave once marked by London's walls and still known as "the City," a small school chapel was erected around the year 1850. It soon began to function as a parish, although for much of its existence it was designated a "chapel-of-ease" to nearby St. Mary Moorfields (which was briefly the pro-cathedral of the new Diocese of Westminster). As of this writing, St. Joseph's, Bunhill Row continues to operate, albeit in rather unusual administrative circumstances. It is now named for the nearby street that continues on past the old Bunhill Fields graveyard ("bone hill"), famous for "Nonconformist" burials of luminaries such as John Bunyan (*The Pilgrim's Progress*), Isaac Watts ("O God Our Help In Ages Past" and many other hymns), and Susanna Wesley (mother of John and Charles, founders of Methodism).[1] The property where St. Joseph's is located had been purchased in 1815 by a Catholic charitable group as a site for a school and orphanage, and indeed a school operated on the property until 1977.[2]*

The current worship space is a garden-level room partly below ground in the former school that replaced earlier buildings in 1901. Most of the rest of the property, including what had been the parish priest's residence, has been leased out to various social-service agencies, both Catholic and secular. What is visible at street level is a small enclosed "quiet garden," which fills what was once a car park, a large sign above the first-floor windows of the old school pointing simply to the "Catholic Church" below, and a somewhat incongruous "pedimented gate" added during a refurbishing in 1993 at the top of a set of steps leading down into the church entrance. Inside, a traditionally arranged sanctuary provides "beauty and a sense of holiness,"[3] *as well as nods to the chapel's past, preserving two stained glass windows from the original St. Mary Moorfields church as well as gifts and memorials of past parishioners. Although public housing with working-class residents and immigrants from over thirty different countries are nearby, the property is increasingly surrounded by tech firms, offices, and high-end housing; the prospect of large financial gains from its sale remains an ongoing temptation for the archdiocese.*[4]

For about fifteen years, St. Joseph's has had no resident priest, but has been able, owing to the strength of the Pastoral Council and Finance Committee revitalized under its last resident, to convince the Archdiocese of Westminster that it remains a viable community of perhaps 150 active members. The parish priest of St. Mary Moorfields is now the official priest-administrator, chair of the Pastoral Council, and frequent presider at Sunday Mass. His own parish church, successor to the former pro-cathedral, stands a few blocks away within the City of London, although St. Joseph's remains officially an "independent parish" of the Islington deanery. Among the distinctive activities that the community has carried on since becoming a "priestless parish" are ongoing attempts to invite all parishioners to share reflections on Scripture as well as relevant social issues, occasional parishioner-led Services of the Word and Communion, and a Carmelite spirituality group. The parish community has also been active in the community-organizing alliance Citizens UK, as well as a neighborhood ecumenical association including representation from several other Christian congregations in the area. St. Joseph's has even included ecumenical representation on its own Pastoral Council.

ST. JOSEPH'S MAY seem an odd choice for the topic of this chapter—sacred place. Yet the oddities may help to focus some important questions about *location* that parishes in many parts of the world are facing. With the parish description here at hand it will be useful to open the discussion by underlining a few points about the links between parish communities and physical places. We can begin with another word origin, this time for "church." The Greek word *ekklesia*—root of the words for "church" in several European languages—meant an "assembly" of the people, and so was clearly originally focused on the *community*. English, however, with several other Germanic languages, derived "church" from the Greek phrase *kyriakon doma* ("house of the Lord"), which just as clearly brought attention to the buildings in which Christians worship.[5] This word history—though it is only part of a long process by which the believing community, the building, and the clerical institution became conflated with each other—preserves an important perspective: the *place* where the community worships (most especially where it celebrates the Eucharist) belongs to the Lord, acts as a "Christian landmark," and becomes "holy ground."

In this connection, it is worth noting that the history of the St. Joseph's property encompasses several important moments in the reestablishment of the official Roman Catholic presence in England following more than two centuries of legal exclusion after the reign of Queen Mary I. These include the period of increasing "Catholic Emancipation" in the later eighteenth and early nineteenth centuries, the influx of Catholic Irish in the early decades of the nineteenth century, the reestablishment of the English Catholic hierarchy by Pope Pius IX in 1850, and the building of many schools and churches in the opening years of the twentieth century (including not only the current St. Joseph's building, but also the "new" St. Mary Moorfields and even Westminster Cathedral, home to the Roman Catholic archdiocese since 1903[6]). St. Joseph's is thus located on land with an identifiable and significant Catholic history. Having begun as a functional space for a school and orphanage made necessary by immediate circumstances, the property was then so shaped by its Catholic usage that it became a landmark that even now contributes to the shape of the neighborhood around it: the school needed a chapel, which attracted people who became regular worshipers, which led to the designation as a sort of extension of the nearest parish, which eventually led to separate parish status. Later generations, responding to the presence of an established community, carried on its memories, habits, and customs and added their own marks. Such interaction between parish and territory has been a regular historical phenomenon for parishes all over the world. As one observer has noted, "The territory structured the parish but, it is often forgotten, the parish also structured the territory."[7]

Other powerful influences have taken over the cityscape in more recent years, and St. Joseph's finds itself on the edge of a revitalized area pressing into its territory. Yet even in these new circumstances, a diverse congregation of newcomers has joined the remnants of the more traditional community and found comfort and purpose: the preservation and enhancement of an ongoing tradition and a role as providers of a quiet oasis in the midst of a teeming modern metropolis. In these ways, St. Joseph's Bunhill Row has become a sacred place, a symbol of the community that gathers there in continuity with Catholics reaching back two centuries. The place has helped to form and preserve the community, and the community has helped to form and preserve the place. Yet St. Joseph's displays even more clearly than other parishes (for whom it is also—always—true) that this vital connection, despite its longevity, is as tenuous as it has been tenacious.

PARISH AS TERRITORY

Throughout these chapters, my first assumption about the essence of parish has settled on the *community* of believers. Particularly in emphasizing the "sojourning" metaphor, *location* has not been nearly so much in view. Yet, from certain traditional perspectives, the connection between parish and place seems obvious. Long before it was decreed at the Council of Trent,[8] it had been the custom in much of Europe for the parish to be understood in a territorial way, at least regarding each significant location (a village, a neighborhood) having its own associated parish church. In the opening chapter, I wrote of my own childhood experience of the parish church as the *omphalos*—the "navel" or the center point of meaning—of my young life. Much later I was introduced to the phenomenon—known to many American Catholics who grew up in large Northeastern cities—of using the parish as a geographical marker: "Oh, you're from Dorchester? Which parish?" The physical plant of a typical American parish—almost invariably including at least the church, the rectory, the school, and the convent—was a sign of identity for Catholics, a landmark even for non-Catholics, and a reliable anchor for the community of care that parishioners learned to rely on.

In his now-classic pre–Vatican II article in pastoral theology, "Peaceful Reflections on the Parochial Principle," renowned twentieth-century theologian Karl Rahner, SJ, discussed the pastoral importance of the *spatial* way in which tradition and law have primarily conceived the Church and its world-wide administration. Rahner writes,

> The reason for this spatial structure of the church is a very profound one precisely because of its primitive nature, and is easily comprehensible: the Church's pastoral care is concerned with the *whole* man [*sic*] and with men insofar as they form a "people" which as such is to enter into the Kingdom of God. Both of these purposes are accomplished by addressing man as a being with a home.[9]

This way of understanding the parish helps Rahner to see a particularly crucial role for it amid "modern communization" in which the individual person "is left to the tender mercies of anonymous, vast, soul-less and brutal collective powers."[10] At its best, as I suggest in chapter 1, the parish as traditionally conceived can be an agent of humanization as well as evangelization in its more literal sense.

On the other hand, territorial definitions require imposed boundaries, and boundaries introduce not only measures of identity and security but also *constraints*. French Canadian Catholics of a certain age in the small city of Biddeford, Maine, recall that as children their "Catholic world" ended at Hill Street, which separated St. Joseph's and St. André's parishes. For years, the "us" versus "them" scenario in their heads had to do with kids from the other side of Hill Street. A question easily arises from the scenario: To what degree did the network of *care and concern* also fail to extend beyond that arbitrary boundary?

With such difficulties at hand, and the first glimmers of what would become movements like Fresh Expressions and City Church decades later, Rahner is able to come to some important forward-looking conclusions (given that the article was written even before the Second Vatican Council was convoked) regarding the ways that territorial parishes fall short of meeting all of the Church's pastoral needs. In one example, he asks,

> If school-children...live more in the school and in youth groups created by these surroundings than in the district of the town where they happen to live at any particular moment (until their parents "move" once more), and if our pastoral work must in its own interest meet them on their *own* ground, where they actually feel "at home," how can the parochial youth group, i.e., the youth of their "district," be the only and decisive meeting point between Church and school-child?[11]

Nearly sixty years later, Laurent Villemin, French priest and theologian, could say with regard to the type that corresponded neatly with a rural town or an urban neighborhood—the sort of territorial parish of which Rahner had already seen the social limitations:

> That pastoral function and that type of parish was intimately tied to what is called the Christian regime, which has well and truly disappeared along with the type of parish that was associated with it.[12]

Villemin cites Henri-Jérome Gagey as pointing out that, in the "plural belonging" of postmodern society, the issue is not the parish itself but rather an irrelevant ideal of parish assemblies as "the beating heart of totalizing natural communities."[13]

Such observations remind us once again of the complexity built into the root image of the *paroikía*. They suggest new metaphors for the *places* associated with parishes, to substitute for the unmovable *rock* or the unresponsive *ark* or the impersonal *service station*. Pope Francis extols the *flexibility* of the parish as a place of evangelization and urges that it use that flexibility to get "in contact with the homes and the lives of its people," taking care that it "does not become a useless structure out of touch with people or a self-absorbed group made up of a chosen few" (*EG* 28). Our contemporary sense of cultural and political impermanence already favors perspectives of *change* and *development*, and that atmosphere makes it particularly relevant to rediscover and revisit the motif of "spiritual sojourn" of which I have made extensive use here. In terms of sacred *place*, this perspective suggests images such as *pilgrimage* (the journey has a destination), *oasis* and *shelter* (there are places of refreshment and safety along the route), and perhaps *compass* or *signpost* (the route is marked or pointed out in both physical and spiritual ways). The parish may indeed be presented as a *territory*, but the point is not to remain there.

At the same time, the stories of very small but engaged communities such as St. Joseph's Bunhill Row urge caution in the ways that lessons taken from the decreasing relevance of territory are turned into plans for reorganizing the Church's pastoral life. Such a community may retain complicated but very real connections to the neighborhood around their church and should remain one of the decisive voices in plans that affect its very existence. Albert Rouet, the former archbishop of Poitiers (who presided over much of the restructuring there that was mentioned in chapter 4), has pointed out that reorganizing territorial parishes simply by combining them keeps the focus on the parish priest and gives him a new way to "shine." In the meantime, the places where formerly distinct parish communities gather are reduced to mere "annexes" or "way-stations,"[14] and the reorganization ends with the parish leadership further from, rather than nearer to, "the people."

The Poitiers approach left significant *locations* in place—it was not a matter of closing churches that still housed viable communities, nor of combining a number of otherwise viable communities for the sake of clerical convenience. Rather, it was the *territories* that were redrawn—now to be called "pastoral sectors"—and the roles of ordained pastoral leaders, lay professionals, and committed community members that were rethought. Subcommunities within the pastoral sectors carried on the essential day-to-day business of the Church in their own particular contexts, under the leadership of their own members commissioned by the archbishop for a set term, in the essential functions of teaching, prayer, service, funding, and general administration. The results, at their best, were networks of small communities that experienced a kind of spiritual renewal and growth that enlivened the whole Church of Poitiers. As Prof. Dr. Reinhard Feiter explains in his appreciative essay on the Poitiers experiment,

> A "discerning of spirits" is required here....Because of this elementary rule [of choosing local leadership] the local community becomes in a fundamental way a community that asks, that prays, that encourages. It becomes above all attentive to others and begins to question itself, to have experiences of being called and confirmed in an area of ministry, and to seek a language for this experience.[15]

Revitalizing and relying on the faith and abilities of all its members will be the way forward for the Church's continued efforts to be present "in the midst of the homes of her sons and daughters" (*CL* 26).

MUST A "PEOPLE" BE IN A "PLACE"?

In the previous two chapters, I have focused first on the *mission* of the parish and then on the role of *community* within that mission. I have considered both dimensions to be essential characteristics of the whole Church, embedded in its origins, doctrines, and practices. They are displayed in a particularly vital and concrete form, though, at the most local levels. Living Christian love requires face-to-face human contact. Originating in the work of the Holy Spirit "in [the] inner being" (Eph 3:16) and in the bonds of *koinonia*, love must be a *practice* and not merely a theological formula or distant ideal. As St. Ignatius of Loyola puts it, "Love ought to be put more in deeds than in words,"[16] and it "consists in a mutual sharing of goods."[17] To encounter such love in Christian community, as gift from God inviting our response, demands engagement within a context that regularly challenges and strengthens our practical abilities to be "one with" each other. In 1 John 4:20 there is a stark reminder: "Those who do not love a brother or sister whom they have seen, cannot love God whom they have not seen." The "recompense" (as St. Paul might put it [see 1 Cor 9:17–18]) of the community that meets the challenge and sustains this practical love is the grace of God going out as example into the world, new seed for the mission to be "rooted and grounded in love."

Living God's love in intimate contact with the real people to whom that love is directed was, of course, at the heart of what Jesus taught his disciples through his preaching, healing, and shared life with them. Yet, although the call to be "nearer to people" (*EG* 28) includes physical presence, it does not specify a geographical location or a single *way* of being present. Jesus also instructed his disciples to "go into the whole world" with their message. The teaching is received, preserved, and passed along by the whole Church at every level, not just by local communities. In our contemporary era, moreover, the worldview of many Christians is profoundly shaped by instant communication, social media, mass transportation, multiple and overlapping community memberships, and an ever-growing sense of individual autonomy. Some Christians, as we have seen, are inclining more toward an understanding of church as a loosely organized network of individuals than as a stably committed and engaged community.

For all these reasons, it is necessary to ask whether the mission of love in some way *requires* that "a certain community of the faithful" (i.e., a particular *embodiment* or *representation* of the whole people of God) be connected to a specific territory or *place* within which it lives its commitment and from which it reaches out. These are the parameters within which much of our contemporary understanding of parish has developed. If place *is* somehow essential, then what exactly is the *relationship* between the *community* and that *place* in which it is found? Seeking an answer to this question reveals further instances of the pilgrim/neighbor tension within the understanding of parish, which can never be completely resolved.[18]

CHRISTIANS AND "SACRED PLACE"[19]

"Place," writes Walter Brueggemann, "is space...where some things have happened which are now remembered and which provide continuity and identity across generations."[20] Regarding its sense of "sacred place," the Church's tradition of prayer and liturgy as well as its overall self-understanding owe much to the Hebrew Bible's reverence for the city of Jerusalem. The stories, psalms, and rituals of ancient Israel show us the depth of meaning and feeling, the gift and the challenge, connected with a "spiritual home." Jerusalem functions as a symbol of unity and strength for the people (Ps 48 is a particularly good example), but also of the sorrow, devastation, and rage of exile (Ps 137), the almost unspeakable joy of the return (Ps 126), and the pious longing to worship in the temple again and again with "brothers and friends" (Ps 122). In the mid-twentieth century, when new parish churches were being consecrated frequently in the United States, a common borrowing from this psalm tradition was the text of Psalm 43:4 enshrined over the doorway, rendered (as Ps 42:4) either in the Latin Vulgate or the Douay-Rheims version of the Psalms: "And I will go in to the altar of God: to God who giveth joy to my youth." Another popular entrance inscription, drawing on the tradition not of Jerusalem but of Bethel (where a rival temple was built during the division of the Israelite kingdom [1 Kgs 12:25–33]), quotes Jacob's dedication after marking the spot where he had his famous dream of the "ladder to heaven": "This is...the house of God, and this is the gate of heaven!" (Gen 28:17).[21]

On the other hand, in the gospel stories of the ministry of Jesus, the position of Jerusalem and its temple is far more ambiguous than in the Hebrew Bible. Although as an infant Jesus is presented in the temple and dedicated to God as the firstborn, it is on this occasion that his passion is first prophesied by Simeon (Luke 2:22–38). Later in the life of the child Jesus, the temple is also the scene of his first encounter (itself quite positive) with the scribes, others of whom will later be his adversaries

(Luke 2:41–51). This story is set against the "great anxiety" (Luke 2:48) of Mary and Joseph as they search for their "lost" child in a place that is both unexpected and deeply familiar ("my Father's house," Luke 2:49). In Jesus's adult ministry, his disagreements with the scribes and Pharisees about the meaning and use of the temple ("You have made it a den of robbers!" Mark 11:17) are understood by the Gospel writers from their conviction that, in Jesus, "something greater than the temple is here" (Matt 12:6). The contrast between the destructibility of the temple and the immortality of the risen Jesus is reflected in several gospel passages,[22] and we even read in the Book of Revelation that the *New* Jerusalem, "coming down out of heaven" (21:10), has no temple, "for its temple is the Lord God almighty and the Lamb" (21:22). As one biblical scholar has put it, "The New Testament finds holy space wherever Christ is or has been."[23]

Elsewhere in the New Testament, there are few hints of how today's Christians should answer the question of the relationship between the local church community and the place in which it is found or the territory with which it is associated. This is only *partly* because of the vast technological and social gap between the first and the twenty-first centuries. While *community* is certainly central to the biblical understanding of church (in ways that I discussed in chapter 4) and physical gathering is taken for granted, its specific *location* is not a matter of concern, and genuine spiritual communion across the breadth of the Roman Empire is clearly in view.[24] As the symbolic treatment of Jerusalem suggests, the earliest generations of Christians were much more focused on the kingdom toward which they were collectively bound than on their present earthly gathering places.[25] Speaking of the physical human body as a "tent," for instance, St. Paul proposes that Christians are awaiting "a building from God, a house not made with hands, eternal in the heavens" (2 Cor 5:1). There is no discussion of "sacred places" that is not linked to this eschatological vision of the triumph of faith, the fulfillment of hope, and the sanctification of believers in the divine presence into eternity.

Nonetheless, the communities that shared this vision were followers of the risen Christ, the Word Incarnate, and continued to exist in *this* world of time and space. Physical meeting was both an anticipation of the kingdom and, in the absence of "virtual space," an unavoidable necessity. Various arrangements for gatherings of Christians are alluded to in the Scripture. In the Acts of the Apostles, we read that following Jesus's ascension, the apostles returned to Jerusalem and "went to the room upstairs where they were staying" (1:13). Within a few verses, the text remarks that "together the crowd numbered about one hundred twenty persons" (1:15), and that when the day of Pentecost came "a sound like the rush of a violent wind...filled the entire house where they were sitting" (2:2). A more public dimension is also attested. As the description of the growing Jerusalem community unfolds, Acts notes, "Day by day, as they spent much time together in the temple, they broke bread at home" (2:46).[26]

The letters of Paul (all but a few of which identify their intended recipients by their city of residence) take for granted a similar pattern of large group meetings and smaller "house church" devotions. In chiding the Corinthians about their faulty eucharistic practice, which amplifies divisions within the community, Paul declares, "When you come together, it is not really to eat the Lord's supper. For when the time comes to eat, each of you goes ahead with your own supper" (1 Cor 11:20–21). He then asks rhetorically, "Do you not have homes to eat and drink in?" (v. 22) and goes on to remind them of the true tradition of the Eucharist, ending with the exhortation, "So then...when you come together to eat, wait for one another" (v. 33).

There are other hints of house-church arrangements involving more than just the resident family. The Jewish Christian couple Prisca and Aquila, along with "the church in their house," are mentioned twice, once when they were residing in Rome (Rom 16:5) and again when they were apparently living at Ephesus but still gathering a small community of Christians around them (1 Cor 16:19). "Give my greetings to the brothers and sisters in Laodicea, and to Nympha and the church in her house," writes Paul to the Colossians (4:15). The letter to Philemon opens with, "Paul...to Philemon, our dear friend and coworker...and to the church in your house" (Philemon 1–2). The intimacy attested by these allusions puts the emphasis back on the *koinonia* experienced among these Christians, but it is easy to imagine that the physical arrangements, particularly in private homes large enough to host a group, would have played a role in the expression of that intimacy.

"CHURCH PLACE" AS "SPIRITUAL HOME"

The twentieth-century discovery of the ruins of an ancient house at Dura-Europos on the Euphrates in what is now Syria—a Roman outpost during the mid-first to mid-second centuries AD—points to another phase in the development of Christian sacred place. The building (which has been called "the world's oldest church"[27]) had the form of a private home but had been renovated to create a larger assembly room with a raised platform at one end and, on the opposite side of the central courtyard, a baptistry thoroughly decorated with a series of Christian motif murals and with a large basin dug into the floor.[28] Thus, about two hundred years after Paul's greetings to and from Aquila and Prisca and "the church at their house," it seems that some houses had been converted to full-time church use—indeed, the first "parish churches."

These origins suggest that the development of dedicated, permanent gathering places was in many ways a clear gain for local Christian communities in all their variation. A house with several rooms could be carefully arranged for specific purposes and would accommodate larger gatherings, perhaps even several simultaneous meetings. No one household would be overly taxed, nor gain undue influence, by hosting the community. Most important of all, the community per se would gain a home that would, by its physical arrangement and its decoration, reflect the people's shared stories and practice. As we experience even now, such a place can hold and contribute to the memories and customs—the culture—of the people who have worshiped there and becomes itself a symbol of their *koinonia*. The house at Dura-Europos probably functioned in this way for only about fifteen years,[29] not long enough to attain the venerability of many still-extant parish churches built in later centuries. Yet, to study its form and its murals today, eighteen hundred years later, is still to gain fascinating insights into the faith and hope of ordinary believers in that time and place.[30]

Many variations contributed to the continued development of local church places in subsequent centuries. In Rome, what might be considered the next step along from the dedicated house church were the "titular churches," privately owned buildings that evolved from house churches to purpose-built meeting places for neighborhood-level Christian communities. Sites associated with the death or burial of particular martyrs (notably Peter and Paul) were frequented for worship at shrines that gradually became increasingly elaborate. Under the Emperor Constantine, building projects began that included—often in locations already associated with worship—basilicas large enough to gather many urban neighborhood communities together in one place with their local bishop (some of which—much altered architecturally over the centuries—remain to this day).[31]

Further afield from Rome and somewhat later in the development, the chapels or churches of monasteries often became important gathering places for Christians in the surrounding locality. As the feudal system gradually emerged in the West amid the ruins of Roman order, especially in some of the kingdoms established by recently Christianized Germanic tribes, proprietary churches (*Eigenkirchen*) were erected by important landlords. These owners then controlled both the tithes paid by the members of the worshiping community (as Christianization continued, nearly all the people of a district) as well as the appointment of the clergy for that community. In part as a countermove by bishops to reestablish some ecclesiastical control, other "baptismal churches" were erected as the official sites for the celebration of that sacrament. Later still, particularly as new urban areas in Europe began to develop, guilds and sodalities—pious associations of laypeople giving mutual spiritual, material, social support, and prestige to their members—were sometimes wealthy enough to have their own churches or at least elaborate chapels or altars within larger parish churches.[32]

All these developments, however, also help to make apparent the various losses associated with the shift toward physical church buildings. The "settling in" of the pilgrim people would have both signaled and helped to normalize important shifts in beliefs, practices, and perceptions. For one thing, concern for permanent buildings points to the gradual diminishment of a lively expectation that the Lord is "coming soon" (Rev 22:6, 12). The sense of a longer "earthly exile" than the first believers expected did contribute to the communities' spiritual development (broadening and deepening appreciation of the material and symbolic world, for example). It also added, though, a lengthening list of mundane tasks to the churches' purview, from fundraising to maintenance, that are still with us today. In doing so, it also necessitated more elaborate forms of organization, and therefore of authority.

What is more, because "the Church" was now in a specific location, it was vulnerable to becoming objectified apart from the *koinonia*, the network of divine and human relationships of faith, hope, and love, that had brought it into being. Even while allowing the whole community a sense of having a "spiritual home," the appearance of church buildings thus also contributed to the slow process of transposing the value of the gathered community of believers with the place of gathering and the institutional framework that supported it. A simple inventory of the ways we now commonly speak of and imagine "going to church" would reveal what this trend has hardened into, consequently pushing many people further away from a sense of full participation in the community. It has been a very long road from Dura-Europos to the proprietary churches of the Middle Ages and on to the "service-station" parishes of late twentieth-century America, but the route can still be traced.

This trajectory might seem to argue that the traditional territorial parish centered on a church building was a mistaken and dangerous organizational choice. Such a conclusion might suit some of the narratives that favor looser affiliations of individual Christians with no permanent physical location at all. (This could describe some versions of the Fresh Expressions and "urban pastoral" approaches mentioned in chapter 4, but rejection of elaborate institutions and buildings has been standard in criticisms of Catholic practice since before the Reformation.) Yet this line of reasoning passes over many advantages both practical and symbolic that were gained in the early centuries, many of which remain and are easily taken for granted. More importantly, abandoning the basic parish model too readily would also mean abandoning millennia-old roots of still-vital religious cultures that continue even now to provide both comfort and challenge to believers and would-be believers. In this way, a "progressive" move to "greater freedom" from literal church structures could become a disguise for another form of the refusal to listen to a whole community, the failure to hear what the Spirit might be saying, the assumption that we cannot read the signs of the times in unexpected places.[33]

On the other hand, there is also real danger that the memories associated with a "spiritual home" could be idealized into a romantic fantasy that leads only to frustration and internal conflict. Spiritual depth can be found in a community's sense of place only when that place has been allowed to develop into a true *icon*. I mean this in much the same way as when, in chapter 4, I proposed the community itself as an icon of *koinonia*—a sacred image, carrying the awareness of both the genuine beauty and gift *and* the real sinfulness and suffering of the community. In this case, the image would carry, as well, a serious invitation to the community to rediscover its pilgrimage toward God's reign. That onward journey is what gives perspective to any physical attachments Christians might develop, a grounding in eschatology by which "we recognize that the present place is emphatically not the end of the world."[34]

As in every aspect of a "parish of the people," what is needed in questions affecting the status of a parish's "place" is the community's honest self-awareness, supported by open dialogue and prayerful discernment. Fostering the conditions for this kind of exchange is an urgent priority for the leaders of parish communities, long before they face the need for practical decisions.

THE PARISH AS "HOLY GROUND"

An icon, as the Orthodox and Eastern Catholic traditions are particularly aware, is an image created and venerated in a way that renders it *sacramental*: a material object forms a doorway or a bridge to sacred reality and draws those who use it deeper into the presence of God.[35] The principle applies to many different aspects of the physical universe (as when Jacob declares that Bethel is "the gateway of heaven") but is relevant to religious objects in obvious ways, not only in the popular devotions of many Latin Rite Catholics but in official rituals such as that used to consecrate new church buildings for sacred use. In that ceremony, which was entirely revised after Vatican II, chrism (the same oil used in confirmation and in holy orders) is used to anoint the walls of the church with crosses in twelve different places and is applied liberally to the altar table (and, in the case of the old rite, a traditional stone altar, lighted on fire), to mark the sacred character of the place.[36] From then on, tradition invites parishioners to bless themselves with holy water as a reminder of their baptism whenever they enter the building, and many older Catholics may still observe the custom of making the Sign of the Cross even if they simply pass the church on the street.

There is a rather startling reversal of messaging between such customary veneration and the trope, "It's only a building," frequently offered in response to the resistance of alarmed parishioners during church closure procedures. The marked contrast (and the smugness with which the excuse is sometimes offered) helps to explain why resistance has so often arisen in the first place. The stubborn reluctance of some parish communities to relinquish their "spiritual home" has been seen in reorganization contexts time and time again. It is an important reminder of another essential aspect of an icon: as a symbol, it doesn't merely point in one distinct direction, but gives access to many "layers" of reality at once. These multiple meanings are the primary reason a clerical insistence on official ritual as the "true purpose" of church buildings so often rings hollow to long-time parishioners. It is also why, when that insistence prevails, it can become a contributor to the deadening of once-lively community participation.

"If they want the Eucharist," grumbled one beset pastor of a merging parish community, "they will go where the Eucharist is offered!" But an iconic parish church is more than mere space in which to celebrate Mass and the sacraments. Certainly, it is beyond question that the sacramental life of the Church, culminating in the Eucharist, is essential to the meaning of the parish, and that a primary *function* of the parish church building is the celebration of those sacraments. But *function* is only one of the many layers of meaning presented by the physical parish in its sacramental character. The church building is a monument—often quite literally—to the faith, hopes, dedication, and countless contributions of its founding members and all those who have sustained it since. They are the living Body of Christ that the Eucharist nourishes, "the temple of the living God" (2 Cor 6:16), a "spiritual house" built of "living stones" (1 Pet 2:5). Further, the building carries marks not only of the history of its own use and renovation, but of the wider cultural and religious history of its people—in its architectural style; in the patron saints or wondrous stories that are portrayed in its windows, paintings, and statuary; in the decorative devices and colors chosen. A parish church, whether it will, should, or even can continue in use, is always a marker of a place on earth where a faithful community has proclaimed God's presence and action among them in palpable forms. (Anglican Bishop John Inge, with his "relational view of place," describes sacred places as "the seat of relations or the place of meeting and activity in the interaction between God and the world."[37]) This helps to explain why it has been suggested that a church can be "read," or that the *de*-consecration of one could be appropriately observed with a version of the funeral rite.[38]

We can now understand how the place where a parish community gathers provides an enriching context for the Eucharist that actualizes and proclaims the community's *koinonia*. That context is created, and the place is consecrated by an essentially *sacramental* outlook of the community that understands its iconic nature. These believers look to the incarnate Christ in order to see God "in the flesh." Having thus encountered God "sacramentally" in their shared faith, they continue to experience this encounter in the physical place that is dedicated to it—in the light and sound and ritual gesture that stimulate their senses, in the ways they themselves participate in the rites, in how they relate to others who also take part, and in the memories and meanings they form from it all. In the midst of this web of sensual experience and sacred meaning, they deepen their reverence for the material world and their own essential place within it. Yet they also begin to learn how to "hold lightly" the material gift that is drawing them ever deeper into the knowledge and love of God, who will ultimately fulfill the meaning that is growing here on this "holy ground."

It is within this already sacramental environment that the sacrament of the Eucharist is received. The context gives that word its richest meaning. Parishioners do not merely line up to do what is expected or to take advantage of a service that is offered. Rather, they *open* themselves, physically and spiritually, to welcome Christ sacramentally into a life already shaped by his sacramental presence in the community and in the place where they gather. To receive the sacrament in this way is truly to "receive communion," an encounter of unity, however imperfect, with Christ himself and with the other members of the community. Of course, the encounter is not limited to those who share that physical place, even though the place is essential to it. Through the Eucharist, Christ extends the sacramental *koinonia* from one sacred place to the next, creating bonds of divine love among all the local communities and with the whole universal Church. The communities will be constantly reminded of these bonds and all they signify whenever they meet on their own "holy ground." Bishop Inge summarizes:

> Holy places are…associated with holy people to whom and in whom something of the glory of God has been revealed. The existence of such holy places should facilitate a sacramental perception and serve as a reminder that all time and place belong to God in Christ—the part is set aside on behalf of, rather than instead of, the whole.[39]

"HOLY GROUND," THE EARTH, AND THE CHURCH'S MISSION

As is affirmed by Brueggemann, Inge, Rumsey, and many others, a community's connection to a specific *place*—however temporary or enduring it may prove to be—is a living verification of a biblical perspective that finds the Spirit of God present and accessible through the peculiar history and characteristics of that location. John Zizioulas, in his discussion on *koinonia*, broadens this basic insight dramatically by considering the *whole* context of the Church:

> Sensitivity to the integrity of creation has not been traditionally part of the Christian mission. We now realize that it ought to be. The Church as *koinonia* relates also to the animal and the material world as a whole. Perhaps the most urgent mission of the Church today is to become conscious of and to proclaim in the strongest terms the fact that there is an intrinsic *koinonia* between the human being and its natural environment, a *koinonia* that must be brought into the Church's very being in order to receive its fullness.[40]

This theological insight prefigures and resonates with that of Pope Francis in *Laudato Si'* ("On Care for Our Common Home"), with all its references to earlier papal uses of the terms *integral development* and *human ecology* (*LS*, esp. 3–6, 16). Francis's description of the relationship between Indigenous communities and their land sets the standard that is then applied to all of humanity:

> For them, land is not a commodity but rather a gift from God and from their ancestors who rest there, a sacred space with which they need to interact if they are to maintain their identity and values. When they remain on their land, they themselves care for it best. (*LS* 146)

This interaction between *place* and a community's relationship with God is put in a nutshell in *Querida Amazonia*: "In a cultural reality like the Amazon region…daily existence is always cosmic."[41] The line of reasoning, then, has moved from human community with the Trinity (*koinonia*) to its broad ecological context in creation and back to a specific application with cosmic ramifications.

The principle itself may strike many people, especially in the "developed world," as hopelessly romantic and irrelevant to contemporary life. From Francis's perspective, this reaction illustrates the point exactly: the chasm that has already been opened between many societies and their physical surroundings is related both to heedless environmental degradation and to the diminishment of human culture and, by implication, to the loss of a sense of the divine.

> Culture is more than what we have inherited from the past; it is also, and above all, a living, dynamic and participatory present reality, which cannot be excluded as we rethink the relationship between human beings and the environment. A consumerist vision of human beings, encouraged by the mechanisms of today's globalized economy, has a levelling effect on cultures, diminishing the immense variety which is the heritage of all humanity.…New processes taking shape cannot always fit into frameworks imported from outside; they need to be based in the local culture itself. (*LS* 143–44)

Francis is not simply emphasizing negative spiritual aspects of globalization. His presentation of what being "based in the local culture" can look like circles us back to the kinds of communities that, embedded in their cultures spiritually and physically, parishes of the people might be. Through "a network of solidarity and belonging," claims the pope, "any place can turn from being a hell on earth into the setting for a dignified life" (*LS* 148).

> Society is also enriched by a countless array of organizations which work to promote the common good and to defend the environment, whether natural or urban.…Around these community actions, relationships develop or are recovered, and a new social fabric emerges. Thus, a community can break out of the indifference induced by consumerism. These actions cultivate a shared identity, with a story which can be remembered and handed on. In this way, the world, and the quality of life of the poorest, are cared for, with a sense of solidarity which is at the same time aware that we live in a common home which God has entrusted to us. (*LS* 232)

Included in this picture of the "*koinonia* of creation" are not only the poor but even those who may find it most difficult to shift their attitudes toward *physical place* because of the benefits they derive from modern technology. Francis also notes, "The ecological conversion needed to bring about lasting change is also a community conversion" (*LS* 219).

Pope Francis's focus here addresses the greatest danger that could arise from a distorted image of the parish as a "spiritual home." A parish community that forgets its wider context and its "neighbor" dimension, that is entirely involved with itself, that looks outward only in defensiveness and fear, is one that mistakes its own roots in the gospel of Christ. The parish as a spiritual home, we recall, is a community of sojourners—not so much like a fortress as like the desert encampment of ancient Israel (as in Exod 19:2)[42] (yet with a new solicitude, bequeathed by its Master, for the "lepers" who were once pushed to the outer edge—see Lev 13:45–46). What the contemporary understanding of parish can draw particularly from these reflections on *place* is the possibility of participating, not *despite* its localness but *through* it, in a "network of solidarity and belonging." From the parish's own "holy ground" this network is extended into a worldwide witness of missionary disciples, living by a Christian vision of wholeness with deep physical and practical implications for humanity today.

Chapter 6

THE PARISH AND THE LARGER CHURCH

The global need not stifle, nor the particular prove barren.

Pope Francis, *Evangelii Gaudium* 235

THE PEOPLE AND THE BISHOP

St. Thomas Aquinas Church on the island of Jamaica (where "parish" is most recognizable to ordinary people as the term for the island's fourteen governmental regions) is a small community in the Archdiocese of Kingston with a weekly Mass attendance of perhaps three hundred persons. Situated in the northeastern corner of the capital, where urban streets give way to the winding roads, ragged forests, and rural hamlets of the Blue Mountains, Aquinas came into being in 1962 as a Catholic student center just off the main campus of the University of the West Indies. At the time, the Jesuit mission region of Jamaica and the Archdiocese of Kingston were nearly indistinguishable ecclesiastical entities; both could take credit for the creation of the student center. A durable, adaptable structure was built, with worship space on the ground floor and provision upstairs for a small apartment, chaplain's office, and student meeting rooms.

As time went on, the collaboration of Jesuit priests with students, staff, and faculty of the university, as well as other residents of the area, resulted in a viable community of worship and service. Though favored and frequently visited by the archbishop (at first an American missionary, but within a few years a native Jamaican), the community at Aquinas both operated and understood itself as "independent" within the structure of the archdiocese. This perception was eventually made official when the Aquinas community petitioned the archbishop to be established as "St. Thomas Aquinas Parish." It was given canonical status as both a "personal" parish (to which any Catholic connected to the University had the right to belong) and a "territorial" parish (with an area carved out of the adjacent SS Peter and Paul Parish). The conferral of parish status recognized the community, which had already become much more diverse than the university community alone and would now include several neighborhoods of "working poor" residents. Aquinas became one of only a few parishes in the archdiocese that was financially self-sustaining and also one of even fewer that regularly gathered parishioners from both extremes of Jamaica's badly divided socioeconomic structure.

The creation of the new parish brought to the fore some complex underlying social tensions that would continue to flare occasionally in the decades that followed. One of these involved the distinctions and overlaps between the Aquinas community (some, but not all, of whom were delighted to have "their own church") and the community at SS Peter and Paul, whose church was situated about two miles away in a more affluent neighborhood near the archbishop's residence and chancery. All of St. Thomas Aquinas's territory had previously belonged to SS Peter and Paul, but the division had excluded from Aquinas one wealthy neighborhood that many saw as belonging geographically to the new parish. Despite the fact that many Kingston Catholics had no qualms about attending and donating to a parish other than their territorially assigned one, and the "traffic" between the two communities was steady and usually quite amicable, the "manipulated map" was still remembered and mentioned decades later.

SS Peter and Paul actually had relinquished to its daughter parish another geographically isolated neighborhood, this one quite poor. It was just far enough away from Aquinas Center to make frequent attendance by its residents dependent on public transportation, which was irregular at best and an unwelcome expense for some would-be parishioners. After years of relative neglect, this area was "adopted" by the rector of the archdiocesan seminary (also located adjacent to the university campus) who saw it as an opportunity to train the seminarians for evangelization and outreach. Yet another new parish church, Christ the King, was established there. But after the seminarians were sent instead to Trinidad, those parishioners were returned to the pastoral care of St. Thomas Aquinas without much planning or consultation. Dissatisfaction was the general result, with parishioners finding that the priest at Aquinas was hard-pressed to provide the level of attention that they had gotten used to.

Closer to Aquinas Center itself, another tension developed between members of the university community and more affluent attendees, on the one hand, and on the other, parishioners who lived in the much poorer neighborhoods on the opposite side of the parish property. Among the latter group were an increasing number of "squatters" who had begun to occupy "captured land" adjacent to the Center—land that legally belonged to the University Hospital across the road from Aquinas. About ten years after the parish was established, a Jesuit pastor focused a great deal of attention on this extremely poor and often violent neighborhood. He established a center for social services there, with decidedly mixed reactions—from wholehearted involvement to grumbling disagreement—from the "regular" parishioners. Long after that pastor had moved on and his center had been more or less abandoned, the proper approach to ministry to people from "the Common" was a source of sometimes bitter disagreement among parishioners.

While the lay community developed its own set of dynamics that either dealt with or covered over these and other tensions, the leadership priorities at St. Thomas Aquinas shifted significantly several times over the years. Sometime after the activist pastor, the parish was put in the care of the Passionist order, who used much of the office and meeting space on the second floor of the Center for a "house of studies" for several of their own seminarians. Direct work with university students shifted to a small office on the campus itself. After the house of studies was also closed, the new pastor (another Jesuit) was pulled back into concentrating on the plight of the very poor in the parish when a powerful hurricane tore up the whole island. When that pastor retired, a team of several Jesuits were sent to see what more could be accomplished by studying the needs and possibilities of the whole parish area and working together on several pastoral and social development projects. That effort faltered largely for lack of a sufficient cadre of priests to keep it going. Subsequent Jesuit, archdiocesan, and Dominican leadership have brought a series of other initiatives and focuses. Through it all, the community has carried on with the week-to-week business of "church."

Although the Aquinas community was, in fact, initiated by the action of the archdiocese and its Jesuit collaborators, it has proven durable across many changes of leadership and circumstances. It has also taken its place happily enough within the structure and practice of the Archdiocese of Kingston. Truly, that practice has been such that neither Aquinas nor any of the other parishes across the eastern half of Jamaica have ever had much opportunity to ignore the reality of belonging to a larger ecclesial body. In many ways this has been very good, even essential, for the many small and somewhat isolated communities of the archdiocese. Although transportation is always a challenge, the archdiocese is compact enough geographically and outnumbered enough by other Christian denominations to have developed a culture that values frequent large gatherings of ordinary parishioners. For many years there was a tradition of an annual "diocesan synod" that gathered the clergy and lay representatives from every parish for reports and deliberations about the priorities and initiatives of the archdiocese. This was preceded by several days of "renewal"—preaching, music, and liturgy open to all—and an official opening Mass at the National Arena. During the following week, synod delegates converged on Aquinas Center, which was transformed for that week into the hub of archdiocesan activity. At each synod, new initiatives were agreed upon that shaped the work of archdiocesan offices and individual parishes for the rest of the year. Parishioners of Aquinas generally welcomed the synod meetings with appropriate excitement, but also quickly grew weary of the disruption of the parish routine.

Even at more ordinary times of the year, parishioners were used to interacting with various archdiocesan organizations and agencies. Many parish functions and activities were overseen or at least "animated" by archdiocesan counterparts. This arrangement, however, was not without its problems, as archdiocesan umbrella groups were not always very accommodating toward parishes that developed their own responses to community-level situations. For example, the archdiocesan altar servers' group at one point would not allow girls to participate in its activities, but female altar servers had long been the custom at Aquinas. Likewise, in dealing with the popular charismatic prayer movement, the archdiocese favored a single large meeting at one of the centrally located parishes. At Aquinas, however, lay parishioners led another weekly gathering that attracted many of the working class and poor—parishioners and non-Catholics alike—from the neighborhoods nearby the church. For some of these attendees, uninformed about the intricacies of Catholic governance, that Tuesday evening gathering was enough to consider themselves "members of Aquinas." Despite all the opportunities parishioners have had for contact with the archdiocese, and the pride with which they have participated, it has often been clear that for participants like these, the archbishop's "higher" level seemed very far away from the immediacy and relevance of "church."

PARISH "COMMUNITY" AND DIOCESAN "LOCAL CHURCH"

THESE RECOLLECTIONS PRESENT the question—lived in many different ways under vastly different circumstances around the world—of the relationship between the parish community and the diocese within which the parish exists. St. Thomas Aquinas Church demonstrates one distinctive approach to this relationship, with its goals and advantages on the one hand but also its limitations and problems on the other. This chapter will look more closely at what the parish's place within the diocese—and therefore within the structures of the universal Church—is meant to signify theologically and accomplish pastorally. I will attempt here to point in directions that seem more promising for the development and flourishing of communities of missionary disciples throughout the Church.

Just as the individual members of a parish cannot be Christians "by themselves," so the parish as Catholic community cannot be "on its own." It must be—in theological principle, by institutional mandate, and in lived experience—integrated into and accessible to the larger Church. The parish is generally the entry point to the Church for all those otherwise "individual" believers. Alongside being "rooted and grounded in love," this relationship to the entire Body of Christ is of the greatest consequence for a Catholic understanding of local church community. Indeed, among the many places in the New Testament in which Church *unity* is a central concern, the Letter to the Ephesians dedicates most of its fourth chapter to this question, and makes use of this concept of the Body of Christ as the principle of unity:

> The gifts he gave were that some would be apostles, some prophets, some evangelists, some pastors and teachers, to equip the saints for the work of ministry, for building up the body of Christ, until all of us come to the unity of the faith and of the knowledge of the Son of God, to maturity, to the measure of the full stature of Christ. (Eph 4:11–13)

Recall, too, that this letter as well as the Letter to the Colossians was addressed to "the saints and faithful brothers and sisters in Christ," and is concerned with the broader Church beyond these specific communities.

The Church's concern with *unity* and its foundation in the sacramental presence of the risen Christ is clear even in the earliest memories of the believers. An important *contemporary* point of reference for these concerns is the 1992 letter "On Some Aspects of the Church Understood as Communion," from the Congregation for the Doctrine of the Faith,[1] cited earlier in chapter 4. The letter mirrors the theology of Joseph Ratzinger, the future Pope Benedict XVI, who was cardinal prefect of the Congregation at the time,[2] and presents two distinct but inseparable dimensions of "communion" (*koinonia*). "Vertical" or "invisible" communion is understood as the bond "of each human being with the Father through Christ in the Holy Spirit, and with the others who are fellow sharers in the divine nature." "Horizontal" communion is described as "the visible communion in the teaching of the Apostles, in the sacraments and in the hierarchical order." "This link between the invisible and visible elements of ecclesial communion," the letter goes on to explain, "constitutes the Church as the *Sacrament* of salvation"—relying on the basic understanding of a sacrament as a sign that brings together the material and the spiritual.[3] Here, the point of insisting on the *visible* communion is to emphasize the role of the hierarchy in maintaining the unity of the whole Church. The collegiality of the bishops who are "in communion" with the pope, the Bishop of Rome, is founded on the bishops' succession to the office of the Twelve Apostles and on *their* communion with Jesus.

Except to note that it is long and complex, the history of the development of administrative structures associated with the episcopal exercise of this ministry of unity (such as the diocese) need not delay the discussion here. It is important to note, though, that this institutional dimension—the aspect of the Church that allows all these essential relationships to be passed on again and again, without having to be reinvented constantly—has been the source of important tensions throughout the Church's history. There is irony in this, of course, since the goal is unity; yet the struggle to bring together the joy of deeply felt spiritual identity with the demanding discipleship that empowers it is still familiar to Christians today. Paul's letters to the Christians in Corinth and in the region of Galatia, as the itinerant apostle struggles for recognition of his authority in Christ over the local churches that he has established, are poignant examples. "I do not mean to imply that we lord it over your faith; rather, we are workers with you for your joy, because you stand firm in the faith," he explains to the confused and offended Corinthians after changing his plans to visit them again (2 Cor 1:24). At a point of greater frustration in addressing the Galatians, who were being wooed by other Christians who wanted them to keep the whole Mosaic Law, Paul writes, "[When] I first announced the gospel to you...you did not scorn or despise me, but welcomed me as an angel of God, as Christ Jesus. What has become of the goodwill you felt?" (Gal 4:13–15). Paul had only moral authority to fall back on, but he uses it to great effect in passages like these. At times, though, we might easily imagine him wishing that he had access to more institutional tools, all for the good work of keeping these scattered and sometimes unruly churches focused on the full wonder of the message he has shared with them.

Today, many among those who *do* have such tools—diocesan bishops, chancery officials, and the many professionals who staff their offices—prefer to read Paul's letters as addressed to "diocesan" churches encompassing multiple groups of Christians in and around a given city.[4] The individual households—some large enough to host Christians from outside the house, others smaller both in numbers and in resources[5]—seem to correspond to what we call "parishes" today. From the diocesan perspective, the relationship of the whole region to its specific communities can be cast in rather functional and clerical terms. Canon law may describe the parish as a "community," but in declaring it to be among the "juridic persons" in the Church (can. 515.3), "that is, subjects in canon law of obligations and rights which correspond to their nature" (can. 113.2), the law also decrees, "In all juridic affairs the pastor represents the parish according to the norm of law" (can. 532). Furthermore, "It is only for the diocesan bishop to erect, suppress, or alter parishes" (can. 515.2). Within this legal perspective, attempts by parishes to claim and develop their particular local style and subculture (based on the faith lives of the laypeople who make up the network of relationships that give the parish its substance as a "stable community") can sometimes seem to clerics like dangerous overreach, likely to breed confusion and disunity.

Those who approach the question of the parish's place in the structure of the Church from this perspective see it confirmed in Vatican II's discussion of the local church in *Lumen Gentium*, the Dogmatic Constitution on the Church. One favored line reminds the readers that "Every legitimate celebration of the Eucharist is regulated by the bishop" (*LG* 26). However, a longer block of material immediately preceding this sentence gives a rather different impression of how the Council is imagining the pastoral landscape:

> This Church of Christ is really present in all legitimately organized local groups [*congregationibus localibus*] of the faithful, which, in so far as they are united to their pastors, are also quite appropriately called Churches in the New

> Testament. For these are in fact, in their own localities, the new People called by God, in the power of the Holy Spirit and as the result of full conviction (cf. 1 Thess 1:5). In them the faithful are gathered together through the preaching of the Gospel of Christ, and the mystery of the Lord's Supper is celebrated, "so that, by means of the flesh and blood of the Lord the whole brotherhood of the Body may be welded together."[6] In each altar community, under the sacred ministry of the bishop, a symbol is to be seen of that charity and "unity of the mystical body, without which there can be no salvation."[7] In these communities, though they may often be small and poor, or existing in the diaspora, Christ is present through whose power and influence the One, Holy, Catholic and Apostolic Church is constituted. For "the sharing in the body and blood of Christ has no other effect than to accomplish our transformation into that which we receive."[8]

It is the reference to the "altar community," and even more specifically the mention of the actual receiving of the Eucharist, which make it clear that this passage also carries forward the more simple and direct statement of a previous document. Regarding parishes, the Council's Constitution on the Sacred Liturgy (*Sacrosanctum Concilium*) had written that "in some manner they represent the visible Church constituted throughout the world" (*SC* 42). This role is taken up, according to *Sacrosanctum*, because since ancient times it has become "impossible for the bishop always and everywhere to preside over the whole flock in his Church." One might venture to say that as the pastor represents the bishop, the parish represents the diocese. This establishes as a pastoral priority, singled out in *Sacrosanctum*, that "efforts also must be made to encourage a sense of community within the parish, above all in the common celebration of the Sunday Mass" (*SC* 42).

When this crucial perspective is missing, with its tying together of the mission and dignity of parish and diocese, the relationship to the diocese can, from the viewpoint of the parish communities, seem distant (if not actually *external*), arbitrary, out of touch. Very little in the Church's current crises has helped to soften that impression. To challenge the dysfunction in the relationship, what most needs to be addressed is the legalistic attitude toward the parish community. Beyond its status as "*juridical* person" (which, as we have seen, points most directly to the pastor and the bishop) the parish must also be seen as a *koinonia* of "*human* persons," and therefore a *moral* and *pastoral* entity. In fact, this aspect shows us the original, underlying reality, given the origins of local Christian communities that we have been consulting all along.[9]

This shift in perspective is more attitudinal than structural or legal, at least initially. A bishop may indeed control canonically the creation or suppression of a parish. However, equally crucial to pastoral dynamism and compassionate presence are careful respect for the community and its entire context, as well as a willingness to read carefully the social structures and overlapping networks of relationship (both religious and secular) that already connect parishioners or would-be parishioners to each other, the Church, and the larger world. The question, "*Whose* is the parish?" that has brought dioceses to civil court on many occasions (often so that Catholics can argue vehemently against one another[10]) might arise less frequently and divisively if the multiple layers of meaning and reality in a parish (*beyond* its apparent "usefulness" to a diocesan pastoral plan) were more systemically recognized. This attitude, moreover, would go far toward allowing the parish to assume its proper role in a truly "synodal" Church, that is, believers in Christ "journeying together and reflecting together" in a way that "effectively enacts and manifests the nature of the Church as the pilgrim and missionary People of God."[11]

PARISH, DIOCESE, AND THE "COMMUNITY OF COMMUNITIES"

A sociological study published by Tricia Colleen Bruce in 2017 discusses the canonical entity called the "personal parish," attempting to imagine the ideal cooperation between diocese and parish.[12] What Bruce has noticed is that a natural tension exists within the parish system between "place" (the location of the church building or the area from which it draws its attendees) and "purpose" (the spiritual and social reasons why any of those members may attend church in the first place). Organizing primarily according to place (the "territorial system") prioritizes the location and assumes that parishioners will attend regardless of the style of worship or the other activities taking place. Organizing according to purpose puts the emphasis on some unifying characteristic, or a small group of strongly related ones, and assumes that those who attend will share that identifying mark. Bruce contends that "the proportion of dioceses with personal parishes grows each year,"[13] and finds support in this trend for her assertion that "the US Catholic Church reconciles place and purpose through a higher-order outlook on community: one that is managed across dioceses, rather than within single parishes."[14]

Bruce claims that the resolution of this tension is accomplished at the diocesan level, where the optimal balance of personal and territorial parishes can be most efficiently determined and can allow for the regional church to serve both those who respond best to the Church when they experience it as a nearby and integrated feature of their ordinary lives, and those whose response is strengthened by a strong and specific liturgical, spiritual, or social mission. It does seem, though, that for this system to work in a way that serves the underlying mission and community of "parishes of the people" requires that the diocese be strongly and purposefully ordered toward listening to and cooperating with both the existing communities of the faithful (whether independent of parish or developing within parishes) and those whose participation in the Church's mission and community life may have been marginalized, intentionally or by negligence.

Beyond Bruce's focus on the choice between personal or territorial parish structures, it is worth the time to reflect here on the kind of support that dioceses might give to all the face-to-face communities within their purview. It is well established by now—through the Scriptures, basic moral convictions, sacramental practice, and a host of related reflections—that, indeed, these communities are of great value to the Church. Is it not, then, incumbent on the bishops to employ the Church's two thousand years of experience, and accumulated wisdom and talent, to devise means for active communities to go on living in communion with the larger Church? In many situations, current strong canonical preferences (such as a resident ordained pastor, and ordination restricted to celibate men with extensive seminary education) create seemingly insurmountable barriers. Yet ancient practice, more recent "experimental" or "emergency" measures, and a host of current but atypical arrangements in various places could all be starting points for broader approaches toward the Church's future. The existence of these models honors the contributions of local church communities as highly valuable and very much worthy of the hard work of listening and discernment required for the establishment of new or revived practices or structures. This *humble listening* on the part of those who discern the Church's mission at the diocesan level is the counterpart to the listening that the parish community itself has to do in shaping its outreach according to the broader community within which it exists. So, rather than creating "master plans" laced with insufficient engagement with the daily reality of its local communities, dioceses would be well advised to carefully *learn* that concrete reality through careful attention to how its decision-makers become present to those communities.

Bruce's sociological perspective may help us to get more concrete with regard to the required pastoral listening. Discussing the concept of "social capital" (as she explains, "advantages derived from one's social network"),[15] she supplies two contrasting but complementary terms that describe the community-building work of parish and diocese. "Bonding capital" Bruce sees as the contribution of parishes. It is "inward looking" and "solidifies current group identities and exclusivity."[16] "Bridging capital," on the other hand—providing connections with "dissimilar others"—is supplied by dioceses as Bruce sees it.[17] It is important to underscore the importance of both forces, and the mutuality of the relationship Bruce describes. Parishes "bond" Catholics together by attending to the *koinonia*, with all the practical measures that keep strong the community's recognition of Christ's presence, and their own response to it. This includes, of course, fostering face-to-face meeting and opportunities for genuine mutual listening—essential work in every sort of parish (not only the *personal* parishes that are Bruce's focus). The diocese, too, undertakes this work, primarily in its support of the parishes themselves, but also through groups such as the various "lay ecclesial movements" that often meet and operate on both parish *and* diocesan levels.

The "bridging" role is similarly shared across all levels and is seldom completely distinct from "bonding." Diocesan meetings, conferences, and longer-term associations (those that bring together, for example, parish music ministers or parish business managers) are clearly meant to *bridge* those who perform similar services in parishes that may have quite different memberships and situations. (For this reason, Bruce speaks quite rightly of a *diocesan* "community of communities."[18]) Yet they do so in the hope that these representatives of different parish communities will find ways to *bond* that will broaden their horizons with regard to the Church and its mission. It is quite possible, though, for such bonding to counteract some of the intended bridging, by creating isolated elites who come to be seen as the "chosen representatives" of many who cannot participate at the broader level. In this case, bridging again becomes the work of the parish, which must continue to try to close the gaps that open between its "better connected" and "less widely known" members. In the end, it seems necessary to conclude that the Church must not leave bridging exclusively to the more distant structure of the diocese. Rather, bridging should be a crucial element of every local Christian community, however it may be composed.

From this perspective, one of the crucial roles of the parish within the larger Church can be made explicit. The parish is in the position to call its diocese, and thereby the whole Church, to *listen* to local communities and especially to the "hidden margins" with which these communities have—or at least are *called* to have—contact.

CHURCH LEADERSHIP TOWARD "PARISHES OF THE PEOPLE"

Laity and Clergy in Collaboration. My emphasis in this chapter, and indeed throughout the book, has been on what could perhaps be called an ecclesiological "turn toward the community." Rather than interpreting the traditional structures of the Church as an organization that calls forth communities (or, what would be even more improper, individual believers), I have preferred to understand the *physically local*, or "face-to-face," community as the original center of the Church's mission and focus. This is not an *anti*-clerical move—as per certain skeptical perspectives that I have already discussed—even though it may require a significant shift of attitude toward both the formation and the "privileges" of the clergy. I find, rather, that this emphasis on stable communities is strongly suggested by the physical character of the eucharistic celebration around which they gather daily and weekly all over the world.

Basic sacramental doctrine understands this celebration as the *central* act of the Church, and yet Catholics know intuitively (despite the proliferation, especially in the COVID era, of TV and online Masses) that physical presence is *essential* to its full meaning. This means that even in an era when technology could allow for an evolution of eucharistic practice toward a standard of "electronic attendance," the meaning of the sacrament could never make such an allowance. If traditional arrangements of leadership can no longer accommodate the need of the people of God for eucharistic participation, then more flexibility must be introduced in the structures and customs of leadership, *not* in the frequency or quality of presence of the Eucharist itself.

Leadership, both clerical and lay, is more crucial than ever when the institutional structures are required to be *fluid* rather than to bear the whole weight of keeping the community together. When the community is prioritized because it is the natural location of the Eucharist, lay leadership can likewise emerge naturally as the best source of an authentic local perspective. As Pope Francis makes clear in his response to the Synod on the Amazon,

> For the Church to achieve a renewed inculturation of the Gospel in the Amazon region, she needs to listen to its ancestral wisdom, listen once more to the voice of its elders, recognize the values present in the way of life of the original communities, and recover the rich stories of its peoples.[19]

This kind of leadership is already present for the Church—either purely in potential or, more likely, as acknowledged and effective in other sectors of the community's life. Its emergence allows ordained or other professional leaders who occupy positions representative of the larger Church to focus more intentionally on the "bridging" and "empowerment" tasks that are proper to those roles (and which can become particularly clear in the ministry of the sacraments).

The development of genuine leadership roles for the laity has been progressing, albeit often haltingly, since the Council's many overtures to a new way of understanding mutual responsibility within the Body of Christ. The laity has an explicit share in the threefold ministry of Christ as Priest, Prophet, and King (see *LG* 31). The laity and clergy together receive in equal measure the "universal call to holiness" (see *LG* 39ff.). The proper share of the laity in the apostolic mission of the Church is far more than as assistants to the clergy.[20] With all members of the people of God, those whose vocation is to family and to work toward a just and flourishing world are called to be missionary disciples of Christ in that world.[21] For all these reasons, the authority of the laity, exercised in large part within the local communities that they above all others animate, is theirs even when elements of the clergy are indifferent, hesitant, or resistant. It is precisely because lay authority does *not* derive from the authority of the clergy, but is rather given them by the Spirit of Christ in the midst of the Church, that mutual *collaboration* is so essential (see *AA* 3). For either group—or any part of either group—to attempt to exercise its authority in isolation from or in defiance of the rest of the Church is a theological contradiction: "For in the one Spirit we were all baptized into one body—Jews or Greeks, slaves or free—and we were all made to drink of one Spirit" (1 Cor 12:13).

Since the Council, one of the services that many parish communities have been providing for the Church at large, usually without any notion that they are doing so, is an ongoing development of the *theology of pastoral leadership*. This has become part of the local contribution to the Church by virtue of rapidly changing social conditions, the widely varied effects of those changes within church communities, the ongoing need for creative solutions to attendant problems, and the flexibility introduced by the Council and postconciliar developments. Whether the isolation of some communities leads to a desire for regional collaboration, or shifting demographics lead to the creation of sprawling new parishes or the merging of multiple older ones, there is a dynamism in local cooperation that is constantly creating new kinds of leaders. Whether a scarcity of priestly vocations leaves once-traditional tasks and projects undone, or one of many vibrant lay movements sparks the interest of numerous parishioners in the "New Evangelization" or outreach work toward social justice, new kinds of training are devised. When particularly motivated individuals find themselves drawn into education and training as directors of religious education or parish life coordinators or rural catechists or leaders and promoters of prayer groups or retreat movements, new kinds of interaction among laity and clergy emerge. In the midst of it all, there are previously unfamiliar tensions to be resolved, and new identities to be understood and claimed and fitted into the Church's reality.

Almost none of this is being or could be finalized at the diocesan level alone, because even for the problems and needs to be addressed, they have to come to light in the day-to-day lives of real parish communities. All of this work changes expectations, creates contexts, sparks reflection, and produces new insights about what leadership in Christ's Church is and requires. All such reflection and insight is "practical theology" as it becomes increasingly conscious of itself. And such theology is gradually able to fill in the areas that have been hitherto unaddressed or addressed by inadequate assumptions based on old paradigms that no longer fit the local realities of the people of God.

Servant Leadership. Because of their practical and mutual nature, these leadership developments already rely implicitly on the model of leadership insisted upon by Jesus in his interaction with the first disciples. As it happens, though, deep reflection on that model was inserted into the context of Vatican II before the Council even met, by theologians who were already attempting to read "the signs of the times." Prominent among them was Yves Congar, OP, already a highly respected ecclesiologist within the Nouvelle Théologie movement in France before the Council, who as a theological consultant to the bishops ended up having an outsized influence on many of the outcomes of the Council. Just prior to its meeting, he wrote his reflections on Jesus's insistence on "servant leadership" and how it has fared in the Church's history. He published them in 1963 as *Pour une Église Servante et Pauvre*, literally "Toward a Poor and Servant-Like Church," published in English as *Power and Poverty in the Church.*[22]

Congar takes as his theme the message of gospel passages like Matthew 18:4–5: "Whoever becomes humble like this child is the greatest in the kingdom of heaven. Whoever welcomes one such child in my name welcomes me." Congar notes that the honor of being "the greatest" is not given for the sake of the humble disciples, nor for the sake of the child, but because of the name of Jesus. The dignity of Jesus, of the child, and of the disciple alike is received from the One whom Jesus calls "Father."[23] "In Jesus Christ," writes Congar, "God has revealed himself leaning toward us and over us, Gift of Love, Grace."[24] For a priest to preside at the Eucharist *in persona Christi*—in the role of Christ himself—cannot, then, be a source of personal pride, power, or control (regardless of what the priest believes about his own interior disposition) but rather must be to sacramentalize for the whole community that inclination toward God's people, that quality of being "love poured out." This is not something that can remain on the level of a legally or ritually adequate fulfillment of prescribed duties! In a parish, the pastor's mandate is to gather as Jesus gathers, listen as Jesus listens, and love as Jesus loves.

Congar also notices that at the very moment Jesus calls the apostles *friends* rather than *servants*, he also calls them to "wash each other's feet" as Jesus, the master and teacher, has done.[25] The gesture could be seen as a mere metaphor, but in the Gospel of John it is as real and solemn and central to the action at the Last Supper as the Eucharist is in the Synoptic Gospels. Its position in the narrative precludes an interpretation that allows us to nullify its radical meaning by substituting some other "more dignified" role for a pastor on the grounds that "this, too, is service." Peter, the fisherman, was so startled and scandalized by what he saw Jesus doing that he once again presumed to "correct" Jesus. But Jesus made it clear: if there is no truly humble service, there is no share in the kingdom. This radicality and literalness is undoubtedly what Pope Francis has intended to retrieve by his nearly-as-scandalous insistence on washing not just the decorously presented feet of approved Christian men, but also the truly "needy feet" of prisoners, including non-Christians, women, and children as well as others customarily excluded from the annual *pro forma* rite on Holy Thursday evening.[26]

Congar seems to have anticipated Pope Francis's program by half a century when he writes of what it will take to "restore clerics to the full truth of their position as servant members [of the Church]."[27] The point, he hastens to emphasize, is not at all to undermine the hierarchical structure of the Church. Rather, Congar shows that it is well within Catholic tradition to set aside ways of exercising leadership that "have served for a moment," in order to better express the life of Christ in the world.[28] He addresses both temptations and needs of the Church in our times that are, if anything, even clearer now than they were when he wrote:

> For the Church as for each one of us, health does not consist only in being oneself, but in realizing the truth of one's relationships with others. It is a Church-in-dialogue that will also be a poor Church, a servant Church, a Church with good news for humanity—less *of* the world and more *for* the world![29]

Servant leadership points us back toward a Church that, at all levels, is able to live its mission of love by listening, discerning, and reading the signs of the times.

One approach to revisioning the relationships between ordained leadership and the people of a parish could be expressed in terms of replacing a "mediation" role for an *empowerment* role. As noted earlier, Vatican II emphasizes that all members of the Church share, according to their own calling and situation, in the threefold ministry of Christ. Traditionally, this ministry is defined by the three key roles in ancient Israelite society as described in the Hebrew Bible: Prophet, Priest, and King. They were understood as *God's* roles in creation—to teach, to sanctify, to rule—shared with those who lead God's people. Christians have naturally seen them as fulfilled in Christ, and in Catholic tradition they are referred to in Latin as Christ's *munera*—a wonderfully rich word that can mean many things including both "gift" and "duty." The theology of how Christ's triple office applies to priests and bishops in the Church is, not surprisingly, very well developed. It is well-rehearsed even in Vatican II's *Lumen Gentium.* What this dogmatic constitution adds, however, is the application to *all* the faithful who share Christ's life in Baptism and Eucharist. The ordained priest who exercises Christ's ministry is therefore no longer to be understood merely as a "middleman" between God and other believers but must build up participation in the mission by *each and all.* The *munera* can thus be understood in a way that assumes a *cooperative* ministry rather than an *exclusive* one.

The priestly or sanctifying ministry, which *Lumen Gentium* describes as Christ's "function of offering spiritual worship for the glory of God and the salvation of [humanity]" (*LG* 34), provides the sacramental context for all development in the Church. It is the work of the whole community: "It is through the sacraments and the exercise of the virtues that the sacred nature and organic structure of the priestly community is brought into operation" (*LG* 11). While administering the sacraments is the specific task of ordained leaders, the reception of the sacraments is essential to the *empowerment* of missionary disciples throughout the Church. That is why *Sacrosanctum Concilium*, as I have noted before, offers this image as "the pre-eminent manifestation of the Church":

> ...full active participation of all God's holy people in these liturgical celebrations, especially in the same eucharist, in a single prayer, at one altar, at which there presides the bishop surrounded by his college of priests and by his ministers. (*SC* 41)

On this model, the sacraments cannot be treated as the "possessions" of clerical leaders over against the lay faithful (never an ideal, but often a strong temptation), nor are they to be distributed as if in an act of charity toward their recipients.[30] Rather, they are to be given as a steward makes supplies available to the household.[31] Where this attitude toward sacraments is encouraged by the practice of clergy at both the diocesan and parish levels, the people of the various communities can begin to see that even in this most clearly "clerical" sphere of Church life, all are essential partners in the one enterprise of the Church's mission. Such a shift in perspective can begin to bear fruit in parish communities even before any resolution of the serious tensions felt throughout the Church regarding who can and should be admitted to the ordained priesthood itself.

Similarly, the prophetic or teaching ministry—already more clearly shared in partnership than the other *munera*—can come to be regarded as the ongoing process of mutual listening, reflecting, and relating, between the official magisterium and all the faithful. I have already examined this process as a necessary characteristic of the Church as it seeks to understand itself more fully as the people of God, read the signs of the times, and reach out to the world around it. Obviously, as with all the elements of the threefold ministry, teaching involves a variety of gifts and offices exercised according to their own requirements, but always in cooperation with one another in the work of Christ (recall Eph 4:11–13, quoted earlier in the chapter).

In the parish, the fruit of such cooperation can be seen as various local leaders—clerics and laypersons—share with each other their knowledge and experience and their perception of what it is to live Christ's love specifically in this time and place. As each learns what the others are able to tell about the gifts and challenges of the community as a whole, they will also be able to facilitate the often subtle but always crucial conversation among those leaders, the community or communities they lead, and the realities of the larger Church. Ordained and professional leaders who come to the community from the outside can learn something of living as the members of this community live, can come to know and share their struggles, to understand the *cultures* that coexist in this local church. If this kind of work is undertaken in mutual respect and growing love, it can foster the *agency* and *coresponsibility* within the community that are the bedrock of a "Church of the people," mirroring Christian collaboration to the whole community and beyond.

The "kingly," or governing, ministry—in keeping with the same considerations of conciliar insights, listening, and presence—can be seen in general as the full reception of Jesus's teaching about leadership, as discussed by Congar and reflected in much of the artistic and liturgical tradition. Even at its most triumphant, the kingship of Christ is never legitimately separated from the reality of the cross. As Congar explains,

> Because their life belongs entirely to Christ, is entirely from him and for him, the disciples can only ascend [to the level of "first" or "greatest"] by lowering themselves, following Christ along the way of descent, of self-giving and loss of self, by which St. Paul has traced God's victorious path from death on the cross, and the tomb, to glory.[32]

This sort of "royal attitude" is what would allow parish priests to be the point of connection of local communities with the local (diocesan) church and, through the diocesan bishop, with the universal Church. Since Pope Francis's revival and reapplication of the term, we can now label the sort of relationship that can emerge as a "synodal" one, in which members of the Church at all levels "walk together" in living out the Church's mission. The clerical role is not diminished but revivified in this genuine imitation of Christ. Priests and bishops offer the faithful an honest witnessing of their own living faith, spiritual encouragement and prayer, and personal support. Their vision of the mission is constantly being nourished and renewed by their ongoing relationships of respect and openness to the laity, and their forward-looking guidance on matters practical, strategic, and logistical. They govern the Church by rejoicing in, taking account of, and calling into service *all* the gifts the Spirit pours out in the local communities.

"THE WHOLE IS GREATER THAN THE PART"

The call to live in the love of Christ is not a vague and distant notion, but is concrete, personal, and transformative. Pope Francis's image of the polyhedron, discussed earlier in chapter 4, addresses the apparent tension between the personal (and cultural) calling and its universal application. As I mentioned in the previous discussion, Francis's explanation of the principle "the whole is greater than the parts" must be carefully grasped to avoid misapplying it within Church institutions. As we have seen, "the parts" must each be allowed their proper weight and shape within the whole. When that happens, it becomes clear that, in contributing their unique attributes, they ensure that the whole does, indeed, become greater than the parts that compose it:

> It is the convergence of peoples who, within the universal order, maintain their own individuality; it is the sum total of persons within a society which pursues the common good, which truly has a place for everyone. (*EG* 236)

Two of the most important details of Francis's image are that each surface of the polyhedron is "irregular," and that each retains its unique shape as it comes together with all the other surfaces. Very importantly, because the polyhedron is not a sphere, each point on the various surfaces maintains its own unique distance from the center of the whole figure. Some other details follow from these two: the center, by itself, is no longer completely expressive of the whole. It cannot be described simply by its distance from *any* point on the surface but must be understood specifically in its unique relationship to *each* point. Likewise, although it is crucial to the whole that every piece be accommodated in a way that connects *all* the edges of each surface, it is not the sole function of any one surface to "fit itself" into the whole. That "fitting" must be the work of *each* surface for itself and of *all* the surfaces for each other. In other words, if there are pieces that "don't fit," that lack of fit describes not just a single piece that is "out of place," but all the other pieces as well, that might have to be rearranged to accommodate the one that has not yet been properly placed.

When we enter the world of the Church's social dynamics through the doorway of this metaphor, we can see more clearly that particular persons, as well as particular communities—ultimately the building blocks of the local church that are constituent parts of the universal Church—are not to be simply ignored, forced to conform, or expelled if some aspect of their reality runs counter to a uniform and "smooth" image of the Church. Such an approach to difference favors the "center" of the institution and mistakes it for the whole, while overlooking the importance of the parts in their particularity. This would be to miss Francis's meaning entirely. Rather, in the "polyhedronal church," it is the function of local communities to hold up, for all to see, those persons, cultural features, and spiritual insights that most need to be "fitted into" the whole. The Church can only be "greater than its parts" if it has found room for all of them within itself. The image of the polyhedron helps us to imagine the final outcome of the Church's mission of love.

In discussing the place of the parish within the whole, the "larger Church" has to be understood in its fullness—not merely as a clerical institutional structure, but as the whole network of tradition, ways of life, and relationships (human and divine) that is concretized in the local church on both the diocesan and parish community levels. As Francis spoke of it in one of his earliest interviews after his election to the papacy,

> This church with which we should be thinking is the home of all, not a small chapel that can hold only a small group of selected people. We must not reduce the bosom of the universal church to a nest protecting our mediocrity. And the church is Mother; the church is fruitful. It must be.[33]

This way of understanding how the Church is urged away from its own complacency and on toward genuine life-giving ministry is directly relevant to the parish community, in what it undertakes but most especially in how it understands.

This broader vision, though—now authorized at least in outline by both an ecumenical council (Vatican II) and a pontiff (Francis)—raises thorny problems for the Church in terms of diversity and inclusivity. In the immediate aftermath of Vatican II, although the Council had cast its gaze on many of the specific challenges in the world of its day, a great deal of energy was turned to questions of cooperation between laity and clergy, "dialoguing" across differences (with special attention to Orthodox Christianity) and, more recently, the inclusion of the "Global South" within the power structures of the Church. But as important as such efforts have been, they have also kept the more fundamental questions hidden until recently. If the Church is to be a *whole* that is capable of embracing, celebrating, and learning from its *parts*, how will it face its deeply engrained *clericalism* and the unexamined theological excesses that support it? How will it come to terms, across its many cultures and social histories, with Jesus's own reverence for and empowering of women? Will its recognition that its growth and vitality now reside substantially in former "mission" territories lead it to confront legacies of racism where that sin continues to mislead and divide? Can it continue down the path, onto which Pope Francis has stepped, that leads to "respect, compassion, and sensitivity"[34] toward those with same-sex attraction? Of all these real issues, local parish communities all over the world have genuine and concrete experience, as well as scars, burdens, and pain, to share with their sisters and brothers across the whole Church, the whole Body of Christ.

THE PARISH AS "THE FACE OF THE CHURCH"

As I observed in chapter 4, sociologists have called the parish an "intermediate group," charged with face-to-face ministry yet usually still too large for such ministry to involve the *whole* local community on every occasion. In a variety of ways, the community constantly looks both "inward" and "beyond" itself, toward the specific groupings that do allow regular face-to-face encounter even beyond liturgical and sacramental gatherings, and even beyond formal parish membership. At the very least, this view includes all baptized Catholics within the reach of the parish, whether active, "casual," or inactive. As we have already seen, to establish a culture of careful listening among the faithful, the view needs also to take in the network of community organizations within which the parish operates. This leads outward even further, touching other persons who are connected through the social networks of parish members. In all these ways, the parish community comes to understand "who" they are, in terms of interconnected groups of persons, and "where" they are, in terms of the physical, virtual, and social "locations" that are most influential in shaping the community's character and concerns.

Similarly, the parish looks outward toward the larger vital connections within the universal Church that guard it from becoming a parochial "museum of local folklore" (see *EG* 234). Such connections include, of course, the ordained pastors who represent the parish to the bishop and the diocese, and likewise represent the diocese to parishioners. The internal view described above, having identified local leaders of all sorts—professional and voluntary, formal and informal—connects the parish further to networks of pastoral leaders and practitioners of a wide array of skills and endeavors that can further the parish's missionary discipleship. This puts the local community in contact with the full diocesan "community of communities" and—depending on the state of various associations, gatherings, and networks of communication—with parishes, dioceses, movements, and church projects all over the world. Some of these contacts will be able to evolve into strong ongoing connections and opportunities for cooperation, based on the character and engaged membership of the parish.

All these interactions broaden the context of the parish in increasingly larger circles and keep the members of local communities alive to the invitation of the *whole* Christian tradition and the *whole* human family, deepening their practice of *mutual* listening, respect, and loving action. Such development and connection for a single parish helps the whole Church to continue its reflection on love begun by St. Paul (see 1 Cor 13:4–7). We might say, love *gathers, opens, includes, bridges.* It does not *wall-off, exclude,* or *guard.* Love is *flexible,* not *bound* by *habits* or *fears.* The constant invitation to wider circles *forms parishioners as Christian disciples.* If this kind of integration is the goal, the parish becomes a manifestation of the Church's fullness within a particular time and place. To see and experience this parish is to encounter the Church in a particularly personal and concrete way, but a way that is also "official," "institutional," and therefore more than "accidentally representative" of what the Church is and does. Even the *process* toward such a goal, not only its completion (which, almost by definition, may never be reached), allows the parish to become "the face of the Church."

Chapter 7

PARISH
A Vision Forward

> The call to review and renew our parishes has not yet sufficed to bring them nearer to people, to make them environments of living communion and participation, and to make them completely mission-oriented.
>
> Pope Francis, *Evangelii Gaudium* 28

"LAST SUNDAY"

At a parish church in central Massachusetts that I will call St. Philip's, on a recent Sunday near the end of Ordinary Time, I joined a congregation of between 100 and 150 people in a space designed for probably four times that number. Nearly all had arrived by car, parking across the street on the playground of the former parish school. (Though still parish property, the school is now being operated privately. Next door, the former convent still holds its place within the old parish "compound," now serving as diocesan offices.) As I arrived by the same means, we all streamed together across the small side street, onto the walk, into the front or side doors that all lead into the ample narthex.

Inside was the customary furniture for this transitional space: racks holding the weekly bulletin and various other publications, boxes for donations of food and clothing, a table that in other times might have been staffed with someone overseeing sign-ups for a parish activity or two. There were ushers saying hello as people arrived, and a server preparing various details for the Mass about to begin. There were also some newer rituals being observed, with many of those entering pulling on masks as they stepped in from the outdoors or stopping by the hand sanitizer dispensers installed near the traditional holy water fonts (which had not yet been refilled, even though permission had been granted for their customary use to resume).

Inside the church, the atmosphere was a rather informal mix of busy preparation, conversation of various kinds, listless waiting, and silent prayer. One of the ushers conferred with the organist at the front of the church. The general chatter was most concentrated in the front section of pews—quiet casual greetings among those accustomed to meeting at church, with an occasional enthusiastic outburst from friends reconnecting unexpectedly, and some "pillars of the community" checking in with more "peripheral" members that they happened to recognize: "How's your husband? He hasn't been with you lately." "Not so well, I'm afraid." "Please tell him we're praying for him!" In the back section, the attendees were less engaged with the gathering conversations, but most seemed present to where they were, and several were using their more physically isolated spots in the nave to assume traditional postures of evidently earnest prayer.

The congregation that was rapidly gathering, finding seats in all corners of the space, was made up largely of older white parishioners, with a smattering of people of color and a few families with children. When the Mass began, it seemed that the presiding priest was known to the people and greeted some of them on the way in; I noted that he spoke English with a Latin accent, and I wondered if he were the priest assigned to work primarily with the Brazilian immigrant community. That hunch seemed partly confirmed by the personal way in which he referred, during later announcements, to the Masses and ministries offered at nearby St. Barnabas (now joined with St. Philip's under one pastor), where the Brazilian community gathers.

It was a simple, ordinary experience of Sunday Mass, but so much about what I observed that morning spoke to me of the transitional period in which the Church is living. In the northeastern United States, the pandemic struck as many parishioners were getting used to the long period of ever-more-obvious decline that set in as wave after wave of disclosures about abuse—in the United States and around the world—washed over church communities. They were accustomed to seeing fewer young people at Mass and the enrollment of smaller numbers in religious ed programs. They had suffered through closures and mergers; they knew about twinning and collaboratives. They may have come to understand that their diocese was supplementing its shrinking cadre of parish priests with new arrivals from other parts of the globe, often West Africa or India or, less typically, South American countries such as Colombia (as is the case here in the Diocese of Worcester). They tolerated the appearance of priests they had little or no opportunity to meet and get to know, because the priests drove in from elsewhere to help or remained only a short time in the parish before being sent to another parish where the need was greater.

After the months-long hiatus when no in-person Masses were being held, all these effects seemed to be intensified as some people began to return. There are places where part of the reaction has been a kind of "tightened inner circle" to protect what is left of a previous identity and to provide as much practical help as possible for keeping parish life going. Often enough, though, even that can be accompanied by a new atmosphere of welcome to those who were not immediately recognized—"It's good to have you here!" A sense of determination to carry on seems to compete with both the joy of the celebration of faith itself and the confusion and discouragement that could break through to dominance at any given moment.

VISION OR FANTASY?

As I HOPED TO emphasize in the first chapter of this book, it has not been part of my intention to offer anything like a blueprint or model for creating "the ideal parish." Rather, I have hoped to evoke a vision of where the "sojourning believers" of the parish's original image should aspire to arrive. As I conclude these reflections, I will attempt here to underscore the main lines of this vision, the most important challenges and obstacles that are present now or may be foreseen, and some of the tools, skills, and habits that are already available for coming closer to realizing the vision. That it is possible to move closer to or further away from its realization is part of what distinguishes such a vision from pure fantasy. Further distinctions come from the ways it can be linked to the steady tradition of the Church and to the reputable lines of discussion and argumentation that have been discernible in the more recent life of the Church. As opposed to a fantasy, the vision is also robust enough to survive and even thrive in a variety of contexts in which parish communities may find themselves, whether declining or increasing in power and membership; whether experiencing lagging, adequate, or abundant clerical vocations; whether enjoying plenty or deficient material resources; whether accustomed to cultural dominance or struggling to find their voices in the world and in the Church.

THE TIMES, THE POSSIBLE, AND THE NECESSARY

During the time that I have been at work on this book, six million people have died in the COVID-19 pandemic, well over nine hundred thousand in the United States alone—numbers that continue to grow. This horrendous death toll will certainly remain a historical marker in the future for many cultural changes as well, some of which are now gradually coming into view. Because customary social gatherings and activities of all sorts have been greatly curtailed or reconfigured in the face of the disease, communities are disrupted and probably permanently transformed. For the Church, the crisis of communities and leadership outlined in chapter 1 has been exacerbated by pandemic emergency measures that have tested the perseverance of tentative and stalwart parishioners alike.

Recall that one of the features of the broader cultural crisis is the increasing alienation of many people around the world from specific *institutions* of many kinds, and a corresponding lack of trust in most institutional arrangements. Far from being exempt from this trend, the Church has been particularly vulnerable. This is not only because of its grievous self-inflicted wounds—division, pride, fear, and abuse—which are real enough. It is also because of the growing attraction, in the world at large, of populist models that diminish genuine community and commitment to it, and that encourage conformity to ideology over the kind of open relationship that requires listening and allows for growth. In the same moment, Christian personhood—not the "autonomous individual" but rather the individual within a cultural context and a network of relationships—seems less and less comprehensible in postmodern culture.[1]

Anti-institutionalism was being amply demonstrated long before the COVID pandemic but has been strongly confirmed by the restive response of significant numbers of people in various parts of the world who are strongly challenging government emergency measures put in place to stem the tide of the virus. Yet both the self-organization even of such resistance, as well as the many more positive instances of humane outreach and innovation in the face of the restrictions suggest some light still on the horizon, despite the decline of commitments to large scale institutions. The elements of community that are most responsive to local situations, local participation, local energy, and initiative *can* continue and even flourish. This realization has a number of implications for *parish communities.*

Of particular significance, these signs of the times reveal the necessity of parishioners *owning* the mission and being able to *see locally* the results of their own missionary discipleship. This is a particular challenge in that this local mission remains genuine only in connection with the universal. Here, I refer not only to clerical structures but to the very way that local communities perceive *why* and *how* they live "rooted and grounded in love." Ownership of the mission so understood, though, is what seems most lacking in a certain type of online emergency substitute for church attendance.

In some ways, the COVID crisis has facilitated another long-term tendency, very much related to the decline in institutional commitment, which might be called "consumer religion" that offers a "product" already packaged for electronic consumption by various media outlets long before the pandemic. Recorded or live-streamed Masses and other services available via the internet exploded in popularity during the height of the pandemic. It was noted, as well, that while many Catholics did indeed use the new online possibilities to remain connected to their own parish communities, many others treated the smorgasbord of online offerings in a way similar to their entertainment choices, logging in to more professionally produced or higher-profile Masses, whether presided at by the pope or another "celebrity cleric" far away from home. While TV Masses and certain kinds of online content have long been available, they have usually been thought of as something for "the shut-ins" (before we *all* became homebound!) and not in nearly the variety, frequency, or quality that started to become available during the pandemic.

It remains to be seen whether widespread interest in "electronic religion" is sustainable over the long run. In the meantime, many parishes are finding the burdens of maintaining operations with radically reduced participation and shrinking financial contributions to be insupportable. A "return to normal," if it can indeed happen, may take too long for some of the former structures to survive. If, instead, many people do take the opportunity to "get their religion" via the internet, they will be replacing their public expression of faith with an individual act that has more in common with diversion and entertainment than with worship. Moreover, the responsibility for its content will be placed almost entirely in the hands of "spiritual providers" (very often clerics who, due to pandemic precautions, appear alone at "center stage") at the very time when community ownership is becoming more crucial to the local church. Rather than providing the hope and empowerment that are capable of inspiring missionary discipleship, such developments in public worship can easily feed a kind of desperation, a paralysis that sets in while we wait for a return of accustomed circumstances that will very likely never be reestablished just as they were. Such a loss of hope would, at best, allow temporary measures and contingencies of all sorts to dictate the shape of the mission for the future. Personal consolation—a refuge from trying social situations—could rise among pastoral priorities, to the detriment of nurturing an evangelizing community.

The real work of parish is different from such a crisis-driven approach. It is about seeking to clarify God's call in a new situation and *in that light* attempting to build or renew the structures that will enable a community's faithful response. So, out of some dangerous temptations emerges an important general principle: let the *mission*—prayerfully discerned—seek out the tools by which it can be accomplished, rather than letting whatever tools we have handy tell us what the mission is. ("If all you have is a hammer, every problem looks like a nail," runs the adage.) This is the principle that was used to create criteria for the multiple "pastoral teams" within the sectors established in the Archdiocese of Poitiers (as seen in chapter 4). The pastoral councils in each sector asked, Can this group of people, who wish to identify themselves as a local church community, take on the basic work of prayer, teaching, service, management, and leadership that is essential to such a community? Can they sustain it within the real conditions of their time and place? The principle is just as applicable to healthy, even growing, communities as it is to situations of huge, crumbling infrastructure in the hands of severely diminished communities. In the end, perhaps the most crucial question for parishes in the time of the COVID pandemic, and all the other elements of crisis they face, is this: How may we use the tools available amid these crises to stimulate a community process of spiritual discernment about *how* to remain "rooted and grounded in love," even here and now?

To give their due to the many uncertain responses that have been generated in widely differing circumstances worldwide, this discernment process has not been entirely neglected over the past twenty years. The question of how to revitalize parishes, taken up in the many ways that have been noted throughout these chapters, and in countless others, has, of course, been the focus of passion, urgency, prayer, and discernment. The mergers, collaboratives, and pastoral teams, the "liquid parishes," "Fresh Expressions," and "urban pastoral" projects, the "shrines as parishes" and "parishes as shrines" have all emerged from consideration of local circumstances and local problems, from dioceses and parishes groping for their way, along many different pathways. Yet, as Pope Francis has noted (see the epigraph for this chapter), parishes still fall short of being focused on their real mission.

A SIGN *FOR* THE TIMES

The parish community is already a *sign of the times*, for parishioners and others, as it displays the pressures and losses of the multiple crises it faces. Yet, with full attention to this mission, parishes could also be, and in many instances are becoming, "signs *for* the times," signs of the life of the Spirit in a seriously wanting world. To make such a transition in times like ours, though, will require (as, truly, has been a running refrain here) continuing commitment to intense *pastoral listening*. Crucially, this approach must include both the tools and methods of social analysis (allowing parish leadership to remain aware of general trends and contexts) *and* the sort of personal attentiveness that has already allowed countless dynamic parish communities to slowly build up networks of face-to-face contact and relationship.

As the vignettes at the beginning of each chapter of this book have been meant to suggest, Catholic parishes have always exhibited enormous variety, not only in location and ethnic diversity, but also in terms of their understanding of the mission they are called to embody and especially in terms of the conditions and situations within which they must accomplish that embodiment. As I began to map out the project of creating this book, a long-time friend asked me whether part of what I envisaged was creating a kind of "taxonomy" of parishes around the world—that is, a charting of all the different types of parishes, their characteristics, and the differences between them. If anything has become clear in the intervening four years since that remark was made, it is the breadth of variety even within a single region (let alone worldwide!), as well as the breathtaking pace of change, that renders such charting an impossible exercise (and ultimately not very helpful). It is, once again, *flexibility* and a willingness to privilege the image of *pilgrimage* that need to replace everywhere the image of a rockbound immobility. Yet, local communities do have their Rock. It is Jesus, "the radiant face of God's mercy."[2] The relationship of *this* Face to the parish as a "face of the Church"—the face of the Body of Christ—provides the image under which I summarize and conclude these discussions with some remarks about the essential characteristics that the Church can look for, can foster and nourish, in its parishes.

REPRISE: WHAT IS A PARISH?

The parish is the logical structure in the Church to be the location of the most practical forms of evangelization—that day-to-day modeling of Ephesians' prayer for the Church to be "rooted and grounded in love" that I have returned to throughout these chapters. That grounding begins in the life of sacraments and prayer that welcomes each believer into both a face-to-face community of faith and a worldwide Church called to embody the love of Christ in the world. That endless love itself continually calls for action in service of humanity, a direct response to the love that is poured out upon it. It is this acting out of loving service that continually nourishes faith in Christ and occasions its proclamation by way of the believers giving "reason for the hope" that guides their lives.

This, though, is really an *outsider's* view of parish community. We have seen how much internal work lies within the kind of community that can become a living witness to Christ in the world. Its members must grow continually more accustomed to sharing their insights with each other and challenging one another with their differences. This is not work merely for the personal level: through it the whole community grows the pastoral listening skills that empower a culture of openness, patience, and diversity as they continue to discern what exactly the *Love* that calls them is asking of them at any given moment.

Such a community culture is impossible without the *humility* that is fostered in the spirit of "servant leadership." This attitude can no longer be understood as pertaining, if at all, to the clerical leaders only. Rather, within the pilgrim Church it must be exercised by all members of the community on behalf of one another, in keeping with Jesus's instruction to his disciples: "Whoever wants to be first must be last of all and servant of all" (Mark 9:35). In this way, the community life of the parish will bear fruit not only for itself, not only for the larger community in whose midst it is a living witness, but also the larger Church. It is to the larger Church that the parish community's commitment to humble, evangelical love and its habits of listening and discernment can present perspectives and insights that challenge broader ecclesial structures in the same way the local communities themselves are challenged. Certainly, such "grassroots" challenges are already part of the tradition of the Church and have borne great fruit at various times in the past, from the local churches of the early centuries to *Devotio Moderna* in the late Middle Ages, to the popular religiosity observable globally in our own day, to the demands for accountability and renewed Christian culture coming from parishes all over the world that have been affected by the crises of sexual and power abuse. The kind of urgency that can be inspired by parish communities rooted and grounded in love reflect growing habits of dialogue as well as the more responsible level of ecclesial decision-making addressed in the challenges that are already being made.

Parishes, being strengthened by attention to their own mission, can focus their calls for accountability in the whole Church on elements that either empower or obstruct the continuation of that very mission of love. This is no more than the parish recognizing—and calling the larger Church to recognize—its role as an integral "surface in the polyhedron," to overcome an inaccurately discouraging view of the local community's status and influence. This recognition, though, also requires an end to clericalism, so that communities are understood, respected, and cherished for themselves rather than simply as a tool for the ministry of the ordained. It demands a sharing of leadership responsibility, so that the faithful voice of the community is truly heard and heeded. That communal voice, in turn, must express the broad *inclusion* of all persons too easily marginalized and alienated from what should be the embodied love of Christ, so that no voices are absent from the dialog and from the ministry of service that it generates and sustains.

What is called for in this vision for the parish—while hopefully "radical" in the true sense of the word, as it deals with where the local church community is most genuinely "rooted"—is not a replacement for a previous role for parishes. Rather, it is a revitalization of the tradition established in the early Church and adapted in endless ways through the centuries. It is a tradition that encompasses the Christian people's intuitive grasp of the faith to which they are committed (*sensus fidelium*). It sets out the role of their communities in sustaining that faith and making it fruitful. It urges the role of their ordained leadership in guiding, nourishing, and encouraging the loving way of life which that same faith generates. In fulfilling their proper part in the Church's leadership, the ordained serve the "visible communion" described by the Congregation for the Doctrine of the Faith.[3] The parish community, for its part, serves an "invisible communion" (*koinonia*) of a more general kind. This community itself—not its priest, its territory, or any part of its infrastructure—is the true heart of the *paroikía*, the parish. St. Ignatius of Antioch, having written, "Wherever the bishop shall appear, there let the multitude [of the people] also be," went on to conclude, "Even as, wherever Jesus Christ is, there is the Catholic Church."[4] Under circumstances more like our own, he might well have written, "Where God's people are, there is the Church"—that is to say, "Where the Holy Spirit dwells, as promised by Christ to his disciples, there is the Church." To be the communities of sojourning believers, Christ's pilgrim people, parishes need "only" to be the places of relationship where the Spirit dwells in the hearts of believers, joining them to one another in the Church, wherever and whatever their situation, "as it was in the beginning."

SEMPER RENOVANDA (SEE *LG* 8)

Attempting to draw useful conclusions for a theology of parish at our time in history has frequently reminded me of an artist trying to capture a sunrise or some other rapidly changing scene. In addition to the trauma of the COVID pandemic, the time I have spent working on these chapters has also seen rapid developments in the conversation about local church. In an era that sees the Church straining toward epochal change in the midst of historic challenges, guidelines and encouragements for that change are more and more ready to hand.

Pope Francis himself has certainly not been silent (indeed, some might say, he would hardly *be* "himself" if he had been!). Just as the outbreak of the virus was becoming known, in February 2020 his response to the controversial Amazon Synod was issued in the apostolic exhortation *Querida Amazonia,* to which I have referred several times. There, the pope continues to lay the groundwork needed for regional churches and local communities to be able to take up the Church's universal mission in their own territories and with their own cultural resources and authentic inspirations. Some saw it as having fallen short of the hopes that many had formed in light of the synod's own document—hopes for explicit moves toward the ordination of qualified married men as priests or the fruition of the pope's clear interest in the provision of women deacons. Yet the pope made the unprecedented move of associating the synod's own document with his post-synodal exhortation. In doing so, he made it part of the official papal response, keeping many hopes alive within the strong encouragement given for the local churches of the Amazon to continue reflecting deeply and acting accordingly.

Months later, in October 2020, the pope issued his encyclical *Fratelli Tutti*, On Fraternity and Social Friendship. Invoking the Saint of Assisi as he had done so many times before (most notably in his 2015 encyclical, *Laudato Si'*, On Care for Our Common Home), Francis provides further resources toward his vision of "a poor church for the poor." Noting the rapidly multiplying contemporary attacks on mutual love as a social force, he turns his focus toward *how* to *love* despite such a social context. As I have noted continually, the mission to witness to Love in our local communities requires *listening* and *dialogue*. Pope Francis laments that listening in love is a disappearing skill in the contemporary world (*FT* 48–49).[5] In discussing the need for "political clarity," however, he declares,

> Here, economic negotiations do not work. Something else is required: an exchange of gifts for the common good. It may seem naïve and utopian, yet we cannot renounce this lofty aim. (*FT* 190)

Claiming for all humanity the vision that is also located at the heart of the mission of parish, Pope Francis continues to call the Church forward to meet the challenge.

The pope has not been alone in strengthening the parish's call to mission. In July 2020, the Vatican Congregation for the Clergy issued its instruction, "The Pastoral Conversion of the Parish Community in the Service of the Evangelizing Mission of the Church" (also previously cited in these chapters). It calls parish priests and their parishioners to a more intentional embrace of the parish's mission, addressing "situations…[that] represent a valuable opportunity for pastoral conversion that is essentially missionary."[6] At about the same time, the Implementation Advisory Group of the Australian Catholic Church, through its Governance Review Project Team, released the draft "The Light from the Southern Cross: Promoting Co-responsible Governance in the

Catholic Church in Australia." LSC, as it came to be called, is an instrument for continuing discussion that was finalized in August 2020 as part of an intensive response, across the whole membership of the Church in Australia, to the Royal Commission's report on sexual abuse in the church. It includes numerous recommendations for reform in church governance, particularly emphasizing accountability and coresponsibility among clergy and laity in the Church throughout Australia and, by implication, worldwide.[7]

The announcement of "Synod 2021–2023: For a Synodal Church," quickly dubbed the "Synod on Synodality," was officially opened on October 9, 2021. This synod emerged from Pope Francis's frequent return to the theme of synodality and his issuing of new rules for the processes to be followed in calling a general assembly of the Synod of Bishops. It is an attempt to move toward a permanent ecclesial structure that not only continues to give weight to collegiality among the bishops but encourages and indeed positively requires consultation, discussion, and pastoral listening at all levels of the Church. In such a process, the impact of the parish on the wider Church can move from "theoretical," or at best "indirect," toward a much more visible and traceable input of local communities in the discernment of the larger Church.[8]

Each of these documents on its own, though only one is specifically about the culture of *parish* communities, offer important insights that are directly relevant to the topics I have been discussing here. Together, and with the many others of their type that could be added to the list, they mark out something of a trajectory. The signs of the times are fearsome, and they require both serious attention and vigorous response. In keeping with a Church that is coming to understand again its quality of being constantly reshaped with and in the Spirit of Christ, the proper response is, once again, a "moving target." What is clear, though, is that it will involve the structures of pastoral listening that will provide the flexibility that Pope Francis called for when he wrote of parishes in *Evangelii Gaudium* as his pontificate was just beginning.

NEXT SUNDAY...

The most difficult challenge to be acknowledged at the end of this book of pastoral theological reflection on the parish is the dreaded practical question, "What are we to do next week in our own parishes?" It is easy enough to speak of one idea following from the next, one inspiration building on this text or that, one insight leading inexorably to a certain conclusion. But what are we to do in the face of our real parish communities, with all their history and tradition, all their resources and talents, all their nitty-gritty problems and petty foibles, all of their small and specific encounters with the enormous challenges that we all know are there? What are we to do with a community of children, young adults, middle-aged persons, and elderly, who are seekers and neophytes together with life-long committed Christians, and in many places represent a challenging mix of cultures (both ethnic and generational)? Is any of this talk about pilgrimage, the people, the mission, community, sacred place, and the structures of the Church in any way *real*? If it is, what now?

The first point is "attendance": *be there!* If the parish community is, for better or worse, the true face of the Church, which is the face of Christ, who is the face of the God of mercy, let us at least begin by gazing on that face, by taking with utter seriousness that little pocket in the web of human life into which our God has placed us.

The second point is "attention": *understand* what this community *is*, even when it is difficult to *see* that reality. It is, in fact, God's *people* as they are being formed by their *gathering* as the Body of Christ, their *hearing* of the word of God proclaimed in their midst, their *sharing* of the nourishment of the Eucharist, and their *going out* as Christians into the world. In each of these aspects, the people of God shows its face to the world.

The third point is "reflection": *consider*, *pray*, *discern* with and on behalf of your community. This can be accomplished, for great good, by dwelling on such questions as these: What are the particular gifts of this community, and what does my own membership contribute? What is still lacking here, how am I part of this lack, and how can I begin to address it with the rest of the community? What can I contribute *now*—where and how?

The fourth point is "commitment": finding the specific place and community with whom I can attend to all of these duties *now* within the Church, and with whom I can imagine establishing lasting relationships that are rooted and grounded in love.

CONCLUSION

The parish appears to be a more or less accidental structure initially named for the Christian conviction that worldly communities of believers are very temporary arrangements. As time went on, however, both the complexity and the ubiquity of the parish showed it to be anything but accidental in terms of what it offers to the Church—a local embodiment in every place where Christians dwell. On that basis, the parish has become an apparently indispensable church structure, erected as much with reference to its location and its buildings as to its people. For a time, it nearly lost completely its original sense of itself as a "sojourning community," on the move toward the reign of God. But in the crisis of the moment, as the parish seems to be crumbling out from under the Church that relies on it, it is rediscovering some of its most crucial original character—its sense of community and of mission. It has been my contention in this book that this rediscovery brings with it the possibility of revitalizing the other qualities—structure and place—that without their connection to community and mission were becoming the death of parish. Can the parish really be all these apparently contradictory things at once? The practical answers to that question will have to unfold in the ongoing history of Christ's Church. But looking carefully at each of these aspects from a theological perspective, I contend, will help us to understand what practical steps might best be taken to reveal a complex unity in what might otherwise seem a shear impossibility.

NOTES

1. WHY PARISH? WHY THEOLOGY? WHY NOW?

1. Second Vatican Council, *Apostolicam Actuositatem*: Decree on the Apostolate of the Laity (November 18, 1965), no. 10, https://www.vatican.va/archive/hist_councils/ii_vatican_council/documents/vat-ii_decree_19651118_apostolicam-actuositatem_en.html.

2. *Omphalos* comes from the Greek word for "navel," and was used to refer to a rounded stone venerated at the ancient shrine of Apollo at Delphi, representing the "navel" of the earth. In English, it has come to refer to anything considered to be a "hub," "center," or "point of origin." (My friends and former parishioners in Kingston, Jamaica, would occasionally refer to the place where they were born as "where mi navel-string bury"—literally, "where they buried my umbilical cord"!)

3. See Second Vatican Council, *Gaudium et Spes*, Pastoral Constitution on the Church in the Modern World (December 7, 1965), no. 1 (hereafter cited in text and notes as *GS*), https://www.vatican.va/archive/hist_councils/ii_vatican_council/documents/vat-ii_const_19651207_gaudium-et-spes_en.html.

4. Code of Canon Law (CIC) (Vatican: 1983), c. 374, https://www.vatican.va/archive/cod-iuris-canonici/eng/documents/cic_lib2-cann368-430_en.html#Art._1 (hereafter cited in text and notes as *CIC*).

5. As the Vatican website translation is redundant at this point, I have borrowed the words in brackets from *The Code of Canon Law: A Text and Commentary* (Mahwah, NJ: Paulist Press, 1985), c. 515.1. (The problem is caused by the prevalence of the word *pastor* in some areas of the English-speaking world, the United States especially, for the office that is more widely referred to in the Church as "parish priest.")

6. See, e.g., Acts 8:4, 25; 9:32–35, 42–43; 11:19–26.

7. For application of the designation "church" for these apostolic communities, see Second Vatican Council, Dogmatic Constitution on the Church, *Lumen Gentium* (November 21, 1964), no. 26, https://www.vatican.va/archive/hist_councils/ii_vatican_council/documents/vat-ii_const_19641121_lumen-gentium_en.html (hereafter cited in the text and notes as *LG*). There is ongoing debate about whether it is legitimate to consider these communities the forerunners of our *parishes* rather than of our *dioceses*. See, e.g., Francis Cardinal George, OMI, "The Parish in the Mission of the Church," in *What Is a Parish? Canonical, Pastoral, and Theological Perspectives*, ed. Thomas A. Baima (Chicago: Hillenbrand, 2011), 18–38 (esp. 30–33). I would argue, however, that what has most evolved in the Church is not its reliance on face-to-face local communities but rather the shape of the ministry of bishops regarding the pastoral care of these communities. See chap. 6 for further discussion of this question.

8. See 1 Pet 1:1–2, 17–21; 2:11–12. Eph 2:19, on the other hand, insists that Christians are "no longer strangers and aliens," in its eagerness to emphasize the ideal *unity* between the Jews as "the household of God" and the Gentile converts whom the letter specifically addresses.

9. Clement, "Letter to the Corinthians," no. 1, John Keith, trans., in *Ante-Nicene Fathers*, vol. 9, ed. Allan Menzies (Buffalo, NY: Christian Literature Publishing Co., 1896). Revised and edited for New Advent by Kevin Knight, https://www.newadvent.org/fathers/1010.htm.

10. The basic meanings of the Greek word *paroikía* are well explained in Gerhard Kittel and Gerhard Friedrich, eds., *Theological Dictionary of the New Testament*, tran. and abridged Geoffrey W. Bromiley (Grand Rapids: Eerdmans, 1985), 707–9. For a very thorough investigation of several related Greek words and their uses in the early Church, and the ecclesial developments they suggest (outlined in the following paragraphs here), see Alex Blöchlinger, *The Modern Parish Community* (New York: Kenedy, 1965), 21–38.

11. In many parts of the United States, this was extensively chronicled by journalists representing a wide range of local and national news media, particularly during the decade between 2004 and 2014. Among the many books and scholarly articles that analyzed the issue, an interesting set of case studies from the Boston area was included in John Seitz, *No Closure: Catholic Practice and Boston's Parish Shutdowns* (Cambridge, MA: Harvard University Press, 2011). One brief case study based on my own research is included in chap. 2 below.

12. Pew Research Center: Religion and Public Life, "In U.S., Decline of Christianity Continues at Rapid Pace: An Update on America's Changing Religious Landscape," October 17, 2019, https://www.pewforum.org/2019/10/17/in-u-s-decline-of-christianity-continues-at-rapid-pace/.

13. Callum G. Brown, *The Death of Christian Britain: Understanding Secularisation 1800–2000*, 2nd ed. (Abingdon, Oxon, UK: Routledge, 2009), 198.

14. For examples of the now extensive literature regarding the Fresh Expressions movement, see Graham Cray et al., *Mission-Shaped Church: Church Planting and Fresh Expressions of Church in a Changing Context* (London: Church House Publishing, 2004) and Michael Moynagh, *Church for Every Context* (London: SCM Press, 2012). I will examine this movement further in chap. 3 below.

15. Matthias Sellmann, "Seven Characteristics of a Future-Proof Parish: The Approach of the Center for Applied Pastoral Research," in *Envisioning Futures for the Catholic Church*, ed. Staf Hellemans and Peter Jonkers, Cultural Heritage and Contemporary Change, series VIII, Christian Philosophical Studies, vol. 23 (Washington, DC: Council for Research in Values and Philosophy, 2018), 231–32.

16. Sellmann, "Seven Characteristics," 250.

17. Sellmann makes frequent use of this and similar terminology; see, e.g., 240–45.

18. Pope Francis, *Evangelii Gaudium*, Apostolic Exhortation on the Proclamation of the Gospel in Today's World (November 24, 2013), no. 24, http://www.vatican.va/content/francesco/en/apost_exhortations/documents/papa-francesco_esortazione-ap_20131124_evangelii-gaudium.html (hereafter cited in text and notes as *EG*).

19. John Paul II, apostolic exhortation *Christifideles Laici* (December 30, 1988), no. 26, http://www.vatican.va/content/john-paul-ii/en/apost_exhortations/documents/hf_jp-ii_exh_30121988_christifideles-laici.html (hereafter cited in notes and text as *CL*). Pope John Paul refers here to a sentence from Vatican II, *Sacrosanctum Concilium*, Constitution on the Sacred Liturgy, no. 42.

20. Two of the best-known such works are Tom Corcoran and Michael White, *Rebuilt: Awakening the Faithful, Reaching the Lost, and Making Church Matter* (Notre Dame, IN: Ave Maria, 2013) and James Mallon, *Divine Renovation: From a Maintenance to a Missional Parish* (Toronto: Novalis, 2014). Earlier, Thomas P. Sweetser's books, including

The Parish as Covenant: A Call to Pastoral Partnership (Lanham, MD: Sheed and Ward, 2001) and *Keeping the Covenant: Taking Parish to the Next Level* (New York: Crossroad, 2007) served a similar purpose, though based on much wider experience and research. Paul Wilkes took a more superficial but informative and engaging narrative approach in *Excellent Catholic Parishes: The Guide to Best Places and Practices* (Mahwah, NJ: Paulist Press, 2001).

21. For Francis's action, see Pope Francis, "*Traditionis Custodes*: Papal *Motu Proprio* on the Use of the Roman Liturgy Prior to the Reform of 1970" (July 16, 2021), https://www.vatican.va/content/francesco/en/motu_proprio/documents/20210716-motu-proprio-traditionis-custodes.html. For a good display of the polarization involved, see Michael Brendan Dougherty, "Pope Francis Is Tearing the Catholic Church Apart," Opinion: Guest Essay, *New York Times*, August 12, 2021, https://www.nytimes.com/2021/08/12/opinion/pope-francis-latin-mass.html, and "The Latin Mass and the Foes of Pope Francis," Opinion: Letters, *New York Times*, August 29, 2021, https://www.nytimes.com/2021/08/29/opinion/letters/francis-church.html.

22. For a discussion of the Church's part in systemic American racism, see Rev. Bryan Massingale, *Racial Justice and the Catholic Church* (Maryknoll, NY: Orbis, 2010).

23. For an example of this phenomenon with regard to the Church, see Rod Dreher, *The Benedict Option: A Strategy for Christians in a Post-Christian Nation* (New York: Sentinel, 2017).

24. For various aspects of this general description, see Biko Agozino, "Trumpism and Authoritarian Populism," Ctheory.net, 2016; Thomas Friedman, "Why Are So Many Political Parties Blowing Up?," Opinion, *New York Times*, June 26, 2018; Pipa Norris, "It's Not Just Trump," *Washington Post*, March 11, 2016; Dalibor Rohac, Liz Kennedy, and Vikrama Singh, *Drivers of Authoritarian Populism in the United States: A Primer*, Americanprogress.org, 2018, among many other commentaries.

25. For in-depth theological analysis of contemporary sociopolitical crises and the role of the Church, see Matthew T. Eggemeier and Peter Joseph Fritz, *Send Lazarus: Catholicism and the Crises of Neoliberalism* (New York: Fordham University Press, 2020); for a related work with emphasis on community action, see Eggemeier and Fritz, *The Politics of Mercy: Catholic Life in an Era of Inequality, Racism, and Violence* (Chestnut Ridge, NY: Crossroad/Herder and Herder, 2020).

26. *LG* 4, referencing St. Cyprian, St. Augustine, and St. John Damascene.

27. *LG* 7, with reference to Eph 4:23.

28. See the description of the parish and its mission in John Paul II, *CL* 25–27, and in other documents he quotes there, including Vatican II, *Sacrosanctum Concilium* 42 and *Apostolicam Actuositatem* 10.

29. See, e.g., *EG* 28.

2. THE PARISH AND A THEOLOGY OF THE PEOPLE

1. Lucio Gera, "Apuntes para una interpretación de la Iglesia argentina" (first published 1970), in *Escritos Teologico-Pastorales de Lucio Gera*, ed. Virginia Azcuy et al., vol. 1 (Buenos Aires: Agape, 2006), 527.

2. Austen Ivereigh, *Wounded Shepherd: Pope Francis and His Struggle to Convert the Catholic Church* (New York: Henry Holt, 2019), 149–50, describes this work in some detail.

3. See Ignatius of Loyola, *Spiritual Exercises*, nos. 230, 233, and 234. One contemporary edition is David L. Fleming, ed., *Draw Me into Your Friendship: The Spiritual Exercises—a Literal Translation and a Contemporary Reading* (St. Louis: Institute of Jesuit Sources, 1996).

4. Photographs of the *encuentro* posters and the video *40 Años de la Diócesis*, documenting the 2018 meetings, can be viewed on the diocesan Facebook page, "Diócesis de San Miguel," accessed October 2, 2021, https://www.facebook.com/diocesissanmiguel/photos and https://www.facebook.com/diocesissanmiguel/videos/278420729469082.

5. Ivereigh, *Wounded Shepherd*, 150–52, gives an engaging first-hand account of this mission effort and the group reflection following it.

6. *CL* 26 (see chap. 1 for additional comment on this passage).

7. On "Responding to the New Signs of the Times" in the context of theology of the people, see Rafael Luciani, *Pope Francis and the Theology of the People* (Maryknoll, NY: Orbis, 2017), 37–62.

8. A concise example of his reasoning, in the form of a commentary on the Argentinian bishops' "San Miguel document," can be found in Gera, "Apuntes para una interpretación," 526–32.

9. See Rafael Tello, *Fundamentos de una Nueva Evangelización* (Buenos Aires: Agape Libros, 2015), 81–87, where the author describes

el cristianismo popular. Likewise, in *La Nueva Evangelización: Escritos Teológico-Pastorales*, vol. 1 (Buenos Aires: Agape Libros, 2008), 26–32, describes the "non-conceptual way" (*camino non-conceptual*) in which the people grasp revealed truth.

10. Detailed summaries of this historical trajectory of ToP can be found in Luciani, *Pope Francis and the Theology of the People*, 63–102, and in Emilce Cuda, *Para Leer a Francisco: Teología, Ética y Política* (Buenos Aires: Manantial, 2016), 67–100.

11. See Juan Carlos Scannone, "Pope Francis and the Theology of the People," *Theological Studies* 77, no. 1 (2016): 124–25. Cuda, *Para Leer a Francisco*, 87–100, focuses on various theologians' (including Gera and Gutierrez) interpretations of culture as it is treated in *GS* and in the document from CELAM's 1979 Puebla conference.

12. Tello, *La Nueva Evangelización*, 1:101. Tello also refers here directly to *GS* 53. This idea of culture is also related to Gera's idea, cited above, of "the people" as an agent and source of theological understanding.

13. See Luciani, *Pope Francis and the Theology of the People*, xvii–xviii.

14. Episcopal Conference of Latin America (CELAM), "Final Document," Fifth General Conference of Latin American Bishops, Aparecida, Brazil (May 2007), no. 367. Official English translation, https://www.celam.org/aparecida/Ingles.pdf (hereafter cited as "Aparecida").

15. Tello, *La Nueva Evangelización*, 1:57: "Y esto, que no sólo la fe influye en la cultura sino que también la cultura influye grande y *determinantemente* en la vida Cristiana, hay que tenerlo muy en cuenta" (my English translation in the text.)

16. Luciani, *Pope Francis and the Theology of the People*, 20–21.

17. Pope Francis, *Let Us Dream: The Path to a Better Future*, ed. Austen Ivereigh (New York: Simon and Schuster, 2020), 97.

18. Francis, *Let Us Dream*, 97.

19. Francis, *Let Us Dream*, 100.

20. Francis, *Let Us Dream*, 101.

21. Francis, *Let Us Dream*, 103.

22. Francis, *Let Us Dream*, 101.

23. Francis, *Let Us Dream*, 97.

24. See *LG* 10–13, 31, and 34–36.

25. Pope Francis, "Address Commemorating the 50th Anniversary of the Institution of the Synod of Bishops," October 17, 2015, https://

www.vatican.va/content/francesco/en/speeches/2015/october/documents/papa-francesco_20151017_50-anniversario-sinodo.html. The quotation in the first and second lines of the excerpt is from *EG* 171.

26. See Francis, "Address Commemorating 50th Anniversary," and *LG* 35. For the context of the teaching on *papal* infallibility, see First Vatican Council, First Dogmatic Constitution on the Church of Christ, *Pastor Aeternus* (July 18, 1870), chap. IV; and *LG* 18, 25, and appendix 3–4.

27. Clemens Sedmak, *A Church of the Poor: Pope Francis and the Transformation of Orthodoxy* (Maryknoll, NY: Orbis, 2016), 174. His phrase "the chaos of reality" is an allusion to the writing of Jesuit ethicist James Keenan, who has defined *mercy* as "the willingness to enter into the chaos of others." See James F. Keenan, *The Works of Mercy: The Heart of Catholicism* (Lanham, MD: Rowman and Littlefield, 2008), 4.

28. The full context of Matt 5:3 in the Beatitudes (5:3–12) reveals the simplistic nature of the "everyone is included" approach. See also the alternate version in Luke 6:20–26, as well as Matt 11:5, 28–30; 19:21; Mark 12:38–44; Luke 4:18; 7:22; 14:13; 16:19–31; and James 2:5–7.

29. The acknowledged beginning of an ongoing series of modern papal encyclicals on social justice was Leo XIII, *Rerum Novarum* (May 15, 1891). The term "preferential option for the poor" (which originates in CELAM documents in the 1960s) first appeared in a papal encyclical in John Paul II, *Sollicitudo Rei Socialis* (December 30, 1987), no. 42. This was issued to mark the twentieth anniversary of another social encyclical, Paul VI, *Populorum Progressio* (March 26, 1967), which (in no. 22) quoted fourth-century bishop St. Ambrose as saying, "The earth belongs to everyone, not to the rich!"

30. Pope Francis, "Welcome Ceremony: Address of the Holy Father," La Paz, Bolivia (July 8, 2015), https://www.vatican.va/content/francesco/en/speeches/2015/july/documents/papa-francesco_20150708_bolivia-benvenuto.html.

31. Pope Francis, "Address to a Meeting with Priests, Consecrated Men and Women and Seminarians," Santiago [Chile] Cathedral (January 16, 2018), https://www.vatican.va/content/francesco/en/speeches/2018/january/documents/papa-francesco_20180116_cile-santiago-religiosi.html.

32. Aparecida 1 (and many other places). This phrase, taken from the stated theme of the Aparecida meeting, can be found throughout the document.

33. Aparecida 4. "Seeds of the Word" is a reference to the final document of CELAM's 3rd General Conference at Puebla, Mexico, in 1979: Documento de Puebla, III Conferencia General del Episcopado Latinoamericano, 401, which itself alludes to *GS* 57, https://issuu.com/iglesia.cl/docs/documento_conclusivo_puebla.

34. Pope Francis, "Address of the Holy Father Pope Francis," Audience to Representatives of the Communications Media (March 16, 2013), http://www.vatican.va/content/francesco/en/speeches/2013/march/documents/papa-francesco_20130316_rappresentanti-media.html.

35. *EG* 120. Luciani, *Pope Francis and the Theology of the People*, xvii, comments on the vulnerability of *agency* within the pope's critique of globalization: "Our globalized world tends to render us incapable as agents; that is, it relativizes the absolute value of people and their cultures and thus suppresses the diversity that gives human relevance and meaning to everyday life."

36. Pope Francis, apostolic exhortation *Querida Amazonia* (February 2, 2020), no. 7, http://www.vatican.va/content/francesco/en/apost_exhortations/documents/papa-francesco_esortazione-ap_20200202_querida-amazonia.html.

37. Michael Paulson, "65 Parishes to Be Closed: News Brings Despair, Relief," *Boston Globe*, May 26, 2004, A1. See also Michael Paulson and Bella English, "O'Malley Will Keep Open Two Parishes Set for Closing," *Boston Globe*, December 15, 2004, A1, where, seven months later, the figure mentioned is eighty-three parishes slated for closure. Several of those decisions were ultimately reversed.

38. Joanna Massey, "Consolidation Prods Parishes to Take Stock: Churches around Region Building Case for Survival," *Boston Globe*, February 8, 2004, A1.

39. The earliest such story was published on the day after the announcements: Marcella Bombardieri and Erica Noonan, "The Waiting Ends with a Letter: Emotions High at Local Parishes," *Boston Globe*, May 26, 2004, A1.

40. The following broad sketch of this cluster of parishes was constructed from information and perspectives gathered during numerous conversations and listening sessions with parishioners and former parishioners. I have chosen to use pseudonyms for the communities involved because the full stories are very complex, the nuances and details of the struggle are of great significance to those who lived

through it, and available space does not allow for more than an illustration of the primary point regarding lack of collaborative approaches in this early example of parish reconfiguration.

41. See Thomas Sweetser, *The Parish as Covenant: A Call to Pastoral Partnership* (Lanham, MD: Sheed and Ward, 2001).

42. Michael Paulson, "O'Malley Seeks Review of Closings; Acknowledges Laity's Unrest on Parishes," *Boston Globe*, October 8, 2004, A1. See also Paulson and English, "O'Malley Will Keep Open Two Parishes," *Boston Globe*, December 15, 2004, A1.

43. Pope Francis, "Video Message of the Holy Father Francis to the Participants in the Virtual Continental Congress of Religious Life, Organized by CLAR" (August 13, 2021), https://www.vatican.va/content/francesco/en/messages/pont-messages/2021/documents/20210813-videomessaggio-americalatina.html.

44. Pontifical Council for Justice and Peace, *Compendium of the Social Doctrine of the Church* (Vatican City: Libreria Editrice Vaticana, 2004), no. 160.

45. In this regard, see the much-debated passage of Pope Francis, apostolic exhortation *Amoris Laetitia*: "On Love in the Family" (March 19, 2016), no. 305: "A pastor cannot feel that it is enough simply to apply moral laws to those living in 'irregular' situations, as if they were stones to throw at people's lives."

46. Regarding this authority, see William Clark, *A Voice of Their Own: The Authority of the Local Parish* (Collegeville, MN: Liturgical Press, 2005).

47. See 1 Pet 3:15.

3. THE PARISH AND THE MISSION OF THE CHURCH

1. This is a pseudonym for an actual parish in the Chicago area that I researched from 2011 to 2013. A fuller description of the merger presented here, with comparison to a less successful process and with practical theological conclusions, can be found in William A. Clark, SJ, "Toward a Culture of Dynamic Community: Parish Consolidation and Collaborative Leadership," in *Collaborative Parish Leadership: Contexts, Models, Theology*, ed. William A. Clark and Daniel Gast (Lanham, MD: Lexington Books, 2017), 75–102.

2. Usually rendered "basic Christian communities" or simply "base communities" in English, this term has resonances of both "most simple" and "most foundational."

3. Bruce Saunders, "Purposefully Going: The Parish as a Community in Mission," in *The Parish—People, Place and Ministry: A Theological and Practical Exploration*, ed. Malcolm Torry (Norwich, UK: Canterbury Press, 2004), 115.

4. Jorge Mario Bergoglio (Pope Francis), *Nuestra Fe Es Revolucionaria*, ed. Virginia Bonard (Buenos Aires: Planeta, 2013), 199–200.

5. On the questions of the authorship and audience of Ephesians, see Margaret Y. McDonald, *Colossians—Ephesians*, Sacra Pagina, vol. 17, ed. Daniel Harrington, SJ (Collegeville, MN: Liturgical/Michael Glazier, 2000), 14–18. See also Raymond Collins, "Ephesians," in *The Paulist Biblical Commentary*, ed. J. E. A. Chiu, et al. (Mahwah, NJ: Paulist Press, 2018), 1400–1403. With regard to "circular" letters, see the instruction at Col 4:17.

6. For examples of this call to immediate and practical love, see Rom 12:9–21; 1 Cor 13:1–13; 2 Cor 8:1–15; Gal 5:22–26; Phil 2:1–4; 1 Thess 4:9–12; Philemon 4–16.

7. Cf. Saunders, "Purposefully Going," 120: "The Church's mission task cascades from the nature and purpose of God."

8. As noted above in chap. 1, n. 24, the term itself is rejected as a description of the Church in Eph 2:19, but in an entirely different context than its use in other New Testament passages.

9. The breadth of this title, beyond "the Twelve," is demonstrated in Pauline passages such as Rom 16:7; 1 Cor 9:1–2; 2 Cor 12:11–13; and Gal 1:17.

10. One of Paul's famous paeans to the Church's unity in diversity, listing some of these gifts and offices, can be found in Eph 4:11–16. As for the mission simply to live Christian faith in full view of the world, see Phil 2:14–15.

11. Congregation for the Clergy, "The Pastoral Conversion of the Parish Community in the Service of the Evangelising Mission of The Church" (Vatican City: Holy See Press Office, July 20, 2020), nos. 6–10, takes a more strongly institutional, structural point of view on these communities, describing them almost as if they were the product of a diocesan pastoral plan of the twenty-first century.

12. See Alex Blöchlinger, *The Modern Parish Community* (New York: Kenedy, 1965), 27–28, on the loss of the "sojourner" notion in the transition from Greek to Latin.

13. Yves Congar, *Pour une Église Pauvre et Servante* (Paris: Cerf, 1963), 26. (Translation my own.)

14. "Mémorial du Cinquantenaire de la Fondation de la Paroisse St. Joseph de Biddeford, Maine" (Biddeford, Maine: May 1922), 21. (Translation my own.)

15. See Robert Putnam, *Bowling Alone: The Collapse and Revival of American Community* (New York: Simon and Schuster, 2000), for an application of the concept of "social capital" to late twentieth-century American life. This concept will also be encountered in the work of Tricia Collen Bruce, *Parish and Place: Making Room for Diversity in the American Catholic Church* (New York: Oxford University Press, 2017), cited below and highlighted particularly in chap. 6.

16. This is an important part of the critique of contemporary parish life made by Fr. James Mallon in *Divine Renovation: From a Maintenance to a Missional Parish* (Toronto: Novalis, 2014).

17. See Bruce, *Parish and Place*, who has carefully documented and analyzed this recent phenomenon.

18. See Brett C. Hoover, *The Shared Parish: Latinos, Anglos, and the Future of U.S. Catholicism* (New York: NYU Press, 2014), where the term itself originated and a solid foundation for its study was laid.

19. I have employed this term and concept in Clark, "Toward a Culture of Dynamic Community," and in William A. Clark, "Ark, Fueling Station, or Engaged Community? The Parish in U.S. Catholic Experience," in *Parish under Pressure—Quests for Meaning from a Global Perspective: Germany and the USA in Comparison*, ed. Andreas Henkelmann and Matthias Sellmann (Münster: Aschendorff Verlag, 2012), 83–96.

20. Saunders, "Purposefully Going," 116–17.

21. John Zizioulas, "The Church as Communion," *St. Vladimir's Theological Quarterly* 38, no. 1 (1994): 8.

22. Among many works on aspects of this movement are the Archbishop's Council on Mission and Public Affairs, *Mission-Shaped Church: Church Planting and Fresh Expressions in a Changing Context*, 2nd ed. (London: Church House Publishing, 2009), from which the movement takes its name, and Michael Moynagh, *Church for Every Context: An Introduction to Theology and Practice* (London: SCM Press, 2012).

23. Appreciation to Rev. Robert Heidenreich, Archdiocese of Chicago, who both accompanied me on visits to several dioceses in Germany and himself spent some months of a sabbatical in the Diocese of Essen in 2014. His observations and notes from these experiences have provided important background for this too-brief profile.

24. Center for Applied Pastoral Research (ZAP), *Netzwerk Citykirchen Projekte*, accessed September 12, 2021, https://www.citykirchenprojekte.de/inhalt/zentrum-fuer-angewandte-pastoralforschung-zap.

25. Insights from Fr. Robert Heidenreich, "Diary of Research Visit to Germany: Conversation with Fr. Christian Hennecke," September 2013. Appreciation also to Fr. Hennecke (Diocese of Hildesheim) for insights given to me in conversations over several years and especially in March 2019.

26. Heidenreich, "Diary."

27. See Christian Hennecke and Dieter Tewes, "Small Is Big: The Pastoral Vision behind Small Christian Communities," in *Small Christian Communities: Fresh Stimulus for a Forward-Looking Church*, ed. Klaus Krämer and Klaus Vellguth, One World Theology (Quezon City, Philippines: Claretian Publications, 2013), 2:329–34.

28. An excellent short discussion of this initiative is given in Reinhard Feiter, "The Local Communities of Poitiers: Reflections on Their Reflection," trans. Robert Schreiter, in Clark and Gast, *Collaborative Parish Leadership*, 155–74. Prof. Dr. Feiter relies on two volumes published by original participants in the Poitiers experiment: Albert Rouet et al., *Un Nouveau Visage d'Église: L'Expérience des Communautés Locales à Poitiers* (Paris: Bayard, 2005), and Rouet et al., *Un Goût d'Espérance: Vers un Nouveau Visage d'Église* II (Paris: Bayard, 2008).

29. *CL* 26. The pope quotes first Vatican II's *Lumen Gentium*, then his own *Catechesi Tradendae*, and finally the Code of Canon Law.

30. Saunders, "Purposefully Going," 119.

31. Enrique Eguía Seguí, *De Bergoglio a Francisco: El Sueño de una Iglesia en Salida* (Buenos Aires: Talita Kum Ediciones, 2018) 30. (Translation my own.)

32. Saunders, "Purposefully Going," 119.

33. Pope Francis, apostolic exhortation *Querida Amazonia* (February 2, 2020), no. 7, https://www.vatican.va/content/francesco/en/apost_exhortations/documents/papa-francesco_esortazione-ap_20200202_querida-amazonia.html.

34. See Laurent Villemin, "La paroisse territorial a-t-elle un avenir?" in *Réinventer la paroisse*, ed. Marc Pelchat (Paris: Médiaspaul, 2015), 61–80, and especially his quotation and discussion of the work of Alphonse Borras.

35. Saunders, "Purposefully Going," 118.

36. Saunders, "Purposefully Going," 120.

37. For examples of such invitation in the ministry of Jesus, see Matt 18:2 and Mark 9:36 (a child), Mark 3:3 and Luke 6:8 (a man with a withered hand), Luke 5:19 (a paralytic), and John 8:3 (an accused woman).

38. Saunders, "Purposefully Going," 121.

4. THE PARISH AS COMMUNITY

1. Jacqueline Williams, "In Australia, a Booming Economy with a Tragic Price for Farmers," *New York Times*, May 21, 2018, 8A.

2. "About Us," St. Mary's War Memorial School (West Wyalong, NSW, Australia, 2021), accessed October 16, 2021, https://smwms.nsw.edu.au/about-us.

3. John Zizioulas (Metropolitan John of Pergamon), "The Church as Communion," *St. Vladimir's Theological Quarterly* 38, no. 1 (1994): 5–6.

4. For a slightly expanded explanation of *icon*, see chap. 5, n. 43.

5. See John 14, esp. vv. 5–11 and 26.

6. See Eph 1:22 and Col 1:18 (where Christ is spoken of as "head" and the Church is "the body") and 1 Cor 12:27 and Rom 12:4–5 (where Christ and the members of the Church are united in one body).

7. Zizioulas, "Church as Communion," 7.

8. Zizioulas, "Church as Communion," 8–9.

9. Ignatius of Antioch, "The Epistle of Ignatius to the Ephesians," no. 1, in *Ante-Nicene Fathers*, vol. 1, ed. and trans. Alexander Roberts et al. (Buffalo, NY: Christian Literature Publishing Co., 1885). Revised and edited for New Advent by Kevin Knight, accessed June 21, 2022, http://www.newadvent.org/fathers/0104.htm.

10. For some background details on these developments, see Casiano Floristan, *The Parish: Eucharistic Community*, trans. John F. Byrne (London: Sheed and Ward, 1965), 50–53.

11. See Karl Rahner, "Theology of the Parish," in *The Parish: From Theology to Practice*, ed. Hugo Rahner, trans. Robert Kress (Westminster, MD: Newman Press, 1958), 23–35. See esp. Rahner's "First Thesis" in this work, 25–30.

12. For a helpful treatment of the idea of authority in Orthodox theology, see John Chryssavgis, "Obedience and Authority: Dimensions of a Hierarchical Church," in *Soul Mending: The Art of Spiritual Direction* (Brookline, MA: Holy Cross Orthodox Press, 2000), 101–10, https://www.goarch.org/-/obedience-and-authority-dimensions-of-a-hierarchical-church. The relationship between parishes and the Church authority in Roman Catholicism will be discussed more fully in chap. 6.

13. Congregation for the Doctrine of the Faith (CDF), "Letter to the Bishops of the Catholic Church, On Some Aspects of the Church Understood as Communion" (May 28, 1992), https://www.vatican.va/roman_curia/congregations/cfaith/documents/rc_con_cfaith_doc_28051992_communionis-notio_en.html.

14. CDF, "On Some Aspects of the Church," 10.

15. See Joseph Fox, "The Status of the Parish in the 1983 Code of Canon Law," in *What Is a Parish? Canonical, Pastoral, and Theological Perspectives*, ed. Thomas A. Baima and Lawrence Hennessey (Chicago: Hillenbrand Books, 2011), 48–49.

16. CDF, "On Some Aspects of the Church," 4.

17. Philip J. Murnion, "The Community Called Parish," *Church* 1, no. 4 (Winter 1985): 9.

18. Philip J. Murnion, "Parish: Covenant Community," *Church* 12, no. 1 (Spring 1996): 6.

19. Matthias Sellmann, "Seven Characteristics of a Future-Proof Parish: The Approach of the Center for Applied Pastoral Research," in *Envisioning Futures for the Catholic Church*, ed. Staf Hellemans and Peter Jonkers, Cultural Heritage and Contemporary Change, series VIII, Christian Philosophical Studies, vol. 23 (Washington DC: Council for Research in Values and Philosophy, 2018), 250–51.

20. Sellmann, "Seven Characteristics," 235.

21. Sellmann, "Seven Characteristics," 246–48.

22. See Evelyn Whitehead and James Whitehead, *Community of Faith: Models and Strategies for Developing Christian Communities* (New York: Seabury Press, 1982), 32.

23. Sellmann, "Seven Characteristics," 246.

24. Sellmann, "Seven Characteristics," 247.

25. Sellmann, "Seven Characteristics," 248.

26. Sellmann, "Seven Characteristics," 248.

27. Robert Bellah et al., *Habits of the Heart: Individualism and Commitment in American Life*, updated ed. (Berkeley: University of California Press, 1996), 220–21.

28. St. Augustine of Hippo, Sermon 272, no. 15, in *The Eucharist*, trans. D. Sheerin (Wilmington, DE: Michael Glazier, 1986), 95: "If, therefore, you are the body of Christ and His members, your mystery has been placed on the Lord's table, you receive your mystery. You reply 'Amen' to that which you are, and by replying you consent. For you hear 'The Body of Christ,' and you reply 'Amen.' Be a member of the body of Christ so that your 'Amen' may be true."

29. Sellmann, "Seven Characteristics," 233. The idea calls to mind, of course, Jesus's saying, "For those who want to save their life will lose it, and those who lose their life for my sake, and for the sake of the gospel, will save it" (Mark 8:35, with parallels in all of the other canonical Gospels.)

30. Philip Murnion, "The Parish Community: Theological Questions Arising from Attempts to Implement Vatican II," in *Catholic Theological Society of America: Proceedings of the Thirty-Sixth Annual Convention* (June 10–13, 1981), vol. 36, ed. Luke Salm, FSC (Bronx, NY: Manhattan College, 1982), 49.

31. Murnion, "Community Called Parish," 10–13.

32. Murnion, "Community Called Parish," 12.

33. Murnion, "Community Called Parish," 14.

34. See above, at n. 27.

35. Examples include 2nd Plenary Council of the Philippines (1991), nos. 600–601, and the Catholic Bishops' Conference of the Philippines use of "communion of communities" as part of the theme for the "Year of the Parish" in 2017 (https://www.cbcplaiko.org/2017/01/24/guide-for-the-observance-of-the-year-of-the-parish-as-communion-of-communities/); CELAM, *IV Conferencia General del Episcopado Latinoamericano*, "Conclusiones," no. 58; *EG* 28.

36. A thorough discussion of the relationship between BECs and the parish can be found in John Paul Vandenakker, *Small Christian Communities and the Parish* (Kansas City, MO: Sheed and Ward, 1995).

37. For an excellent summary and evaluation of the Poitiers experiment, see Reinhard Feiter, "The Local Communities of Poitiers: Reflections on Their Reflection," in *Collaborative Parish Leadership: Contexts,*

Models, Theology, ed. William Clark and Daniel Gast (Lanham, MD: Lexington, 2017), 155–74. Feiter relies largely on two volumes of reflections by the former archbishop of Poitiers and others deeply involved in the project. See Albert Rouet et al., *Un nouveau visage d'église: l'expérience des communautés locales à poitiers* (Paris: Bayard, 2005), and Rouet et al., *Un goût d'espérance: vers un nouveau visage d'église*, vol. 2 (Paris: Bayard, 2008).

38. For detailed discussion of the "shared parish" or "multicultural parish," see Brett C. Hoover, *The Shared Parish: Latinos, Anglos, and the Future of U.S. Catholicism* (New York: NYU Press, 2014); also, Hoover, "No Favoritism: Effective Collaborative Leadership Practices in Multicultural Parishes," in Clark and Gast, *Collaborative Parish Leadership*, 103–24.

39. Pope Francis, "Mensaje a los Educadores y Alumnos, Abril 1999," in *Nuestra Fe Es Revolucionaria*, ed. Virginia Bonard (Buenos Aires: Planeta, 2013), 200. "Otra tentación es privilegiar los valores del cerebro sobre los valores del corazón. No es así. Solamente el corazón une e integra. El entendimiento sin el sentir piadoso tiende a dividir. El corazón une la idea con la realidad, el tiempo con el espacio, la vida con la muerte y con la eternidad." (English translation my own.)

5. THE PARISH AND SACRED PLACE

1. For a brief description, see "Bunhill Fields Burial Ground," accessed July 10, 2021, https://www.cityoflondon.gov.uk/things-to-do/city-gardens/find-a-garden/bunhill-fields-burial-ground.

2. Catholic Bishops' Conference of England and Wales, "Bunhill Row—St. Joseph," *Taking Stock: Catholic Churches of England and Wales*, accessed July 9, 2021, https://taking-stock.org.uk/building/bunhill-row-st-joseph/.

3. Catholic Bishops' Conference of England and Wales, "Bunhill Row."

4. Martin Pendergast, "Beyond the Parochial: Parish Realities and a Synodal Church," in *New Blackfriars* 100, no. 1086 (March 2019): 185, https://doi.org/10.1111/nbfr.12442.

5. See "church, n.1 and adj," *OED Online*, December 2021, Oxford University Press, accessed December 31, 2021, https://www.oed.com/view/Entry/32760?rskey=Mwk29i&result=1.

6. See "Roman Catholic Parish of Moorfields" (https://parish.rcdow.org.uk/moorfields/about-the-parish/) and "Westminster Cathedral" (https://westminstercathedral.org.uk/the-cathedral/history-of-the-cathedral/).

7. Laurent Villemin, "La paroisse territorial a-t-elle un avenir?" in *Réinventer la paroisse*, ed. Marc Pelchat (Montreal: Médiaspaul, 2015), 71: "Le territoire a structuré la paroisse mais, oubli-t-on souvent, la paroisse a structuré le territoire." (My English translation in the text.)

8. Council of Trent, sess. 24, chap. 13, in *Canons and Decrees of the Council of Trent*, trans. H. J. Schroeder, OP, reprint ed. (Rockford, IL: TAN Books, 1978), 204.

9. Karl Rahner, "Peaceful Reflections on the Parochial Principle," *Theological Investigations*, vol. 2, *Man in the Church*, trans. Karl-H. Kruger (Baltimore: Helicon Press, 1963), 289.

10. Rahner, "Peaceful Reflections," 288.

11. Rahner, "Peaceful Reflections," 298.

12. Villemin, "La paroisse territorial," 72.

13. Villemin, "La paroisse territorial," 73.

14. Villemin, 66, "La paroisse territorial," citing Albert Rouet, *Un Nouveau Visage de l'Église* (Paris: Bayard, 2005), 27–28.

15. Reinhard Feiter, "The Local Communities of Poitiers: Reflections on Their Reflection," trans. Robert Schreiter, in *Collaborative Parish Leadership: Contexts, Models, Theology*, ed. William A. Clark and Daniel Gast (Lanham, MD: Lexington Books, 2017), 167–68.

16. Ignatius of Loyola, the Spiritual Exercises, no. 230, in *Draw Me into Your Friendship: The Spiritual Exercises, a Literal Translation and a Contemporary Reading*, ed. David Fleming, SJ, trans. Elder Mullan, SJ (St. Louis: Institute of Jesuit Sources, 1996), 174.

17. Spiritual Exercises, no. 231, in Fleming, *Draw Me*, 175.

18. See chap. 3 above, following n. 13.

19. Particularly important background for the reflections in this section is provided by these works: Walter Brueggemann, *The Land: Place as Gift, Promise, and Challenge in Biblical Faith*, Overtures to Biblical Theology Series (London: SPCK, 1978); John Inge, *A Christian Theology of Place* (Burlington, VT: Ashgate, 2003); and Andrew Rumsey, *Parish: An Anglican Theology of Place* (London: SCM Press, 2017).

20. Brueggemann, *The Land*, 5.

21. Rumsey, *Parish*, 20, offers several observations on this story and draws from it the four pillars of his methodology: being, revelation, tradition, and vocation.

22. For prominent examples, see Mark 15:29; Luke 21:5–6; and Acts 6:13–14.

23. W. D. Davies, *The Gospel and the Land* (1974), quoted in Inge, *Christian Theology of Place*, 48. Inge goes on (51–54) to discuss the incarnation as grounding what he later calls "a relational view of place" (78–82) with the incarnate Christ at its center.

24. This is attested to by the elaborate greetings at the end of several of Paul's letters, notably in Rom 16:1–23.

25. Rumsey, *Parish*, 28, in discussing this eschatological emphasis, refers to "the kingdom of heaven" as "God's new place."

26. For other mentions of the early Christian community in Jerusalem gathering in the temple, see Acts 5:42 and Luke 24:53.

27. Michael Peppard, *The World's Oldest Church: Bible, Art, and Ritual at Dura-Europos, Syria* (New Haven, CT: Yale University Press, 2016).

28. Peppard, *World's Oldest Church*, 15–20.

29. Peppard, *World's Oldest Church*, 16.

30. Throughout his book on Dura-Europos, Peppard provides a detailed discussion of ways in which the arrangement of the house and the content of the recovered wall paintings can be "read" for a deeper understanding of third-century Christian belief and practice. Another highly detailed discussion of this type, from a much different era, is presented by Margaret Visser, *The Geometry of Love: Space, Time, Mystery, and Meaning in an Ordinary Church* (New York: North Point Press, 2000).

31. Alex Blöchlinger, *The Modern Parish Community*, trans. Geoffrey Stevens (New York: P. J. Kenedy & Sons, 1965), 46–48, presents a detailed summary of these developments, as does Casiano Floristan, *The Parish: Eucharistic Community*, trans. John F. Byrne (London: Sheed and Ward, 1965), 43–52.

32. See Blöchlinger, *Modern Parish Community*, 50–78, and Floristan, *The Parish*, 53–57.

33. See Congregation for the Clergy, Instruction on "The Pastoral Conversion of the Parish Community in the Service of the Evangelizing Mission of the Church" (June 29, 2020) (Vatican City: Holy See Press

Office), nos. 6–15, for a description of "The Parish in a Contemporary Context" and an argument for "The Value of the Parish Today."

34. Rumsey, *Parish*, 32.

35. For a brief explanation of the purpose of icons in Orthodox understanding, see Linette Martin, *Praying with Icons* (Brewster, MA: Paraclete, 2011), 5–9.

36. See Liturgy Office of England and Wales, *Dedication of a Church and an Altar* (London, 1978), 8, 19. For descriptions and insightful comparisons of this ritual in past and present forms, see John Seitz, *No Closure: Catholic Practice and Boston's Parish Shutdowns* (Cambridge, MA: Harvard University Press, 2011), 70–73, 119–28. Seitz's whole work seeks to understand the resistance of ordinary parishioners to the loss of their parish churches.

37. Inge, *Christian Theology of Place*, 52.

38. See Richard Taylor, *How to Read a Church: A Guide to Symbols and Images in Churches and Cathedrals* (Mahwah, NJ: Paulist Press/HiddenSpring, 2003); and Michael Weldon, *A Struggle for Holy Ground: Reconciliation and the Rites of Parish Closure* (Collegeville, MN: Liturgical Press, 2004).

39. Inge, *Christian Theology of Place*, 89.

40. John Zizioulas (Metropolitan John of Pergamon), "The Church as Communion," *St. Vladimir's Theological Quarterly* 38, no. 1 (1994): 13.

41. Pope Francis, apostolic exhortation *Querida Amazonia* (Rome: February 2, 2020), no. 41.

42. This image may also bring to mind the "field hospital" that Pope Francis has proposed for the Church at large. See Antonio Spadaro, "A Big Heart Open to God: An Interview with Pope Francis," *National Catholic Reporter*, September 30, 2013, https://www.americamagazine.org/faith/2013/09/30/big-heart-open-god-interview-pope-francis.

6. THE PARISH AND THE LARGER CHURCH

1. Congregation for the Doctrine of the Faith (CDF), "Letter to the Bishops of the Catholic Church, On Some Aspects of the Church Understood as Communion" (Vatican City: May 28, 1992), https://

www.vatican.va/roman_curia/congregations/cfaith/documents/rc_con_cfaith_doc_28051992_communionis-notio_en.html.

2. For a discussion of the evolution, within Ratzinger's writings, of the distinctive line of argument presented in the letter, see William Clark, *A Voice of Their Own: The Authority of the Local Parish* (Collegeville, MN: Liturgical Press, 2005), 135–42.

3. CDF, "Letter to Bishops," 4.

4. The Congregation for the Clergy, "The Pastoral Conversion of the Parish Community in the Service of the Evangelising Mission of the Church" (Vatican City: Holy See Press Office, July 20, 2020), no. 6, takes this understanding for granted. See also Joseph Fox, "The Status of the Parish in the 1983 Code of Canon Law," in *What Is a Parish? Canonical, Pastoral, and Theological Perspectives*, ed. Thomas A. Baima and Lawrence Hennessey (Chicago: Hillenbrand Books, 2011), 50n33. By contrast, Alex Blöchlinger, *The Modern Parish Community* (New York: Kenedy, 1965), 38–42, describes a complex process of development.

5. See Paul's discussion of the Corinthians' abuse of the Eucharist, in 1 Cor 11:18–22.

6. A footnote here attributes the quotation to an ancient Mozarabic (Iberian Christian) prayer.

7. A footnote here attributes the quotation to St. Thomas Aquinas's *Summa Theologiae*, III.

8. *LG* 26 (Flannery translation). The final direct quotation is attributed to a sermon of St. Leo the Great.

9. Lawrence Hennessey, "Foreword," in Baima and Hennessey, *What Is a Parish?*, ix, writing with apparent uncertainty on this very point poses a series of questions about the character of the parish, presented as conundrums, that I have been approaching quite directly here.

10. At one point early in the twenty-first century, as controversies raged across the United States over both the sexual abuse settlements and the wave of parish closures, the Diocese of Spokane, facing bankruptcy, argued compellingly against its creditors that it only held parish property in *trust* for the individual communities. At the same time on the other side of the country, the Archdiocese of Boston insisted on its full legal ownership and the right to close and sell parish church buildings regardless of the wishes of parishioners. See John Stucke, "Parishes' Ownership Key to Case," *The Spokesman-Review* (Spokane, WA), May 28, 2005, https://www.spokesman.com/stories/2005/may/28/parishes-ownership-key-to-case/. See also *Akoury v. Roman Catholic*

Archbishop, No. 043803B (Mass. Cmmw. September 14, 2004), accessed December 29, 2021, https://casetext.com/case/akoury-v-roman-catholic-archbishop.

11. Preparatory Document for the 16th Ordinary General Assembly of the Synod of Bishops (Vatican: Holy See Press Office, September 7, 2021), no. 1, https://press.vatican.va/content/salastampa/en/bollettino/pubblico/2021/09/07/210907a.html.

12. Tricia Colleen Bruce, *Parish and Place: Making Room for Diversity in the American Catholic Church* (New York: Oxford University Press, 2017).

13. Bruce, *Parish and Place*, 4.

14. Bruce, *Parish and Place*, 170.

15. Bruce, *Parish and Place*, 176. On "social capital," Bruce refers to work by Robert Putnam and by William Fischel.

16. Bruce, *Parish and Place*, 176–77.

17. Bruce, *Parish and Place*, 177–78.

18. Bruce, *Parish and Place*, 174.

19. Pope Francis, post-synodal apostolic exhortation *Querida Amazonia* (February 2, 2020), no. 70, https://www.vatican.va/content/francesco/en/apost_exhortations/documents/papa-francesco_esortazione-ap_20200202_querida-amazonia.html.

20. See Second Vatican Council, Decree on the Apostolate of the Laity, *Apostolicam Actuositatem* (hereafter cited as *AA*) (November 18, 1965), no. 2 and throughout the document; for example, nos. 7 and 25.

21. Pope Francis, apostolic exhortation *Evangelii Gaudium* (November 24, 2013), no. 120, https://www.vatican.va/content/francesco/en/apost_exhortations/documents/papa-francesco_esortazione-ap_20131124_evangelii-gaudium.html. See also CELAM, "Concluding Document of the Fifth General Conference of the Bishops of Latin America and the Caribbean," Aparecida, Brazil (May 13–31, 2007), nos. 20–32, https://www.celam.org/aparecida/Ingles.pdf.

22. Yves Congar, *Pour une Église Servante et Pauvre*, L'Église aux Cent Visages 8 (Paris: Cerf, 1963). See also Congar, *Power and Poverty in the Church: The Renewal and Understanding of Service* (Mahwah, NJ: Paulist Press, 2016). Citations here are of the original French edition, in my own translation.

23. Congar, *Servante et Pauvre*, 20.

24. Congar, *Servante et Pauvre*, 27.

25. Congar, *Servante et Pauvre*, 27–29, referring to John 13:12–17.

26. Carol Glatz, "Pope Washes Feet of 12 Young Detainees to Serve Them 'from the Heart,'" *National Catholic Reporter*, March 28, 2013, https://www.ncronline.org/news/vatican/pope-washes-feet-12-young-detainees-serve-them-heart.

27. Congar, *Servante et Pauvre*, 135.

28. Congar, *Servante et Pauvre*, 131.

29. Congar, *Servante et Pauvre*, 136.

30. See Pope Francis, Papal Press Conference, "Pope: Abortion Is Murder, the Church Must Be Close and Compassionate, Not Political," *Vatican News*, September 15, 2021, https://www.vaticannews.va/en/pope/news/2021-09/pope-abortion-is-murder-the-church-must-be-compassionate.html.

31. See Matt 24:45. See also Code of Canon Law, can. 843 §1: "Sacred ministers cannot deny the sacraments to those who seek them at appropriate times, are properly disposed, and are not prohibited by law from receiving them."

32. Congar, *Servante et Pauvre*, 23.

33. Pope Francis, *A Big Heart Open to God: A Conversation with Pope Francis*, ed. Antonio Spadaro (New York: HarperOne/America Press, 2013), 27–28.

34. See *Catechism of the Catholic Church*, §2358.

7. PARISH: A VISION FORWARD

1. Pope Francis has written extensively on this theme and has cited many other sources along the way. See, e.g., *EG* 52–75 and *Laudato Si'*, On Care for Our Common Home (May 24, 2015), nos. 43–47 and 115–36.

2. Pope Francis, apostolic letter *Misericordia et Miseria* (November 20, 2016), no. 22, https://www.vatican.va/content/francesco/en/apost_letters/documents/papa-francesco-lettera-ap_20161120_misericordia-et-misera.html. (My thanks to Prof. Peter Fritz, College of the Holy Cross, for recalling this particular image for me.)

3. Congregation for the Doctrine of the Faith (CDF), "Letter to the Bishops of the Catholic Church, On Some Aspects of the Church Understood as Communion" (Vatican City: May 28, 1992), no. 4, https://www.vatican.va/roman_curia/congregations/cfaith/documents/rc_con_cfaith_doc_28051992_communionis-notio_en.html.

4. Ignatius of Antioch. "Epistle to the Smyrneans" 8, in *Ante-Nicene Fathers*, vol. 1., ed. Alexander Roberts, James Donaldson, and A. Cleveland Coxe (Buffalo, NY: Christian Literature Publishing Co., 1885). Revised and edited for New Advent by Kevin Knight, accessed July 5, 2022, http://www.newadvent.org/fathers/0109.htm.

5. Pope Francis, encyclical letter *Fratelli Tutti*, On Fraternity and Social Friendship (October 3, 2020), https://www.vatican.va/content/francesco/en/encyclicals/documents/papa-francesco_20201003_enciclica-fratelli-tutti.html.

6. The Congregation for the Clergy, "The Pastoral Conversion of the Parish Community in the Service of the Evangelising Mission of the Church" (Vatican City: Holy See Press Office, July 20, 2020), no. 2.

7. Australian Catholic Bishops Conference, Implementation Advisory Group, "The Light from the Southern Cross: Promoting Co-responsible Governance in the Catholic Church in Australia" (August 2020), accessed December 31, 2021, https://static1.squarespace.com/static/5acea6725417fc059ddcc33f/t/5f3f79e41aac2871be0fba5c/1597995610389/The+Light+from+the+Southern+Cross+FINAL+%2815+August+2020%29.pdf.

8. See "Synod 2021–2023" (https://www.synod.va/en.html) for the various documents issued by the Vatican regarding the synod.

SUGGESTED READING

THE BOOKS AND articles listed here have had important influences on my thinking and on the shape of this book and are by and large included in the notes for the various chapters. They are listed here not because I necessarily concur with each of their perspectives, but because they represent influential points of view and are useful for a deeper understanding of the various ways in which parishes today are being studied and discussed.

PAPAL, CONCILIAR, AND OTHER CHURCH DOCUMENTS (FOR POPE FRANCIS, SEE SEPARATE SECTION BELOW)

Australian Catholic Bishops Conference (Implementation Advisory Group). "The Light from the Southern Cross: Promoting Co-responsible Governance in the Catholic Church in Australia." August 2020. https://static1.squarespace.com/static/5acea6725417fc059ddcc33f/t/5f3f79e41aac2871be0fba5c/1597995610389/The+Light+from+the+Southern+Cross+FINAL+%2815+August+2020%29.pdf.

Congregation for the Clergy. "The Pastoral Conversion of the Parish Community in the Service of the Evangelising Mission of the Church." Vatican City: Holy See Press Office. July 20, 2020.

Congregation for the Doctrine of the Faith. "Letter to the Bishops of the Catholic Church, On Some Aspects of the Church Understood as Communion." May 28, 1992. https://www.vatican.va/roman_curia/congregations/cfaith/documents/rc_con_cfaith_doc_28051992_communionis-notio_en.html.

Episcopal Conference of Latin America and the Caribbean (CELAM). "Documento de Puebla." III Conferencia General del Episcopado Latinoamericano. Puebla, Mexico. 1979. https://issuu.com/iglesia.cl/docs/documento_conclusivo_puebla.

———. "Final Document." Fifth General Conference of Latin American Bishops. Aparecida, Brazil. May 2007. Official English translation. https://www.celam.org/aparecida/Ingles.pdf.

General Secretariat for the Synod of Bishops. "Preparatory Document for the 16th Ordinary General Assembly of the Synod of Bishops." Vatican: Holy See Press Office. September 7, 2021. https://press.vatican.va/content/salastampa/en/bollettino/pubblico/2021/09/07/210907a.html.

John Paul II. Apostolic exhortation *Christifideles Laici*. December 30, 1988. http://www.vatican.va/content/john-paul-ii/en/apost_exhortations/documents/hf_jp-ii_exh_30121988_christifideles-laici.html.

Second Vatican Council. *Apostolicam Actuositatem*. Decree on the Apostolate of the Laity. November 18, 1965. https://www.vatican.va/archive/hist_councils/ii_vatican_council/documents/vat-ii_decree_19651118_apostolicam-actuositatem_en.html.

———. *Gaudium et Spes*. Pastoral Constitution on the Church in the Modern World. December 7, 1965. https://www.vatican.va/archive/hist_councils/ii_vatican_council/documents/vat-ii_const_19651207_gaudium-et-spes_en.html.

———. *Lumen Gentium*. Dogmatic Constitution on the Church. November 21, 1964. https://www.vatican.va/archive/hist_councils/ii_vatican_council/documents/vat-ii_const_19641121_lumen-gentium_en.html.

———. *Sacrosanctum Concilium*. Constitution on the Sacred Liturgy. December 4, 1963. https://www.vatican.va/archive/hist_councils/ii_vatican_council/documents/vat-ii_const_19631204_sacrosanctum-concilium_en.html.

POPE FRANCIS (INCLUDING BOTH WORKS AUTHORED BY FRANCIS AND WORKS ABOUT HIM)

Bergoglio, Jorge Mario (Pope Francis). *Nuestra Fe Es Revolucionaria.* Edited by Virginia Bonard. Buenos Aires: Planeta, 2013.

Francis. "Address Commemorating the 50th Anniversary of the Institution of the Synod of Bishops." October 17, 2015. https://www.vatican.va/content/francesco/en/speeches/2015/october/documents/papa-francesco_20151017_50-anniversario-sinodo.html.

———. *A Big Heart Open to God: A Conversation with Pope Francis.* Edited by Antonio Spadaro. New York: HarperOne/America Press, 2013.

———. Apostolic exhortation *Querida Amazonia.* February 2, 2020. http://www.vatican.va/content/francesco/en/apost_exhortations/documents/papa-francesco_esortazione-ap_20200202_querida-amazonia.html.

———. Encyclical letter *Fratelli Tutti.* On Fraternity and Social Friendship. October 3, 2020. https://www.vatican.va/content/francesco/en/encyclicals/documents/papa-francesco_20201003_enciclica-fratelli-tutti.html.

———. *Evangelii Gaudium.* Apostolic Exhortation on the Proclamation of the Gospel in Today's World. November 24, 2013. http://www.vatican.va/content/francesco/en/apost_exhortations/documents/papa-francesco_esortazione-ap_20131124_evangelii-gaudium.html.

———. *Let Us Dream: The Path to a Better Future.* Edited by Austen Ivereigh. New York: Simon and Schuster, 2020.

Ivereigh, Austen. *The Great Reformer: Francis and the Making of a Radical Pope.* New York: Henry Holt, 2014.

———. *Wounded Shepherd: Pope Francis and His Struggle to Convert the Catholic Church.* New York: Henry Holt, 2019.

Luciani, Rafael. *Pope Francis and the Theology of the People*. Maryknoll, NY: Orbis, 2017.

Scannone, Juan Carlos, SJ. "Pope Francis and the Theology of the People." *Theological Studies* 77, no. 1 (March 2016): 118–35.

Seguí, Enrique Eguía. *De Bergoglio a Francisco: El Sueño de una Iglesia en Salida*. Buenos Aires: Talita Kum Ediciones, 2018.

PASTORAL AND PRACTICAL STUDIES

Archbishop's Council on Mission and Public Affairs. *Mission-Shaped Church: Church Planting and Fresh Expressions in a Changing Context*. 2nd ed. London: Church House Publishing, 2009.

Baima, Thomas A. and Lawrence Hennessey, eds. *What Is a Parish? Canonical, Pastoral, and Theological Perspectives*. Chicago: Hillenbrand Books, 2011.

Clark, William A. "Ark, Fueling Station, or Engaged Community? The Parish in U.S. Catholic Experience." In *Parish under Pressure—Quests for Meaning from a Global Perspective: Germany and the USA in Comparison*, edited by Andreas Henkelmann and Matthias Sellmann, 83–96. Münster: Aschendorff Verlag, 2012.

Clark, William A., and Daniel Gast, eds. *Collaborative Parish Leadership: Contexts, Models, Theology*. Lanham, MD: Lexington Books, 2017.

Corcoran, Tom, and Michael White. *Rebuilt: Awakening the Faithful, Reaching the Lost, and Making Church Matter*. Notre Dame, IN: Ave Maria Press, 2013.

Dreher, Rod. *The Benedict Option: A Strategy for Christians in a Post-Christian Nation*. New York: Sentinel, 2017.

Eggemeier, Matthew T., and Peter Joseph Fritz. *The Politics of Mercy: Catholic Life in an Era of Inequality, Racism, and Violence*. Chestnut Ridge, NY: Crossroad/Herder and Herder, 2020.

Krämer, Klaus, and Klaus Vellguth. *Small Christian Communities: Fresh Stimulus for a Forward-Looking Church*. One World Theology. Vol. 2. Quezon City, Philippines: Claretian Publications, 2013.

Mallon, James. *Divine Renovation: From a Maintenance to a Missional Parish*. Toronto, ON: Novalis, 2014.

Moynagh, Michael. *Church for Every Context: An Introduction to Theology and Practice*. London: SCM Press, 2012.

Murnion, Philip. "The Community Called Parish." *Church* 1, no. 4 (Winter 1985): 8–14.

———. "Parish: Covenant Community." *Church* 12, no. 1 (Spring 1996): 5–10

———. "The Parish Community: Theological Questions Arising from Attempts to Implement Vatican II." *Catholic Theological Society of America: Proceedings of the Thirty-Sixth Annual Convention* (June 10–13, 1981). Edited by Luke Salm, FSC. 36:39–55. Bronx, NY: Manhattan College, 1982.

Pelchat, Marc, ed. *Réinventer la paroisse*. Paris: Médiaspaul, 2015.

Pendergast, Martin. "Beyond the Parochial: Parish Realities and a Synodal Church." *New Blackfriars*100, no. 1086 (March 2019): 184–95. https://doi.org/10.1111/nbfr.12442.

Rouet, Albert, et al. *Un Goût d'Espérance: Vers un Nouveau Visage d'Église II*. Paris: Bayard, 2008.

———. *Un Nouveau Visage d'Église: L'Expérience des Communautés Locales à Poitiers*. Paris: Bayard, 2005.

Sweetser, Thomas P. *Keeping the Covenant: Taking Parish to the Next Level*. New York: Crossroad, 2007.

———. *The Parish as Covenant: A Call to Pastoral Partnership*. Lanham, MD: Sheed and Ward, 2001.

Taylor, Richard. *How to Read a Church: A Guide to Symbols and Images in Churches and Cathedrals*. Mahwah, NJ: Paulist Press/HiddenSpring, 2003.

Torry, Malcolm, ed. *The Parish—People, Place and Ministry: A Theological and Practical Exploration*. Norwich, UK: Canterbury Press, 2004.

Vandenakker, John Paul. *Small Christian Communities and the Parish*. Kansas City, MO: Sheed and Ward, 1995.

Weldon, Michael. *A Struggle for Holy Ground: Reconciliation and the Rites of Parish Closure*. Collegeville, MN: Liturgical Press, 2004.

Whitehead, Evelyn, and James Whitehead. *Community of Faith: Models and Strategies for Developing Christian Communities*. New York: Seabury Press, 1982.

Wilkes, Paul. *Excellent Catholic Parishes: The Guide to Best Places and Practices.* Mahwah, NJ: Paulist Press, 2001.

SOCIOLOGICAL AND ETHNOGRAPHIC STUDIES

Brown, Callum G. *The Death of Christian Britain: Understanding Secularisation 1800–2000.* 2nd ed. Abingdon, Oxon, UK: Routledge, 2009.

Bruce, Tricia Collen. *Parish and Place: Making Room for Diversity in the American Catholic Church.* New York: Oxford University Press, 2017.

Hoover, Brett C. *The Shared Parish: Latinos, Anglos, and the Future of U.S. Catholicism.* New York: NYU Press, 2014.

Pew Research Center. Religion and Public Life. "In U.S., Decline of Christianity Continues at Rapid Pace: An Update on America's Changing Religious Landscape." October 17, 2019. https://www.pewforum.org/2019/10/17/in-u-s-decline-of-christianity-continues-at-rapid-pace/.

Seitz, John. *No Closure: Catholic Practice and Boston's Parish Shutdowns.* Cambridge, MA: Harvard University Press, 2011.

Sellmann, Matthias. "Seven Characteristics of a Future-Proof Parish: The Approach of the Center for Applied Pastoral Research." In *Envisioning Futures for the Catholic Church*, edited by Staf Hellemans and Peter Jonkers, 231–80. Cultural Heritage and Contemporary Change, series VIII. Christian Philosophical Studies, vol. 23. Washington, DC: Council for Research in Values and Philosophy, 2018.

THEOLOGICAL AND HISTORICAL STUDIES

Blöchlinger, Alex. *The Modern Parish Community.* New York: Kenedy, 1965.

Brueggemann, Walter. *The Land: Place as Gift, Promise, and Challenge in Biblical Faith.* Overtures to Biblical Theology Series. London: SPCK, 1978.

Clark, William A. *A Voice of Their Own: The Authority of the Local Parish*. Collegeville, MN: Liturgical Press, 2005.

Congar, Yves. *Pour une Église Servante et Pauvre*. L'Église aux Cent Visages 8. Paris: Cerf, 1963.

———. *Power and Poverty in the Church: The Renewal and Understanding of Service*. Mahwah, NJ: Paulist Press, 2016.

Cuda, Emilce. *Para Leer a Francisco: Teología, Ética y Política*. Buenos Aires: Manantial, 2016.

Eggemeier, Matthew T., and Peter Joseph Fritz. *Send Lazarus: Catholicism and the Crises of Neoliberalism*. New York: Fordham University Press, 2020.

Floristan, Casiano. *The Parish: Eucharistic Community*. Translated by John F. Byrne. London: Sheed and Ward, 1965.

Gera, Lucio. *Escritos Teologico-Pastorales de Lucio Gera*. Edited by Virginia Azcuy et al. Buenos Aires: Agape, 2006.

Inge, John. *A Christian Theology of Place*. Burlington, VT: Ashgate, 2003.

Peppard, Michael. *The World's Oldest Church: Bible, Art, and Ritual at Dura-Europos, Syria*. New Haven, CT: Yale University Press, 2016.

Rahner, Hugo, ed. *The Parish: From Theology to Practice*. Translated by Robert Kress. Westminster, MD: Newman Press, 1958.

Rahner, Karl. "Peaceful Reflections on the Parochial Principle." In *Theological Investigations*, vol. 2, *Man in the Church*, 283–318. Translated by Karl-H. Kruger. Baltimore: Helicon Press, 1963.

Rumsey, Andrew. *Parish: An Anglican Theology of Place*. London: SCM Press, 2017.

Sedmak, Clemens. *A Church of the Poor: Pope Francis and the Transformation of Orthodoxy*. Maryknoll, NY: Orbis, 2016.

Tello, Rafael. *Fundamentos de una Nueva Evangelización*. Buenos Aires: Agape Libros, 2015.

———. *La Nueva Evangelización: Escritos Teológico-Pastorales*. Vol 1. Buenos Aires: Agape Libros, 2008.

Visser, Margaret. *The Geometry of Love: Space, Time, Mystery, and Meaning in an Ordinary Church*. New York: North Point Press, 2000.

Zizioulas, John. "The Church as Communion." *St. Vladimir's Theological Quarterly* 38, no. 1 (1994): 3–16.

INDEX OF CHURCH DOCUMENTS AND SCRIPTURAL BOOKS

(Listing common titles and abbreviations used)

GENERAL INDEX